MANAGED FUTURES IN THE INSTITUTIONAL PORTFOLIO

WILEY FINANCE EDITIONS

FINANCIAL STATEMENT ANALYSIS
Martin S. Fridson

DYNAMIC ASSET ALLOCATION
David A. Hammer

INTERMARKET TECHNICAL ANALYSIS
John J. Murphy

INVESTING IN INTANGIBLE ASSETS
Russell L. Parr

FORECASTING FINANCIAL MARKETS
Tony Plummer

PORTFOLIO MANAGEMENT FORMULAS
Ralph Vince

TRADING AND INVESTING IN BOND OPTIONS
M. Anthony Wong

THE COMPLETE GUIDE TO CONVERTIBLE SECURITIES WORLDWIDE
Laura A. Zubulake

MANAGED FUTURES IN THE INSTITUTIONAL PORTFOLIO
Charles B. Epstein, Editor

ANALYZING AND FORECASTING FUTURES PRICES
Anthony F. Herbst

CHAOS AND ORDER IN THE CAPITAL MARKETS
Edgar E. Peters

INSIDE THE FINANCIAL FUTURES MARKETS, 3RD EDITION
Mark J. Powers and Mark G. Castelino

RELATIVE DIVIDEND YIELD
Anthony E. Spare, with Nancy Tengler

SELLING SHORT
Joseph A. Walker

THE FOREIGN EXCHANGE AND MONEY MARKETS GUIDE
Julian Walmsley

CORPORATE FINANCIAL RISK MANAGEMENT
Diane B. Wunnicke, David R. Wilson, Brooke Wunnicke

MANAGED FUTURES IN THE INSTITUTIONAL PORTFOLIO

Edited by

Charles B. Epstein

John Wiley & Sons, Inc.
New York • Chichester • Brisbane • Toronto • Singapore

In recognition of the importance of preserving what has been written, it is a policy of John Wiley & Sons, Inc., to have books of enduring value published in the United States printed on acid-free paper, and we exert our best efforts to that end.

Copyright © 1992 by John Wiley & Sons, Inc.

All rights reserved. Published simultaneously in Canada.

Reproduction or translation of any part of this work beyond that permitted by Section 107 or 108 of the 1976 United States Copyright Act without the permission of the copyright owner is unlawful. Requests for permission or further information should be addressed to the Permissions Department, John Wiley & Sons, Inc.

This publication is designed to provide accurate and authoritative information in regard to the subject matter covered. It is sold with the understanding that the publisher is not engaged in rendering legal, accounting, or other professional services. If legal advice or other expert assistance is required, the services of a competent professional person should be sought. *From a Declaration of Principles jointly adopted by a Committee of the American Bar Association and a Committee of Publishers.*

Library of Congress Cataloging-in-Publication Data

Managed futures in the institutional portfolio / [edited] by Charles B. Epstein.
p. cm. — (Wiley finance editions)
Includes index.
ISBN 0-471-52983-4 (acid-free paper)
1. Futures—United States. 2. Institutional investments—United States—Management. 3. Portfolio management—United States.
I. Epstein, Charles B., 1950– II. Series.
HG6024.U6M36 1992
332.64'5—dc20 91-33347

For Laurie, Erin, and Dana

ABOUT THE AUTHORS

Phillip Bennett is chief financial officer of Refco Group, Ltd. and is responsible for the capital management and financial administration of the Group and its subsidiaries.

Prior to joining Refco in 1981, Mr. Bennett was a vice president at the Chase Manhattan Bank where he held various positions involving credit and commercial lending in New York, Toronto, Brussels, and London. Among his positions at Chase was in the bank's commodity lending department. Mr. Bennett is a graduate of Cambridge University.

Joseph P. Collins is a partner in the Chicago law firm of Schiff Hardin and Waite where he specializes in the regulation of the securities, futures, and forward markets. He has served as the vice chairman of the Chicago Bar Association's Futures Law Committee and was also a member of the faculty of the Illinois Institute of Technology—Chicago Kent College of Law's Graduate Program in financial services law.

Mr. Collins holds an AB degree from the College of the Holy Cross and a JD degree from New York University where he was a Root-Tilden Scholar.

Christopher L. Culp is a research associate for Friedberg Commodity Management, Inc. and is pursuing a PhD at the University of Chicago,

Graduate School of Business. He is a graduate of Johns Hopkins University.

Laleen (Lolly) Collins Doerrer is assistant vice president of managed futures/marketing manager with Brody, White & Co, Inc., Chicago. She is responsible for developing CTA evaluation and optimization systems, and identifying new and established trading advisors for Brody, White & Co. She also supervises managed account trading and due diligence procedures.

Ms. Doerrer holds a BS degree in Political Science from Claremont McKenna College and pursued post-graduate studies in political science at the University of Arizona.

Mike Dunmire is the president of Paradigm Partners, Inc., Bellevue, Washington. Previously he was a vice president of the Frank Russell Company where he was responsible for the research and evaluation of "unconventional" money managers for Russell Private Investment clients. Mr. Dunmire has been a partner and director of research at Cable Howse & Ragen; manager of strategic planning at Seafirst Holding Company; director of investment research at Seattle First National Bank; and a vice president and senior security analyst at Bankers Trust Company.

He holds a BS degree from the University of Pennsylvania and an MBA degree from Columbia University. He is a Chartered Financial Analyst.

Diane V. Dygert is a senior associate with the law firm of Schiff Hardin & Waite, Chicago, where she specializes in employee benefits and executive compensation. She received a BS degree from Cornell University in 1984 and a JD degree from the University of Michigan law school in 1987. She began practicing at Schiff Hardin & Waite that same year. Her practice is concentrated in the fiduciary rules concerning employee benefit plans.

Charles B. Epstein is president of Ravinia Associates, a financial marketing consulting firm in Upper Montclair, New Jersey. He was formerly the managing director of marketing for the New York Futures Exchange. His experience also includes positions as vice president of sales at Lind-Waldock, the world's largest futures discount brokerage firm, and at the Chicago Mercantile Exchange where he helped market the exchange's financial futures and options products. He has written for over 30 publications on a variety of financial topics, and also has experience in radio and television.

He holds a BA in journalism and an MA degree in communications from the University of Illinois, Urbana.

Steven H. Hanke is chief economist and director, World Advisory Service, at Friedberg Commodity Management, Inc. of Toronto, Canada, and professor of applied economics at The Johns Hopkins University in Baltimore, Md. He also serves as advisor to the president of Deloitte Ross Tohmatsu International/Eastern Europe in Brussels.

Scott H. Irwin is associate professor at Ohio State University's Department of Agricultural Economics and Rural Sociology. Prior to his appointment at Ohio State, he taught at Purdue University's Department of Agricultural Economics.

Professor Irwin is a frequent contributor to professional publications such as the *Journal of Portfolio Management, Journal of Futures Markets, and the Journal of Financial and Quantitative Analysis and Applied Economics.* In 1988, he received the Distinguished Research Award as the Outstanding Junior Scientist in the Ohio State Agricultural and Development Center. He holds a BS degree from Iowa State University and, received an MS degree in agricultural economics from Purdue University and a PhD degree with a major in agricultural economics from Purdue University. He joined the faculty of Ohio State University in 1985.

David M. Kozak is a partner in the law firm of Chapman & Cutler, Chicago, where he specializes in commodity futures law with particular emphasis in the area of commodity money management. For the past ten years, he has represented commodity pool operators in conjunction with numerous publicly registered and privately offered commodity pools in the United States as well as numerous offshore funds.

David McCarthy is president of McCarthy, McGuirk & Co. of Stockbridge, Mass., a futures and options trading and investment firm. Previously, Mr. McCarthy was a vice president with Rayner & Stonington; deputy manager with Brown Brothers Harriman & Co.; and a management consultant with McKinsey & Co. Mr. McCarthy serves on the investment policy committee of an international managed futures fund and is a visiting assistant professor of finance at Skidmore College, Saratoga Springs, New York. He received his MBA from Stanford University.

Gerald Mangieri is a partner in the New York office of Arthur Andersen & Co. with worldwide tax responsibilities for the capital markets industry which includes broker-dealers, investment banking, commodities, and regulated investment companies. He is also a member of the firm's Consolidated Tax Return Practice Committee. Mr. Mangieri has both a graduate and undergraduate degrees from Fairleigh Dickinson University and is a member of the American Institute for Certified Public Accountants.

Henry Marmer is an associate in the asset management consulting practice with William M. Mercer, Ltd., Toronto, advising pension fund sponsors and other clients on setting investment policies, asset allocation, and other techniques to add value to fund performance. Prior to joining Mercer, Mr. Marmer was a senior investment analyst at the Sun Life Assurance Company of Canada. His responsibilities there included analysis and introduction of investment strategies and techniques to enhance returns to reduce risk and evaluate asset classes for strategic investment decision making. Prior to this, he was a capital markets analyst at the Hudson's Bay Company.

Mr. Marmer has published a number of articles and is a part-time instructor for MBA graduates at the Faculty of Administrative Studies at York University, Toronto. The Toronto Society of Financial Analysts awarded Mr. Marmer the 1990 award for the best paper in Canadian capital markets.

Mr. Marmer received a CFA, a BBA, and an MBA in finance and investments from the Faculty of Administrative Studies at York University.

Pascal I. Magnollay is the director of research and development at Mint Investment Management Company. He joined the firm in 1988 and is responsible for building trading systems for futures, foreign exchange and equities and the daily supervision of the computer operations related to trading. Prior to this, Dr. Magnollay worked at AT&T's Bell Laboratories. He obtained his PhD in particle physics from the University of Texas at Austin.

Peter Matthews is a partner and chief portfolio strategist at Mint Investment Management Company, a commodity trading advisor managing approximately $900 million in client funds. He obtained his MA and PhD in statistics at American University, Washington, DC and his BA degree in economics and mathematics at Carleton University in Ottawa, Canada. Mr. Matthews is on the board of the Managed Futures Association and is chairman of its statistics and standards committee.

Mark H. Mitchell is a managing partner of the Chicago law firm of Chapman & Cutler, and heads the firm's futures practice group. His is an editor of *Commodities Law Letter* and formerly served as counsel to the Commodity Futures Trading Commission in Washington, DC. For over 15 years, he has concentrated his legal practice in representing commodity trading advisors, commodity pools and other clients in the managed futures industry.

Julia Oliver is audit manager in the New York office of Arthur Andersen & Co. and has worked extensively in the commodities and financial services areas. She holds a BA degree in accounting and business administration from Rutgers University and is a member of the American Institute for Certified Public Accountants.

Frank Pusateri is vice president, investments for Prudential Bache Securities, New York. Mr. Pusateri has established a national reputation in managed futures through his development of qualitative and quantitative techniques for evaluating and selecting futures money managers. Mr. Pusateri holds an MBA degree in accounting and finance from the Amos Tuck School of Business Administration and a BA degree in mathematics from Colgate University. In 1991, Mr. Pusateri was awarded the Donchian Award by *Managed Account Reports,* the leading publication of the managed futures industry, for making the most significant contributions to the managed futures industry.

Uttama Savanayana is lecturer at the School of Business Administration at the National Institute of Development Administration in Bangkok, Thailand. Mr. Savanayana has a PhD in Finance from the University of Massachusetts in Amherst, Massachusetts.

Thomas Schneeweis is professor of finance at the University of Massachusetts in Amherst, Massachusetts. He is widely published in the area of derivative markets and is the author (with J. Hill and E. Schwarz) of *Financial Futures; Fundamentals, Strategies, and Applications*. Mr. Schneeweis serves as trustee to a number of investment funds and was the recipient of a Fulbright Research Fellowship in 1990. He holds a PhD in finance from the University of Iowa.

CONTENTS

MANAGED FUTURES IN THE INSTITUTIONAL PORTFOLIO

FOREWORD

A cynic might argue that no modern human endeavor can be taken seriously until it is punctuated with conferences, seminars, associations, magazines, newsletters, and award ceremonies. If that is the case, then the managed futures industry has come of age.

No longer can the futures markets simply be considered a high-risk alternative investment which most Commodity Trading Advisors thought suitable only for the most aggressive clients. The industry has reached the point where both practical experience and academic verification seem to demonstrate that a portfolio of trading advisors can yield returns that provide portfolio diversification as well as competitive reward to risk ratios.

Until now, those institutional clients who have ventured into managed futures have been forced to gain their knowledge from interviews, conferences, newsletters, a few articles, and actual trading experience. Many clients learned their lessons the hard way. It is time for the industry to have a source of information that will allow sophisticated investors to quickly review the viability of managed futures as an investment alternative.

The contributors to this book are to be thanked for taking the time to share with us their knowledge and experience. No price can easily be put on the expertise these authors provide. This is not to say that we now have all the answers, or that this will be the last book written on the topic.

Instead, this book represents a solid beginning. The managed futures industry now enjoys the ability to review the first few chapters of its own history. The 1950s and 1960s saw the emergence of our industry and since the mid-1970s, the rate of growth and change in the managed futures industry has accelerated dramatically. Today, some trading advisors manage in excess of $500 million while clients with $10 million to $20 million futures portfolios are not unique.

In spite of this growing popularity, many of the questions that I hear today are almost the same as yesterday's. They seem to differ only in their order of magnitude. The industry's level of growth and change has created many of the opportunities and problems you will read about in this book. But beware, no end to "The History of the Managed Futures" is in sight.

On the contrary, in this rapidly growing industry, many of us are uncertain as to the roles we will play in the future. One way to resolve this confusion is through quality information. I believe successful investors over the long-term find that information is critical to success.

This book will provide the broad, quality education that clients, investment professionals, and other interested parties need in order to begin asking the right questions. Those of you looking for a mass-produced answer to successful futures investing will be disappointed. Instead, I believe that experience and knowledge offer investors improved odds of success while maximizing the hope that one will not have to repeat the mistakes of others.

FRANK S. PUSATERI

February 1992

PREFACE

As investors pursue higher overall portfolio returns while simultaneously reducing their risk, investment professionals are being called on to research a wider range of instruments and strategies to meet these goals. In the course of this search, investing in a professionally managed futures portfolio has become increasingly popular among institutional investors. While the managed futures industry is considered to be in its formative stages, by late-1991, there was an estimated $20 billion invested in managed futures either through funds, pools, or direct investments. Invariably, many investors are asking: What are managed futures and what is their role in a traditional institutional portfolio?

The purpose of this book is to present both the theoretical basis and practical applications of bringing a managed futures account into an institutional portfolio. While this idea may sound basic, like many other new ideas, it requires some fundamental understanding and familiarity before it will be accepted. Even then, the idea of futures positions being in a pension fund portfolio is still abhorrent to many investment professionals. This is understandable and to some degree even justified since there are certain risk levels for all investors. After all, it was only a decade ago that some pension funds were prohibited from holding equities in their portfolios because they were considered too risky.

Time has a way of leveling risk. The same is certainly true of futures trading regardless of its history as providing viable hedging strategies and its stigma in financial history as being raucous, untoward and destabilizing either economically or politically to the established financial order. That being said, futures are also the ideal contrarian investment and as such, have attracted a wider following from both academics and investment professionals who have decided to see firsthand what is behind the veil of superlatives. For some, this journey has been very rewarding financially and academically stimulating.

This book is organized so the professional investor can get a better idea of both the academic foundation and day-to-day practice of trading through a managed futures account. Chapters 1 through 4 present the key theoretical aspects of managed futures including their potential role as an alternative asset class; alternative investment strategies; and a risk-return analysis using a multi-manager commodity portfolio.

The second section of the book presents the practical aspects of investing in a managed futures account. This section looks at methods of evaluating commodity trading advisors; organizing a commodity pool; fiduciary selection and prohibited transactions under ERISA; accounting and unrelated business income tax issues for managed futures; the consultant's viewpoint of managed futures, including how Canadian pension funds can use managed futures; inflation hedging with unleveraged futures; and a provocative study on the risk comparison between futures and stocks.

I would like to thank all the contributors who took time from their busy schedules and endured numerous writing and editing demands, punctuated by a war in the Persian Gulf, the break-up of the Soviet block and a major recession, to submit their valuable contributions to this book. Each one has been extremely generous with their professional insights and experience. I would also like to thank others who helped with this project: my parents, Joanne and Art Shulman, and my past employers at Lind-Waldock and the Chicago Mercantile Exchange who demonstrated how to turn ideas into action.

CHUCK EPSTEIN

February 1992

1 INTRODUCTION: MANAGED FUTURES COME OF AGE

Charles B. Epstein

There are few new product areas in the financial industry with as much demonstrated growth potential as managed futures. Since the first managed futures program was introduced for individual speculators in 1949, this growing pool of investment capital continues to attract a larger following among both institutional investors and retail customers, it also has developed some persuasive arguments for becoming a permanent feature of a diversified portfolio. By 1991, there was an estimated $20 billion in managed futures programs in the United States, Europe, and Asia attracting a large following from institutional money managers and pension plan sponsors.

Managed futures today are the culmination of the futures industry's uninterrupted growth curve that began in 1968. Traditionally, futures markets have brought together commercial hedgers and speculators in an open, competitive marketplace to determine an asset's price at a single point in time. As these markets became increasingly complex, due to the introduction of new futures contracts, more sophisticated strategies, and international market opportunities, users of the futures markets sought more specialized professional advice in managing their futures market assets.

The increasing popularity of managed futures provides the impetus for this book since the growth of managed futures is inseparably tied to the growth of futures trading and, in many instances, provides some of those same benefits to the institutional investor. The benefits of futures trading range from providing a quick, cost-efficient method of obtaining exposure to a new asset group, to new trading strategies using a combination of the cash and futures markets.

In addition to these benefits, the use of a professionally-managed futures program offers investors some features not commonly found in other investments. Among these benefits are:

- Portfolio diversification that can provide noncorrelated returns to other assets such as stocks, fixed income instruments, cash, and real estate
- Multiple professional trading advisors whose performance, taken in aggregate, can provide greater opportunities for higher returns at lower risk
- Potential access to new investment strategies utilizing the cash, forward, options, and swap markets to supplement the initial futures positions
- Liquidity and mark-to-market reporting
- Products designed with a guaranteed return of a client's original investment.
- Limited liability if the futures program is part of a limited partnership
- Economies of scale as positions are pooled.

Despite these benefits, many of the same stigmas that accompanied the futures markets for years also are cited as reasons why managed futures have not grown even faster. Many institutional investors are still unfamiliar with the mechanics and theory of the futures markets despite their history of providing positive risk management strategies to commercial hedgers since the 1870s.

Preoccupation with these concerns may help explain why, for example, despite the popularity of stock index futures, one expert estimated that of the $40 billion invested in equity index funds at Bankers Trust, its institutional owners only permit 25 percent of that amount to be hedged in stock index futures.

There is also concern that pension funds will encounter significant legal restrictions from the 1974 Employee Retirement Income Security Act (ERISA) when trading managed futures. Some pension plan sponsors have expressed reservations about the use of leverage or the difficulties of explaining the operations of the futures markets to a skeptical board of directors.

Despite these potential drawbacks, an increasing number of tax-exempt institutions and money managers consider managed futures a valuable addition to a diversified portfolio. Funds such as the Eastman-Kodak Pension Fund, the Detroit Firemen's and Policemen's Beneficial Association, the DuPont Pension Fund, State of Alaska Pension Fund, Virginia Retirement System, and AMP, Inc. have been cited in industry publications as investing in managed futures programs.

Today, the most commonly cited reasons for including managed futures in a diversified portfolio include:

- Exposure to a new asset class
- Provides additional diversification to a traditional portfolio
- Provides a means of decreasing overall portfolio volatility
- Serves as an inflation hedge
- Can provide incremental return to the total portfolio.

An overview of these features provides a foundation for the more detailed discussion in subsequent chapters. But first, it is important to examine how managed futures can act to diversify an institutional portfolio. After that, we will look at some of the operational aspects of a managed futures account.

ARE MANAGED FUTURES AN ASSET CLASS?

Modern Portfolio Theory provides the framework for determining whether the returns from managed futures or futures trading alone constitutes a separate and distinct asset class. The argument in favor of futures standing on its own as an asset class can be derived from these general characteristics of managed futures:

- They constitute a recognized broad collection of assets.
- They can be traded to track a predetermined index.
- They present the opportunity for passive management.

Statistically, futures and managed futures provide an expected return, standard deviation, and correlations to other traditional asset classes. While futures certainly possess all of these characteristics, managed futures present some problems requiring them to be considered a distinct asset class.

First, managed futures are comprised of a variable underlying asset group. Most managers trade agricultural commodities, financial futures, energy commodities, and precious metals interchangeably in a single portfolio; there are few purist managers who trade only one commodity group during all market cycles.

Second, managed futures are actively traded and while they may offer the opportunity for passive management, that practice currently is rare. As such, managed futures do not present returns stripped of their active feature. Therefore, it is difficult for the plan sponsor to distinguish investment returns from the individual Commodity Trading Advisor's (CTAs) skills or the characteristics of the underlying futures contracts. Finally, until an industry-accepted performance benchmark evolves, the selection and weighting of a managed futures portfolio will remain subjective.

The Case for Diversification

Managed futures can diversify a portfolio in three distinct areas: by assets, investment strategies and manager styles. By definition, traditional institutional portfolios do not contain either futures or options derivatives except as temporary hedging vehicles. Managed futures provide asset exposure to a different set of assets, often including financial futures such as foreign currencies, interest rate instruments, and stock indexes and, in some cases, actual physical commodities (oil, soybeans, gold, cattle) which would not normally be found in an institutional portfolio. In the case of nonfinancial commodities, futures provide cost-efficient, direct access to the commodity price exposure without ever taking actual physical ownership.

For example, owning timberland or farmland was a popular investment strategy among institutions in the late-1970s, but presented potential liquidity, pricing, and management problems. If the goal of the pension fund was to own and manage the property, the investment was justified. But if the fund was solely concerned about obtaining physical commodity price exposure and inflation protection, using the futures markets may have offered a better alternative.

A hypothetical fund could have purchased lumber or soybean futures, for example, and taken advantage of the following features that are unique to the futures markets:

- Daily settlement in cash for all changes in the value of the futures position (mark-to-market daily pricing)
- Exposure to new trading strategies (short selling, spreading, etc.)
- Standardized contracts
- Trade on a registered exchange via registered brokers
- Concentration of all trading in one location
- Equal access to the market for all participants, regardless of size
- Clearinghouse guarantee.

Aside from diversification by asset class, a plan sponsor could also use managed futures to access an entirely new group of investment managers following a variety of trading methods and styles. When these managers are used in a multi-manager portfolio, the portfolio can be optimized to create a complimentary manager mix, with plan assets deployed according to the client's risk-reward tolerance.

THE STRUCTURE AND COST OF A MANAGED ACCOUNT

Investors can participate in managed futures in three distinct ways: through (1) an individual managed futures account, (2) public futures funds, and (3) private futures pools. To date, institutions that have used managed futures have done so primarily through individual managed accounts and private pools.

The key participants in a managed futures account generally follow the same organizational structure found in an institutional equity trading organization. In a multimanager situation, a Commodity Pool Operator (CPO), defined as a person or firm engaged in organizing limited partnerships, oversees the trading activities of a group of Commodity Trading Advisors (CTAs). CTAs are persons or firms who are given limited power of attorney to trade an investor's equity. At the operational level, trades are given to a Futures Commission Merchant (FCM), or broker, who then executes the trade according to the CTA's direction.

All pools and funds are generally organized as limited partnerships in the United States and in many ways function similarly to mutual funds. Each is constructed to offer more flexibility than partnerships enjoy under the Investment Company Act of 1940. As limited partnerships, funds and pools have several distinct advantages over individually managed accounts.

In a limited partnership, for example, an investor's risk is restricted to his original investment. Additionally, limited partners receive simplified monthly reports and enjoy additional diversification that can only be achieved by pooling the capital of several investors. Limited partnerships also must pay any ongoing costs from an offering, such as audit and legal expenses.

"Fund" generally refers to a public offering registered with the Securities and Exchange Commission (SEC) in which units are publicly offered for a limited period. There is generally no subsequent offering of units once the original period has expired. Funds generally have the smallest minimum investment requirements and as such, have been largely used by individual investors. "Pools" generally refer to private limited partnerships that are subject to securities regulations affecting private placements. Pools are developed by a CPO and are offered by private placement to a limited number of nonaccredited investors and to an unlimited number of accredited investors. (An accredited investor is one who meets pre-defined suitability and income guidelines.)

The aggregate amount of trading capital in a pool is generally lower than that found in funds, but the number of limited partners in a pool is always fewer than those in funds. Because of this structure, pools often have less overhead which can reduce the partner's costs. Another benefit of pools is their ability to limit the maximum number of partners. This gives the general partner greater investment management flexibility. Pools can also accept ongoing investments from the partners once the initial subscription period has ended.

Equally important to the structure of the managed futures investment is manager compensation. As one would expect with any growing market segment, the costs of managed futures trading programs have been decreasing as competition increases and the industry matures. The cost structures in managed futures vary widely, but are generally comprised of management fees, incentive fees, and brokerage fees. Management fees go to the fund manager and are usually established at a fixed monthly rate and charged against net equity in the account. Incentive fees provide another source of manager compensation and usually are based on the fund's new net profits set over the previous high point or over a designated period.

Limited partnerships may charge an up-front sales charge. For example, a charge of 7 percent on units valued at $1000 each will be priced at $1070 or sold at $1000 with an initial net asset value of $930. As an alternative or supplemental approach to provide a selling commission, the general partner can receive a portion of interest income from the pool's U.S. Treasury bills and the commissions paid to the executing broker.

Management fees generally are based on a per annum percentage of the fund's total net assets payable to the trading manager or general partner on a monthly basis. The general partner's compensation can be based on fees, commissions, or both. The CTA is compensated by a combination of new profits and an incentive fee based on new net trading profits. This fee can be paid directly to the individual manager or the overall trading manager in the case of multimanager portfolios. Brokerage or trade execution costs, expressed on a round-turn (buy and sell basis), generally are made payable to the trading manager and are another ongoing expense component in a managed futures fund. All of these costs are delineated in the fund's prospectus or a pool's private placement memorandum.

Funds located outside the United States, known as "offshore funds," generally are organized as a corporate form rather than as limited partnership. Because of this, offshore funds generally issue nonvoting shares in a company formed to invest in participating nonvoting shares of a managed futures fund. These investments are tax-sheltered until they are redeemed. In terms of costs, offshore funds are generally similar to their U.S. counterparts. Reporting requirements are also different, and in some cases more lenient, than in the United States.

In the United States, since the first publicly managed futures funds were introduced in the early-1980s, many administrative costs have fallen. In the early-1980s, commissions per trade were as high as 80 percent of the retail rate which could generate commission expenses ranging from 10 to 12 percent of total equity annually, according to Kenneth Tropin, president of John Henry & Co., a well-known commodity trading advisory firm. Advisory fees ranged from 4 to 6 percent with a 15 percent incentive fee, while typical distribution of Treasury bill interest income saw 80 percent of the assets earning Treasury bill interest and the remainder earning free-credit income for the brokerage firm. Because of this structure, a fund would have to earn 9 percent annually from trading just to break even.

By 1990, advisory fees plus commissions were in the 7 to 8 percent range with all interest income being paid to the client. Many managers have lowered their incentive and management fees thus reducing the break-even costs in public funds from 9 to 10 percent (including interest income) to about 5 to 6 percent.

Traditionally, the differences in the cost structure between public limited partnerships "are closely comparable with, but not identical to, those seen in individual accounts and private pools," according to a 1984 study conducted by Managed Account Reports Consultants. While this study looked at cost structures of funds in the early-1980s, Morton Baratz, who conducted the study, said these cost relationships appear to have remained constant.

But this may be changing. Since the 1980s, the managed futures industry has seen a proliferation of new fund cost structures that have altered the overhead and break-even structure for many funds. At the individual fund level, a major innovation occurred in 1991 with the introduction of the Investor's Advantage Fund, L.P., which back-loaded all management and incentive fees so that all compensation to the General Partner and its manager of fund operations was performance-based. The fund was organized so all management fee compensation is only paid out after the customer receives 100 percent of the prevailing Treasury bill rate. According to the Fund's general partner and trading advisor, Mark Ritchie, and Don Karel, manager of fund operations, this structure is the first of its type and was designed as a "true partner relationship between the investor and the Fund."

In the structure of funds, there also have been new developments such as guarantee funds that use a Letter of Credit, U.S. Treasury bond, or other assurance instrument to secure the investor's original capital over a certain minimum period. The issuer of the Letter of Credit generally charges an annual fee or a fee based on the face amount of the instrument.

Commission expense is another cost element which has been reduced since the 1980s. Commission expense is commonly expressed in two ways: as a percent of equity based on an annual basis; and as a number of trades per million dollars of equity under management.

Tropin said his firm trades accounts with commissions as low as $10 per round-turn with that expense running at 1.6 percent annually. If he places the fund's entire capital in U.S. Treasury bills, he will earn 5 to 6 percent annually without trading. Tropin said that given these reduced expenses, institutional clients could find it easier to achieve positive returns while also taking advantage of the futures market's ability to use interest-bearing collateral to take market positions.

The importance of commissions in manager performance evaluation is crucial. In many cases, the average commission charged by a manager is a reflection of their equity raising system and a portion of their sales overhead.

In a survey conducted by Pusateri and Stapleton (1990), trading advisors whose equity was raised by large brokerage firms had track records reflecting commissions in excess of $50 per round turn. "Substantial trading advisors" had commissions as high as $80 to $90 per round turn. These commission rates were significantly higher than traders who raised their own equity for client accounts and pools which had average commission rates of $25 per round turn. The study showed some had commissions as low as $15.

By examining the commission rates and annual gross commissions as a percent of equity, Pusateri and Stapleton estimated the historical effect of a lower commission rate on an advisor's track record. They concluded that an advisor with a composite track record based on an average commission rate of $75 (including 12 percent of equity in annual commissions) would have increased their annual performance by 8 percent if commissions were reduced to $25. (The 8 percent annual increase is unadjusted for investment of profits and additional fees. Additional profits are withdrawn annually.)

Commission rates also have an effect on the risk-reward ratio. To illustrate how this variable affected performance, see Table 1.1. Based on this data, the authors concluded that few, if any investors would select advisor A. Most would probably pick advisors C or D.

In the example in Table 1.2, the authors adjusted the commissions to reflect a maximum commission rate of $25 per round turn. Based on the advisor's estimate of the average commission rate and average annual commissions as a percent of equity, the changes shown in Table 1.2 would have occurred. As Tables 1.1 and 1.2 show, risk, standard deviation, and peak-to-valley loss show little or no change due to changes in commission rates. But a small (.5 to 1 percent) absolute change in the average monthly return makes "a major difference" in the calculated risk to reward ratios for some of the advisors.

Due to these changes, the status of advisor D and advisor A are changed; D no longer has the best reward to risk ratio and A no longer has the worst. In a reversal of earlier expected behavior, most clients would now pick advisor E as their manager.

While this study focused on the effect commissions have on overall performance, the authors also stressed that improvements can be made

TABLE 1.1. The effect of commission rates on an advisor's track record.

Advisor	A	B	C	D	E
Average Monthly Return	1.6	6.8	3.1	3.5	3.6
Standard Deviation	6.9	23.5	11.7	11.6	12.4
Peak to Valley Loss	28.1	71.6	28.6	35.7	38.7
Reward to Standard Deviation	.23	.29	.26	.31	.29
Rank	5	3	4	1	2
Reward to Drawdown	.06	.09	.11	.10	.09
Rank	5	3	1	2	4

Source: Pusateri and Stapleton.

TABLE 1.2. Advisor performance adjusted for a $25 commission.

Advisor	A	B	C	D	E
Average Monthly Return	2.3	6.8	3.5	3.5	4.8
Standard Deviation	6.9	23.5	11.7	11.6	12.4
Peak to Valley Loss	25.2	71.6	28.1	35.7	30.2
Reward to Standard Deviation	.34	.29	.30	.31	.39
Rank	2	5	4	3	1
Reward to Drawdown	.09	.09	.12	.10	.16
Rank	5	4	2	3	1

Note: Track records for advisors A, C, and E based on average commission rates ranging from $65 to $85 per round turn. Each of the advisors is successful trading at these rates for clients.

in other performance reporting areas. These include interest earnings, which are not being included in some track records, while other performance reports include management fees that do not reflect what is actually paid by a new client.

HISTORY OF MANAGED FUTURES

The managed futures industry in 1991 was estimated to have $20 billion under management, including money placed in both private placements and public funds, according to a study by Managed Account Reports. This figure compares to about $500 million to $800 million estimated to have been under management in 1980 (see Figure 1.1). While the growth over the past decade has been significant, the industry is still considered in its formative stages.

The first publicly managed futures fund, Futures, Inc., was started in 1949 by Richard Donchian, a broker at the securities firm of Hayden Stone. Donchian is considered by many industry professionals to be the creator of the managed futures industry and is credited with developing a systematic approach to futures money management. A key feature of his approach involved the application of moving averages to a trading system. In 1965, the first known managed commodity account was set up by Dunn and Hargitt acting as the CTA. The account totalled $2000 and

FIGURE 1.1. The growth of managed futures.

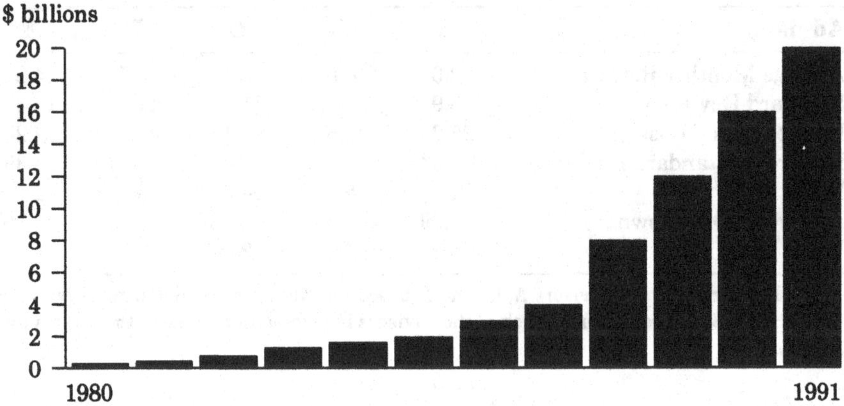

Since 1980 funds invested in managed futures accounts have grown from $650 million to $20 billion. The growth has been especially explosive since 1987, when stock markets plunged; some managed futures funds showed returns of as much as 61% that year.

Source: Managed Account Reports

was traded at Lamson Brothers (now part of Shearson Lehman-Hutton) by a nonbroker CTA.

Throughout the 1960s, exchange-traded commodities were almost exclusively storable, perishable, and agricultural. Product history was made in 1965 when the first perishable commodity, live cattle, began trading on the Chicago Mercantile Exchange. This contract was notable because it broke tradition and opened the realm for new product development by the exchanges in the futures' industry.

By 1967, the first computer testing of commodity trading systems was being conducted and the first commodity price database was created by Dunn & Hargitt. This enabled futures managers to create trading simulations incorporating different commodities, trading styles, and quantitative approaches before actual money was risked in the market.

By 1969, a formal business approach was developed to speculate in the American commodity markets. In that year, Commodities Corporation was founded by a group including Helmut Weymar and Frank

Vannerson in Princeton, New Jersey, with $2.5 million in money under management. An economist named Paul Samuelson (who later was awarded the Nobel prize in Economics in 1970) also provided fundamental trading-oriented research ideas. By 1990, the firm had $240 million in proprietary money and approximately $800 million in customer equity, according to Robert Easton, president and chief executive officer of Commodities Corporation.

By 1971, academics and traders continued to exchange trading ideas and implement them with strict money management practices. In February, Richard Levin, Malcolm Weiner, Mathew Sterling, and Bugs Baer began trading a joint account using methods first developed by Richard Donchian. These methods included diversification over a wide range of futures contracts, intermediate- and long-term trend following, the use of mathematical and technical trend following and adequate capital needed to sustain positions. "These principles represented the basis for most of the successful trend following systems of the past 20 years," according to R. Thomas Northcote, who has been involved in the managed futures industry since 1973.

In September 1972, the futures industry changed dramatically when the Chicago Mercantile Exchange began financial futures trading in seven foreign currencies: Swiss francs, Deutsche marks, British pounds, French francs, Canadian dollars, Japanese yen, and the Dutch guilder. This was the first step in changing the nature of the markets from agricultural commodities to one of providing financial risk management. The change also opened up an entirely new customer base comprised of treasurers and financial managers facing a capital risk.

The remainder of the 1970s saw the introduction of the first quotation machine offered to major traders (Computrend) which allowed traders to create price charts that are crucial to technical analysis; mandatory registration of all futures trading advisors and pool operators with the federal agency responsible for regulating the futures industry, the Commodity Futures Trading Commission (CFTC); the first use of multiple trading systems in a single account (Campbell & Co., 1977); the first large private placement, Nestor Partners by Malcolm Weiner in 1977; and the first use of multiple managers in a single pool, the Thompson McKinnon Futures Fund, in 1978.

By the 1980s, the managed futures industry had enough momentum to build upon the foundation of new product development and an expanded user base which the futures industry had created earlier.

It was also about this time that managed futures began to attract international attention. In early-1982, Ulrich Becker in ContiCommodities' Hamburg, Germany, office, created a trend-following system and began trading customer money on a discretionary basis. Industry estimates say he managed in excess of $30 million. He is widely credited with being the first non-U.S.-based CTA. In July, Dunn & Hargitt created the first offshore pool created by a U.S. CTA.

One of the most significant innovations to come from these advances was the creation of the guarantee fund. Many professionals consider the guarantee fund to be one of the most important developments ever in attracting money into the managed futures industry. As the name implies, a guarantee fund (Figure 1.2) provides a base level of return to participants in a managed futures fund. Because leverage is used in establishing any futures position and any market losses can exceed any investor's initial investment, all futures traders are susceptible to sustaining losses which can exceed their original investment.

The use of a guaranteed return, however, provided an alternative to the cessation of trading that some funds normally incorporate into their policy when certain loss limits are reached. For instance, if a conventionally structured fund sustained a loss of 50 percent of initial trading capital, it could stop trading and refund the remaining equity to investors. The guarantee fund offered a different approach. It provided a guaranteed return of principle, usually at the end of a five- to seven-year period. Investors in a guarantee fund generally receive either the return from the manager's performance or their initial investment, whichever is higher. (See Table 1.3.)

The first public guarantee fund, the Principal Guardian Futures Fund, was offered by Index Futures and James Little in 1987. About one year later, Dean Witter scored one of the most successful managed futures offerings ever when it attracted over $531 million for its $250 million Principal Guaranteed Fund. The firm was forced to return over $280 million to investors. Commodities Corporation served as the CTA.

The guarantee feature was supplemented through the Four Seasons Fund offered by Heinold Asset Management, acting as general partner,

FIGURE 1.2. Sample structure of a guarantee fund.

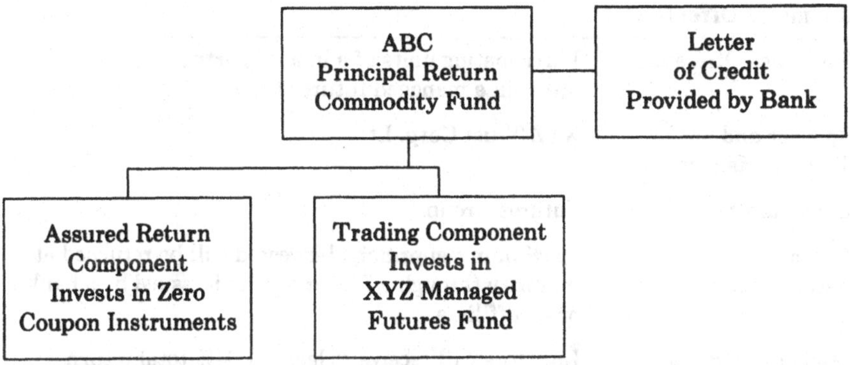

The trading component of the ABC Principal Return Fund will invest in units of the XYZ Managed Futures Fund Ltd.

The XYZ Managed Futures Fund is a limited partnership which seeks to profit form speculative trading of currencies, selected metals and other commodities and financial instruments.

The assurance component will invest in zero coupon instruments that will be pledged to an issuing bank or one of its affiliates to secure the reimbursement obligation of the Fund under the Letter of Credit. At maturity, the zero coupon instruments will be applied to satisfy the reimbursement obligation.

The Fund seeks a high return that permits leverage to control positions in excess of underlying capital.

For funds located outside the U.S., a similar structure exists except that a corporate structure is created which usually issues non-voting shares to the fund's investors.

and RXR of Stamford, Connecticut, as the CTA. This was the first multiasset fund and used stock index and bond futures as surrogates for actual cash market investments. The fund also broke new ground by guaranteeing investors not only a return of their original principal, but also a 5 percent annual return. These conservative features served to attract several pension funds as limited partners.

For investors wishing to participate in a managed futures program without putting up cash to initiate and maintain margin positions, the

TABLE 1.3. Sample terms of offering for a guarantee fund.

Terms of Offering	
Securities Offered:	Participating units of a limited partnership formed to invest in a managed futures fund.
Sponsor and Trading Manager:	XYZ Trust Corp. Ltd.
Consultant:	Futures Group
Principal Assurance:	100% of initial principal invested will be returned at maturity through a Letter of Credit issued by a bank or an affiliate.
Minimum Return Assurance:	Investors will receive at least 17.34% total return (3.25% compounded annually) at maturity regardless of actual trading results, paid at maturity through Letter of Credit.
Minimum Subscription:	U.S. $150,000 (inclusive of sales fee)
Maturity:	Approximately five years from the closing date.
Redemptions:	None in the first three years. Quarterly thereafter at applicable redemption net asset value (with zero instruments valued at lower of market or accrued value). Minimum redemption of U.S. $10,000 with prior written notice.
Sales Fee:	1.2% of investment payable to Sponsor.
Management Fee:	3.5% per annum of the Fund's total net assets payable to the Trading Manager monthly.
Incentive Fee:	15% of cumulative net new trading profit achieved by each Trading Advisor payable to the Trading Manager.
Brokerage Fee:	$25 per round turn trade initiated by Trading Advisors payable to the Trading Manager.
Start-Up Expenses:	Charged to the Fund. Amortized over a five-year-period.
Letter of Credit Fee:	0.5% per annum or face amount of the Letter of Credit.

Kenmar Fund, New York, in June 1990 offered investors the ability to enter a managed account for no cash—just post a Letter of Credit. This was the first time this approach was ever offered.

While these developments have all acted to attract a wider institutional following to the futures markets, one innovation has had such an impact in bringing new attention to the futures industry that it warrants additional attention. That innovation is stock index futures.

The Attraction of Stock Index Futures

Few financial products have had such a revolutionary effect on the capital markets as stock index futures. Since they were introduced in early-1982, stock index futures have popularized a new way of viewing and trading financial assets, while also providing the research impetus to develop new strategies and products worldwide.

The importance of this product area can be traced to a few innovations. First, stock index futures packaged an identifiable asset (an S&P 500 basket of stocks, for example) and allowed them to be traded in a single action. Investors no longer were taking incremental, individual equity positions as they assembled this stock basket. Now, an entire equity asset (as measured by a specific index) was packaged in a single trade. This made it possible to isolate market-wide, or systematic risk.

This product group complimented the huge passive index market in which pension funds seek to match the return of a specific index by purchasing its component equities. Index futures gave these passive quantitative managers a low-cost, effective way to match an index, or by employing active strategies, more ways to outperform the benchmark through the use of equity index futures and options.

In the case of non-U.S. equity portfolios, many of these same strategies are being used with the addition of investing in the host country's currency. By using the foreign currency cash or futures market, the portfolio can be positioned or "tilted" in the direction of a favorable currency move. In early-1992, the Commodity Futures Trading Commission ruled that U.S. pension funds could use Japanese stock indexes (based on the TOPIX and the Nikkei) to compliment their investing strategies in Japan. The continued popularity of passive investing, combined with the proliferation of overseas equity derivatives, will continue to propel the growth of these strategies worldwide.

Yet, despite the importance of these developments, stock index futures were derisively called the "commoditization" of the equities markets by some traditional equity traders who felt the product and its related strategies would jeopardize the status quo of the U.S. financial industry.

One reason for this reaction was that by assuming long or short equity index exposure quickly and cost-efficiently, it became possible to arbitrage price discrepancies between the cash stock market and stock index futures. By using the New York Stock Exchange's electronic order delivery system, called the Designated Order Turnaround (DOT) system (developed in 1975), it was possible to execute the cash side of the trade faster and cheaper than ever before. These two inventions—the DOT system and stock index futures—made stock index arbitrage possible and effectively linked the equity cash and futures markets.

The popularity of stock index arbitrage and the trading of a selected list or "program" of stocks ("program trading") helped focus attention on another essential element of institutional investing: transaction costs. Transaction costs are comprised of commissions, bid-ask spreads, liquidity premiums, and opportunity costs. These costs are much lower using stock index futures than in the cash stock market. (See Figure 1.3.)

Transaction costs have been one of the most important features propelling the institutional popularity of stock index futures and their related strategies, such as index arbitrage, program and basket trading. For example, an investor seeking price exposure to the S&P 500 Index can achieve this via the futures market with a single commission, usually under $15. Many professionals generally agree that stock index futures provide a desired asset exposure at substantially lower cost than using the cash markets. These savings are especially attractive to investors in index funds, which are designed to track a specific market index, such as the Russell 2000 or the S&P 500.

Since the first index fund began trading in 1973, this type of structured investment has become increasingly popular. There is now an estimated $300 billion in index funds. Today, indexing exacerbates liquidity concerns at the New York Stock Exchange and also continues to put downward pressure on equity commissions.

FIGURE 1.3. Transaction costs.

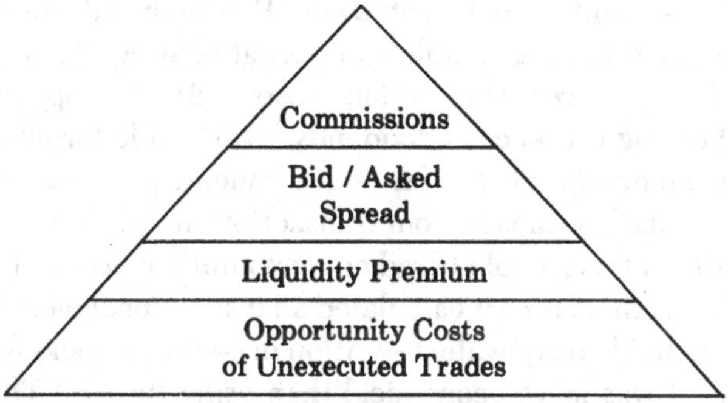

Transaction costs fall into four categories: commissions, the bid-ask spread, a liquidity premium, and the opportunity cost for unexecuted trades. As shown above, the two most commonly discussed transaction costs are commissions and the bid-ask spread because they are easiest to quantify. Opportunity cost, conversely, is the most difficult to value and as a result, it is often not considered as important as the other commission elements.

Source: Salomon Brothers

One of the key components of an efficient program trading strategy is commission costs. A prime component of commission cost is called "market impact," which is defined as the amount of price distortion that occurs when a large order (such as the simultaneous purchase of the 500 stocks in the S&P 500 Index) is executed on the affected market. While market impact is only one price factor affecting an efficiently executed program trade, traders and researchers quickly began to focus on other elements of trade execution costs.

According to a 1991 study by Goldman, Sachs & Co., the approximate cost of buying a $50 million S&P 500 position totals 30 basis points in the cash market versus 8.5 basis points in the futures market. (This amount is comprised of commissions and taxes of 8 basis points and a market impact of 22 basis points for assuming a cash market equity position compared to 1.5 basis points in commissions and taxes and a market impact of 7 basis points in futures.)

These same cost efficiencies exist for investors using the overseas equities markets where stock index futures also are traded. In a

Salomon Brothers Equity and Options Research Report, prepared by Gary Gastineau and John Hornblower, five main advantages of using stock index futures available to international equity investors are highlighted: (1) lower transaction costs, (2) the opportunity to avoid withholding tax on cash dividends, (3) flexible foreign exchange exposure at nominal cost, (4) faster settlement, (5) greater liquidity, and (6) lower market impact from transactions in the futures markets.

In one dramatic example based on a $25 million S&P 500 portfolio, the Salomon Brothers report calculated an institutional money manager would have to hold an equivalent position in common stocks for over 6.5 years before it was more economical than using futures. This calculation was based on rolling the futures position over quarterly at fair-value; a round-turn commission of $30 throughout the holding period; S&P 500 futures contract face value of $135,000 ($500 times the Index with the Index value at 270); futures bid-ask spread of .05; and a common stock commission of 10 cents per share.

Another Salomon Brothers research report states that stock index futures and options offer a low-cost method of changing a portfolio's risk profile without disturbing its underlying position. According to the report, "growing derivative markets are partially responsible for shrinking liquidity in the stock market: The newer instruments compete directly for investment dollars. Investors who do use derivatives to realign equity exposure are taking advantage of this shift in liquidity from one market to another."

Aside from the attraction of lower commissions, an increasing number of managers are using stock index futures as a substitute for assuming actual cash positions. This competition between stock index futures and the cash equity market has highlighted some of the structural deficiencies in equities trading while propelling market and regulatory competition to a higher level.

Fiduciary Obligations

When the law governing tax-exempt pension fund management, the Employee Retirement Income Security Act (ERISA) was passed in 1974, it did not contain any specific ruling on the use of futures in a tax-exempt portfolio. Instead, ERISA's general concern for fiduciary's making an investment decision was that they seek both diversification of plan assets and be prudent.

In June 1979, the Pension and Welfare Benefit Administration division of the U.S. Department of Labor clarified the original Act to elaborate on the permissible transactions allowed under the "prudent man rule." It is this rule that generally governs a fiduciary's responsibility to a pension plan.

Becoming a fiduciary involves a different level of administrative involvement in a tax-exempt fund's management. A fiduciary is defined as anyone with discretionary authority who has control over the assets of a pension plan, or someone who gives investment counsel to the plan.

In a 1979 clarification of the Act, investment guidelines for private plans were detailed, which included a legal list of permissible investments. Under ERISA and its prudent man rule, before a fiduciary makes an investment, they must consider not only the type of investment, but its risk and potential rates of return. Also, all investments must be made for the exclusive benefit of plan participants and their beneficiaries. The ruling also required that if the corporation that administers the pension fund assets (the plan sponsor) is not familiar with the investment characteristics, it must rely on an expert who is familiar with the investment.

The permissibility of using futures and options in a tax-exempt portfolio was covered in the June 1979 ERISA clarification. Three main permissible uses of futures and options were covered in the U.S. Department of Labor's ruling from the plan perspective:

- Futures can be used to diversify plan assets.
- Futures can be used for hedging.
- Futures can be used for speculative purposes to achieve asset appreciation.

With futures permissible in tax-exempt portfolios, trading managers now had to find a way to legally structure their trading and advisory roles. As an example, when Mount Lucas Management Corp., Princeton, New Jersey, was named as a futures fund manager by the Eastman Kodak pension fund, Mount Lucas registered as an investment advisor with the Securities and Exchange Commission, in addition to its previous CFTC registration as a CTA and CPO.

By registering as an investment advisor, Mount Lucas became a fiduciary to a pension plan and was subject to a number of restrictions. These included being subject to due diligence reviews; being responsible for supervising and monitoring investment activities; and also being subject to a group of prohibited transactions. An aspect of a prohibited transaction is avoiding apparent conflicts of interest, such as not being able to participate in commission revenues.

As a fiduciary, an investment manager is individually responsible for certain functions of plan and investment administration, and if a violation occurs, the fiduciary may be forced to make restitution to the pension plan.

THE ROLE OF BANKS IN MANAGED FUTURES

While the managed futures industry expanded its traditional customer base to attract larger numbers of retail and institutional funds, this growth occurred largely without widespread bank participation. Traditionally, U.S. banks were severely restricted by their regulators from engaging in any futures-related activities. This included banks chartered under federal law (national banks), state-chartered banks that were members of the Federal Reserve Board or whose deposits were insured by the Federal Deposit Insurance Corporation (FDIC), and bank holding companies and their affiliates.

These restrictions extended to engaging in protective hedging strategies unless the bank could directly prove the hedge covered direct bank exposures to price fluctuations, such as those in interest rates, precious metals or foreign currencies. Generally, banks were prohibited from engaging in an activity that could jeopardize a bank's safety and soundness, or add risk to deposited funds or ultimately, the national monetary system.

In 1980, however, the Office of the Comptroller of the Currency, the Federal Reserve Board, and the FDIC liberalized their rule interpretations to allow national banks to buy and sell futures for portfolio operations, asset-liability management and dealer-bank trading activities. The regulations have since allowed financial futures (including stock index futures), options on futures and forward contracts to be used in the bank's risk management operations.

Under these guidelines, the responsibility for both creating and monitoring an individual bank's financial futures trading policy and risk exposure resides with the bank's board of directors. Part of this responsibility also includes maintaining a recordkeeping and reporting system for bank management. All of these functions can be done by the bank or its custodian.

The first nationally chartered bank to engage in futures trading was J.P. Morgan, the parent of Morgan Guaranty Bank, which in late-1982 received approval from the U.S. Treasury, Federal Reserve Board, Comptroller of the Currency, and other bank regulators to use the financial futures and precious metals markets to hedge its price exposures in the underlying cash instruments. Since then, other banks such as Northern Trust and Security Pacific have created separate futures operations to accommodate customer trading. But only a few banks—Chase Manhattan, Julius Baer, Union Planters, Manufacturers Hanover, and Chemical Bank—have moved into the managed futures area. Of these, only Chase Manhattan had introduced any managed commodity fund offerings by 1991.

A partial reason for this slow start is due to the strict regulation each banking institution faces. For example, Chase Manhattan, as a registered CTA, is supervised by eight federal regulatory authorities covering banking activities; bank holding company activities; foreign operations securities regulation; and futures regulation. Any U.S. bank acting as a pool sponsor faces similar restrictions. In addition, if the bank engages in customer solicitation outside of the United States, it is subject to local regulations in the appropriate countries where customer solicitation occurs.

While the history in this area is shortlived, the best example of banking activity in the managed commodity fund area is provided by Chase Manhattan which launched its first fund, a $70 million offshore private placement in the last quarter of 1989. The fund traded 15 foreign currencies in the forward foreign exchange markets. Foreign currency futures were not used. The fund initially used three advisors. By early 1991, this same fund employed eight managers who continued their original strategy of only trading foreign exchange forward contracts.

According to a senior Chase Manhattan official, the reason the fund used foreign currency forward markets was because they are more liquid than the futures markets and serve as "an ideal open end-type instrument."

In April 1990, Chase introduced its first guaranteed fund with Chase Manhattan Bank issuing its own Letter of Credit. As in other guaranteed funds, to assure the integrity of the designated principal amount, the funds are invested in zero coupon bonds or U.S. Treasuries, that are pledged to the general partner, or one of its affiliates, to fix the fund's reimbursement obligation as specified in the Letter of Credit. Upon maturity, the guarantee instruments are redeemed to meet the reimbursement obligation. The issuer of a Letter of Credit may also charge a per annum fee or a fee based on the face amount of the instrument.

When a bank decides to move into the managed commodity area, it must first insulate itself from the partnership and its trading activities such as acting as both trader and advisor. This separation is most commonly done through a bank holding company. This is because the bank cannot use pool assets as collateral or acquire an interest in those assets.

Similarly, bank holding companies cannot purchase ownership interest in the pool except for customers who would have sole investment control over those assets.

The Glass-Steagal Act, passed in 1933 as part of Depression-era reform of banking excesses, prevents banks from selling and issuing securities, including futures. Today, banks can trade securities through a subsidiary, usually a trust department, but only as part of "nonbank activities."

Traditionally, bank activities in the managed futures area are limited to issuing Letters of Credit or acting as a guarantor for specific funds. This function is provided by the bank's corporate finance department. But as these products became more innovative, new financing approaches are continuing to develop.

For instance, in order to provide the key feature in guarantee funds, three approaches are commonly used: Letters of Credit; segregating a portion of fund assets in a separate account combined with zero coupon Treasury bills; or a combination of the two approaches. An example of this last approach was the Letter of Credit issued by Citibank to guarantee the principal of the Dean Witter Principal Guaranteed Fund.

Creative financing techniques, combined with asset allocation strategies and revisions in the Glass-Steagal Act should generate increased bank interest in trading, as well as in introducing new managed futures products. For these reasons, a less commonly known institutional banking function—the custodian role—is becoming increasingly important in managed futures.

The Role of the Custodian

For the institutional banking client, all trading transactions—whether they be in stocks, bonds, or futures—are held by a master recordkeeper called the *custodian.* Custody is generally defined as the combination of bank services designed to facilitate the safekeeping, settlement and reporting of a fund's securities transactions both domestically and worldwide. Custody has become increasingly important as more plan sponsors trade internationally and because many foreign markets do not permit the transfer of ownership certificates outside their national borders.

The domestic or global custodian (depending on the scope of the institution's investment activity) is the center of back-office activity between the fund client and the actual money managers. In futures trading where there is a manager-of-manager situation, the custodian interfaces between the master futures manager and the institution.

As described by Fred Settlemeyer, manager of institutional trust services at the Boston Safe Deposit & Trust Co., "the role of the custodian has become increasingly important not only domestically, but on a global basis as well." The need by institutional clients for an "official recordkeeper," information provider and "official calculator of performance" has never been more clearly stated, he said.

Pension plans and endowments are institutions that require sophisticated custody and accounting capabilities. Among the trading and back-office services provided by custodians or master trustees are: safekeeping, price settlement, accounting, performance measurement, securities lending and investment support services. Interestingly, only a handful of custodians are currently capable of providing these services to the managed futures industry on a global basis. Exceptions to this include The Northern Trust Company, Chicago, and Boston Safe.

Both are major forces in the custodian business and in Northern Trust's case, the bank is also a FCM.

The custodian's role is not well understood in the futures industry. This is because few custodians have moved into providing services for futures or managed futures trading. This contrasts with the equities side where custodians provide trade settlement and reporting functions and are responsible for the safekeeping of the individual equity issues. Built upon this core are a number of other services, such as securities lending, performance measurement, performing manager evaluations, and producing an assortment of customized reports that pension plan sponsors require for tax, fiduciary, and manager monitoring requirements.

To fulfill the custodian function, accurate and timely futures trade reporting is essential. To accomplish this, it is important to define the concept of risk in futures trading. Many custodians are familiar with measuring the impact of betas on equity portfolios or fixed income instrument duration. It is also possible to do this with a portfolio containing futures if the advisor's trading characteristics are specified.

In its most basic form, risk assessment includes the use of accrual accounting that is flexible enough to give an accurate daily picture of a futures fund's activity. The custodian handles all the cash transactions and may interface with the various brokers, although the amount of contact varies depending on the custody relationship.

On a daily basis, the custodian oversees all trades being opened or closed, cash activity from various FCMs and daily position reconciliation. From this information, the custodian is in a central position to prepare a variety of reports ranging from individual manager returns to reports on which sectors of the futures markets accounted for losses or gains. The custodian is also in a position to ascertain the performance impact of a futures strategy on an equity position.

To generate more timely reports, many custodians entering the futures area have developed personal computer-to-personal computer links for trade reporting. These, in turn, can be connected to the custodian's mainframe computer. Global custodians are increasingly entering the futures area as their institutional clients become more active in non-U.S. futures and options markets. The first global custodian to provide futures and options trade processing was The Northern Trust.

One key service many custodians provide is performance measurement. Since most custodians are viewed as the chief performance calculator, the custodian must accurately reflect the returns from each asset class in a diversified portfolio so the managers are judged fairly. (Diversified institutional portfolios routinely contain real estate, venture capital, and warrants, in addition to domestic and global bonds and equities.) The problem with attributing performance results from the global custodian's accounting perspective is that each derivative has its own unique return characteristics.

Within the global custody world, performance on futures and options is derived by identifying or calculating the "value added" to a portfolio or underlying group of assets as a result of different derivative trading strategies. Options, for example, are basically considered a liability and carry a negative market value. Alternately, futures have a constantly changing market value so there is also difficulty in computing a return.

These special problems can be overcome by isolating the value-added component from futures and options trading. One approach many consultants and custodians have developed uses performance measurement systems that build up performance from basic levels. For instance, each individual equity sector (small capitalization stocks, blue chips, etc.) provide their own return. Above that are returns from the larger category, such as U.S. or global equities. In the case of Boston Safe, trades in this last category can be delineated by the return they contribute to the U.S. equity component. When using derivitives, the difference between the overall return and the individual market sector could be attributed to the impact of futures and options trading, according to Fred Settlemeyer of Boston Safe. This performance attribution system works well when the assets are clearly categorized within a specific portfolio.

While the performance question remains, bank custodians will continue to develop a growing presence in managed futures simply by virtue of their ability to centralize financial and trade reporting in their client's own language and format. As a result, banks will continue to play a larger role in expanding the uses of managed futures.

THE FUTURE OF MANAGED FUTURES

The growth of managed futures has paralleled the increasing institutionalization of the futures industry. This is evident industry-wide, from the changing composition of the trading floor population and the increasing need for more electronic forms of trading, to the proliferation of more sophisticated trading strategies to assist in asset allocation and the creation of synthetic instruments.

Due to the increasingly complex international marketplace, new trading strategies often require more capital to take advantage of smaller price discrepancies worldwide. As a result, the more established futures managers are linking up with better capitalized investment firms to finance their search for new trading technology and risk capital.

For example, in July 1991, the Blackstone Group, a private merchant bank, formed a new joint venture with the Kenmar Group, a futures trading manager, to access the institutional market. In July 1989, Commodities Corporation, one of the U.S.'s largest futures fund managers, formed a partnership with ORIX Corporation, Japan's largest leasing company, to create ORIX Commodities Corp., one of the first joint venture commodity trading companies created in Japan. ORIX reportedly paid $80 million to purchase 30 percent of Commodities Corporation.

Commodities Corporation is generally recognized as a major force in managed futures. Created in 1969 with $2.5 million in trading capital, by 1991 the corporation had about $1 billion under management ($240 million in proprietary funds and $800 million in customer funds). In 1991, the company employed about 75 traders to manage its combined asset pool.

According to Robert Easton, president and chief executive officer of Commodities Corporation, international trading requires "a presence and a strong trading partner." Easton said that by March 1991, 10 percent of CCA's trading capital was originating from Japan. Easton said he expects the firm to continue to trade across many markets using as many trading approaches as is feasible. The key restraint on seeking global diversification is creating a sufficient pool of speculative capital. For this reason, Easton foresees continued development of "mega-funds" ranging in size from $50 million to $260 million. In 1990, Easton said the company was trading in 60 different futures markets worldwide.

In March 1991, Paul Tudor Jones, of Tudor Investments, New York, formed a joint venture with Nomura Securities Co., the largest securities firm in the world, to supplement their futures trading worldwide. A year earlier, Nomura also began supplementing its worldwide program trading operations. The new venture, Tudor/Nomura Global Trading Partners, was created as a 50/50 partnership initially capitalized at $60 million. Again, some of the same drives prompted the joint venture: the need for more capital, a stronger trading presence worldwide, access to a more extensive sales network, and more resources to develop advanced trading technologies. A senior Nomura official also said the complexity of today's investment world can act to reduce profits. The venture with Tudor is expected to allow Nomura to better cope with that complexity.

Paul Tudor Jones has earned a reputation as one of the world's most successful commodities speculators. Since he began trading customer funds in 1984, Jones has posted a 75 percent compounded annual rate of return and surpassed almost every other investment return during the period. Prior to the Nomura joint venture, Tudor managed about $650 million in customer funds. Jones' trading success is not tied to any one strategy or market, but is a hybrid approach combining fundamental and technical approaches with worldwide cash and futures market asset allocation.

The modern, internationally managed futures fund is emerging as the ultimate trading vehicle—an advanced hedge fund, able to trade worldwide, using any strategy to trade any exchange-listed or off-exchange, hybrid instrument. These new funds will be able to wring trading profits out of any temporary market inefficiency worldwide and engage in arbitrage, whether it be financial, regulatory, or tax-related.

The importance of managed futures is also evident in other areas. On the exchange trading floor, fund managers have increasingly replaced the role of individual speculators and floor locals by providing incremental liquidity across the trading floor. This development also should have an effect on new product introductions as fund managers become more important in providing liquidity to new contracts and electronic trading systems. Futures money managers will continue to be an important new audience not only for futures-specific electronic trading systems, such as Globex, the worldwide after hours trading system being developed by the Chicago Mercantile Exchange, Chicago Board of Trade, and Reuters PLC, but also for other electronic financial technology.

Among the major national wirehouses, managed futures divisions are making greater contributions to their respective firm's overall operating profits. At Dean Witter, for example, one of the nation's four largest brokerage firms, it is estimated that 20 to 25 percent of the firm's overall net income has been generated by the managed futures division. Revenues from this division alone are estimated at $100 million. (Dean Witter originated one of the most successful managed futures offerings ever in July 1988 when it raised $531 million in one day for its $250 million Principal Guaranteed Fund.) Other national wirehouses with larger sales forces also are expected to play an increasing role in offering managed futures programs to all levels of their client base.

Unfortunately, this enviable industry growth also has some detrimental side effects. As the popularity of managed futures increases, many successful managers are facing capacity constraints in terms of the amount of money they can successfully manage vis a vis the size of the individual futures contract markets. While some managed futures experts say the capacity question is overstated, others feel the pool of trading capital may exceed available market opportunities.

The capacity question is a function of both the liquidity of the underlying markets and each manager's own internal investment management abilities. For the industry to continue its successful expansion, it will need both additional individual futures speculators and commercial hedgers. All of these different market participants, with their varying strategies, opinions, timeframes, and capital, will be needed to make the markets more liquid.

Pension funds that have used the financial futures markets should become a major source for this new liquidity as they push for new ways to diversify their portfolios. One new way to achieve this is by including traditional perishable commodities in the portfolio. In anticipation of this, Goldman Sachs introduced its own production-weighted commodity index in April 1991 specifically for institutional investors. The attraction of the Goldman Sachs Commodity Index is that it incorporates a commodity's yield into the Index. In addition, more institutions are using nonexchange-traded financial instruments. This could result in more swap and currency forward market activity, for example, from fund managers who would only use exchange-listed futures for rebalancing or making temporary risk adjustments in their portfolios.

As the futures industry continues to evolve, it will also be accompanied by a debate over manager compensation. As more dynamic managers take on additional risks to achieve superior returns, they will expect higher compensation. Higher fees should encounter more plan sponsor resistance. Because of this, the managed futures industry can expect to see additional pressure for incentive fees to increase at the expense of monthly management fees. For example, incentive fees of 25 or 30 percent would not be uncommon if accompanied by monthly management fees of 1 and 2 percent respectively.

New trading strategies derived from combining artificial intelligence, historical simulations and new applications of tested theory will also be incorporated into the markets. Mount Lucas Management Co. can test an algorithm using historical data going back 30 years. One Chicago proprietary trading firm uses 15 years of tick-by-tick trading data on key markets which are screened by artificial intelligence to discern price patterns over any possible time frame. These historical patterns are then compared against live trading data. Richmond Financial Resources, Richmond, Texas, has also developed an exclusively automated trading operation. Variations of these techniques will soon be used by other firms to manage institutional money.

Finally, there may also be an impetus to re-define who is the actual institutional customer in the managed futures industry. If an increasing number of banks enter the managed commodity markets, the banks themselves could become the institution by issuing their own Letters of Credit, moving daily management of the manager activities inhouse and then selling the services of their multimanager portfolios to their own established client base through their existing bank marketing network. If this scenario develops, banks could replace some of the large wholesale managed futures managers who currently look to the bank to only provide Letters of Credit.

The success of guarantee funds also could become the industry's major product breakthrough in popularizing managed futures to a larger audience. The introduction of new concepts such as this should mark the beginning of an increased acceptance level for managed futures.

The remaining chapters of this book address the theoretical and practical applications of using managed futures. Each chapter's intent is to present a specific aspect of a professionally managed futures program so it can ultimately become a permanent feature of a diversified institutional portfolio.

In preparing these chapters, experts in their respective fields were searched out who were willing to share their knowledge. While certain readers may disagree with some of their conclusions, each chapter provides a starting point for an institutional investor to begin examining how this important new investment class can supplement their ongoing activities.

PART ONE

THE FOUNDATIONS

2 THE POTENTIAL ROLE OF MANAGED FUTURES IN INSTITUTIONAL PENSION PORTFOLIOS

Scott H. Irwin

Managed futures is a relatively new investment alternative. For all practical purposes, this investment did not exist prior to 1975. Investment in managed futures grew substantially during the 1980s. Today, reasonable estimates suggest the investment in managed futures is about $20 billion.

Broadly speaking, managed futures is an investment for the purpose of speculating in futures and options markets. A professional trading advisor (known as a Commodity Trading Advisor or CTA) is employed to manage the trading in futures and options markets. Trading is typically diversified across a number of futures and options contracts and safeguards are built-in to prevent a total loss of capital.

It is useful to divide the managed futures industry into retail and wholesale sectors. The retail sector consists of individual managed accounts and public and private commodity pools. Initial investment in these vehicles may be as small as $5000. Not surprisingly, costs are high for retail investors. The wholesale sector, with substantially lower costs, is dominated by institutional pension plans, best described as a large managed account.

From the perspective of an institutional investor, three basic questions should be answered before investing in a managed futures program:

1. Should managed futures be held in a securities portfolio?
2. What proportions of portfolios should be invested in managed futures?
3. How much will portfolio performance improve with the addition of managed futures?

This chapter reviews the academic evidence regarding each of these questions. First, Modern Portfolio Theory is reviewed because it is the conceptual framework used in nearly all of the academic studies. Second, academic studies of managed futures investment performance are reviewed. Finally, implications of the results of the academic studies for institutional investors are considered.

MODERN PORTFOLIO THEORY

Basic Statistical Concepts

Before delving into Modern Portfolio Theory (MPT), two statistical concepts need to be reviewed. First, MPT significantly emphasizes risk as a component of portfolio analysis. Risk is usually thought of as the possibility or probability of loss. A natural extension of this idea looks at risk as the probability investors will fail to achieve the return they expect on their investment.

This approach to quantifying risk does not measure the possibility of loss alone. Risk is seen as uncertainty. That is, the likelihood that what is expected will fail to happen, whether the outcome is better or worse than expected. So an unexpected return on either the upside or the downside counts in deciding how "risky" an investment is. For example, a return of either 5 or 15 percent, when you expect a return of 10 percent, is equally "risky."

To summarize, an investment whose returns are not likely to depart much, if at all, from its expected or average return is said to have little risk. An investment whose returns are quite volatile from period to period, often departing from the expected or average return, is said to be quite risky.

This method of approaching risk can be quantified by using a statistical measure called the ***standard deviation of returns***. Standard deviation measures the dispersion of returns from period-to-period from the average or mean return. Thus, it indicates the volatility of the investment. The larger the standard deviation of an investment, the less likely you are to get exactly the return you expect, though an investor may get more, instead of less, for any period of time.

The second statistical concept crucial to MPT is the correlation between investment returns. Correlation is the tendency for investment returns to move up and down together. The statistical measure of this tendency is the correlation coefficient, which can take on values between −1 and +1. Interpretation of the correlation coefficient is simple: A negative value means the returns from two investments tend to move in opposite directions. A positive value means that returns tend to move in the same direction. The closer values are to −1 or +1, the more pronounced are the tendencies.

For the purpose of controlling the risk or variability of returns on a portfolio, a negative correlation coefficient is desirable. In fact, the best possible correlation coefficient is −1, which indicates that the returns from two investments always move in exactly opposite directions. Thus, returns for the two investments smooth out portfolio returns by counterbalancing each other. The worst possible correlation coefficient is +1, which indicates that the returns from two investments are perfectly synchronized.

Diversification

The basic premise of MPT is that investors should only be concerned with the expected returns and risks of investment portfolios. An important assumption of MPT is that all investors are risk-averse. In other words, investors want high returns and guaranteed incomes. The theory tells how risk-averse investors should combine individual investments in their portfolios to give them the least risk possible, consistent with the return they seek. To quote Burton Malkiel, "The theory gives a rigorous mathematical justification to the age-old investment maxim that diversification is a sensible strategy for investors wanting to reduce risk."

An example will help illustrate the basics of MPT. Suppose an investor has $10,000 to invest and is considering two investments, A and B. The total returns of A and B over the last four years are shown in Table 2.1. If the entire $10,000 is invested in either A or B, and returns vary in the future as they have in the past, then the expected return per year for either investment is $800, or 8 percent. However, the actual return could be negative due to the risks of either investment. If the investor places half the money in each investment, the expected return will still be $800 per year, or 8 percent, but this return will be much less risky. The same results are graphed in Figure 2.1, where it can be seen that the portfolio's returns are not nearly so volatile as are those of the individual investments.

Why was the portfolio's return in the previous example less risky than either of the individual investments? The reason is that the return on investments A and B did not move in the same direction at the same time. If the return on investments A and B always moved in the same direction and by the same amount, then diversification across the investments would not reduce risk. Thus a crucial factor for constructing portfolios is the degree of correlation between investment returns.

TABLE 2.1. **Rates of return on investment A, investment B, and a portfolio consisting of 50 percent in both investments.**

	Rate of Return (percent)		
Year	A	B	Portfolio
1	20	−10	5
2	−5	25	10
3	19	−5	7
4	−2	22	10
Average Annual Return	8	8	8
Annual Standard Deviation	13	18	3

FIGURE 2.1. Rates of return on investment A, investment B, and portfolio consisting of 50 percent in each investment.

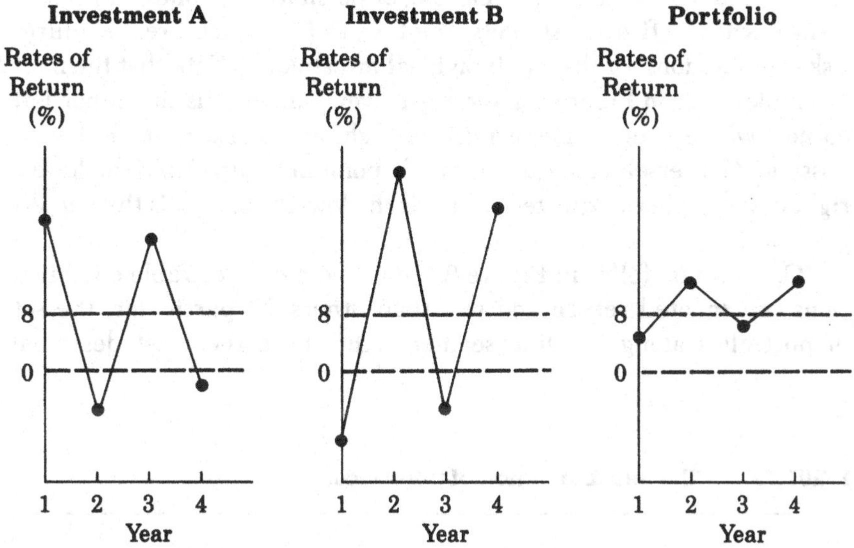

The Efficient Frontier

It should now be clear that portfolios are likely to offer improved return-risk tradeoffs. The example presented in Table 2.1 and Figure 2.1 is a good illustration of basic portfolio diversification. However, the proportions of the two investments (50 percent A and 50 percent B) were selected arbitrarily. MPT suggests a better procedure is to form portfolios that are said to be "efficiently" diversified. An efficient portfolio is a feasible, or possible, portfolio that possesses the following two properties: (1) no other feasible portfolio has the same expected return and a lower risk, and (2) no other feasible portfolio has the same risk level and a higher expected return. All feasible portfolios that do not possess the previous two properties are said to be "inefficient." From the perspective of a risk-averse investor, efficient portfolios "dominate" inefficient portfolios. An example will help demonstrate why this is true.

Figure 2.2 shows the results of efficient and inefficient portfolio diversification for a hypothetical set of five investments. The umbrella-shaped area represents all the feasible, or possible, portfolios that can be formed with the five investments. Points C, D, E, F, and G are the return-risk combinations for the five individual investments. Note that the most desirable point in Figure 2.2 for a risk-averse investor is the upper-left corner, where expected return is the highest and risk is at the lowest possible. Conversely, the least desirable point in Figure 2.2 is the lower-right corner, where expected return is the lowest and risk is the highest possible.

Certain portfolios in Figure 2.2 do have more desirable combinations of expected return and risk than others. In particular, the set of portfolios along the line segment ABC have the most desirable

FIGURE 2.2. The feasible region of portfolios.

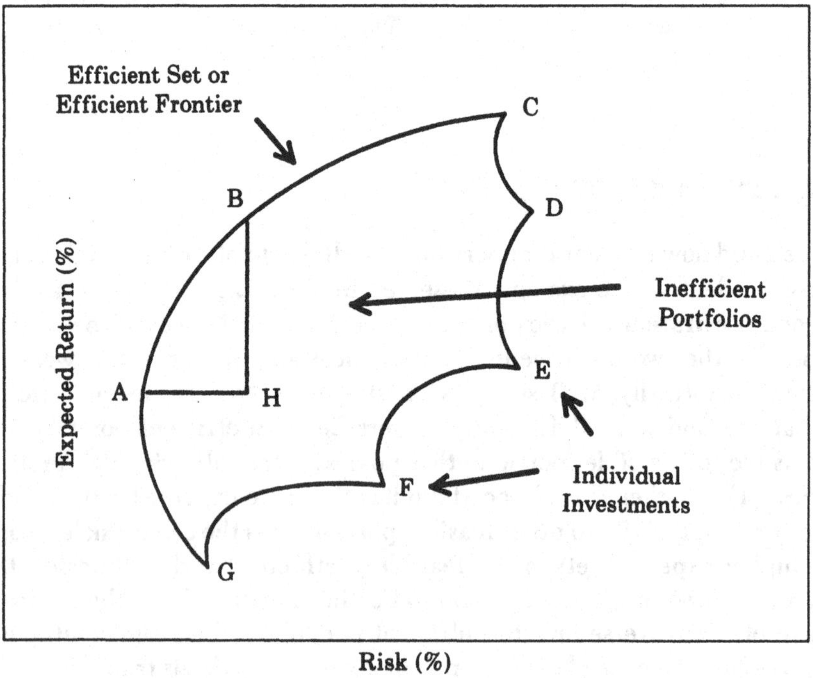

return-risk combinations of all feasible portfolios. This set of efficient portfolios is called the efficient frontier.

Notice that portfolios lying along the efficient frontier do actually dominate all other points in the feasible region (umbrella-shaped area). Consider portfolio H, which does not lie on the efficient frontier even though it is a feasible portfolio. No investor desiring maximum expected return for a given amount of risk would hold portfolio H, since portfolios A and B on the efficient frontier are clearly superior. Efficient portfolio B has the same risk level as portfolio H, but a substantially higher expected return. Efficient portfolio A has the same expected return as portfolio H, but a lower risk level. Therefore, no investor would hold portfolio H, which is said to be "dominated" by portfolios on the efficient frontier.

It is important to be aware of two important characteristics of the efficient frontier. First, the efficient frontier is made up of many possible portfolio "mixes." Point A may be an efficient portfolio that devotes 10 percent to investment G, 30 percent to investment F, and 60 percent to investment D. Point B may be an efficient portfolio that devotes 50 percent to investment D and 50 percent to investment C. Second, each portfolio on the efficient frontier has a different expected return and risk.

Optimal Portfolios

Locating the efficient frontier is the first step of investment decision-making based on MPT. The second step is selecting the efficient portfolio that maximizes an investor's "satisfaction." In more precise terms, this is the selection of an investor's optimal portfolio.

Recall from Figure 2.2 that investor satisfaction is maximized when expected return is the highest and risk is the lowest. However, the optimal portfolio for an individual investor is not simply the efficient portfolio closest to the upper left corner in Figure 2.2. The reason is that investors differ with respect to their preferred tradeoff of expected return and risk. (In more technical terms, investors exhibit different degrees of risk aversion.) Thus, portfolio A in Figure 2.2 may maximize one investor's satisfaction and portfolio B may maximize a different investor's satisfaction. One can think of the efficient frontier as providing a menu of portfolios from which investors make their selections. It is important to emphasize that investors should select only those portfolios on the efficient frontier. To do otherwise, according to MPT, would be inefficient.

The selection of an investor's optimal portfolio can be greatly simplified if borrowing and lending at a risk-free rate of interest is possible. By definition, there is no uncertainty regarding the return to a risk-free asset. A real-world asset that yields a good approximation of a risk-free rate of return is U.S. Treasury bills.

With the existence of a risk-free asset, an investor determines the amount of funds to borrow or lend at the risk-free rate and the amount to invest in a portfolio of risky assets. This situation is illustrated in Figure 2.3. Expected return and risk combinations of the risk-free asset and an arbitrary portfolio S of risky assets are represented by the straight line R_FST. If all funds are lent at the risk-free rate, then the return will be R_F and risk will be zero. If all funds are invested in the portfolio of risky assets S, then the return will be R_s and the risk will be σ_S. If some fraction

FIGURE 2.3. Expected return and risk combinations with a risk-free asset and a portfolio of risky assets.

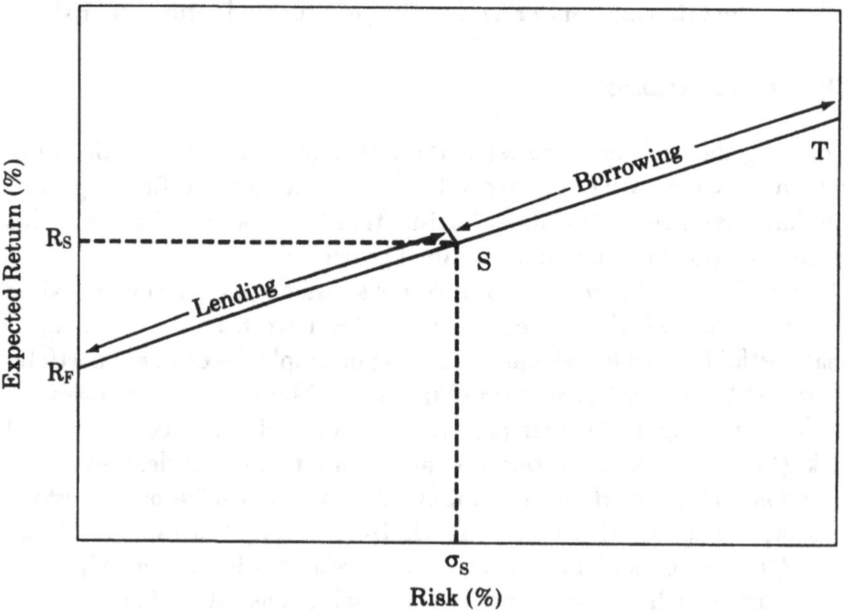

of funds are lent at the risk-free rate and the remainder invested in the portfolio of risky assets, then return-risk combinations are given by line segment R_FS. Note that return and risk for these combinations are between those of the risk-free asset and the portfolio of risky assets. If some fraction of funds are borrowed at the risk-free rate, then return-risk combinations are given by line segment ST. This illustrates the well-known impact of leverage upon investment return and risk.

Now consider the possibility of borrowing and lending at the risk-free rate and investing in an efficient portfolio. Combinations of the risk-free asset and efficient portfolios A, B, and C are represented in Figure 2.4. Portfolios along R_FB are preferred to portfolios along R_FA, because at every point along R_FB expected return is higher relative to risk (and vice versa). For the same reason, portfolios along R_FC are preferred to those along R_FB. In fact, the highest possible expected return for a given level of risk is found along R_FC, the line tangent to the efficient frontier.

FIGURE 2.4. Expected return and risk combinations with a risk-free asset and efficient portfolios.

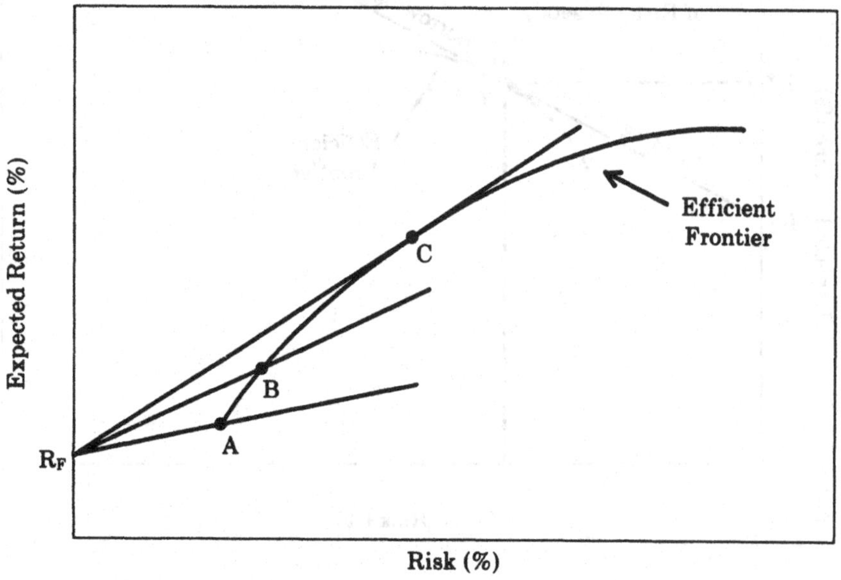

We can now specify the optimal portfolio of risky assets. As shown in Figure 2.5, portfolio C is the optimal portfolio of risky assets because expected return is maximized relative to risk along R_FC. It is important to reiterate that investors *do not* necessarily place all funds in portfolio C. More risk-averse investors may select portfolios along R_FC by lending some fraction of funds at the risk-free rate and investing the remainder in an optimal risky portfolio. Other less risk-averse investors may select portfolios along CD by borrowing funds at the risk-free rate and investing both the original and borrowed funds in the optimal risky portfolio. However, regardless of which combination is selected, the composition of the risky portfolio is precisely the same as that of portfolio C.

FIGURE 2.5. The optimal portfolio of risky assets with borrowing and lending at the risk-free rate.

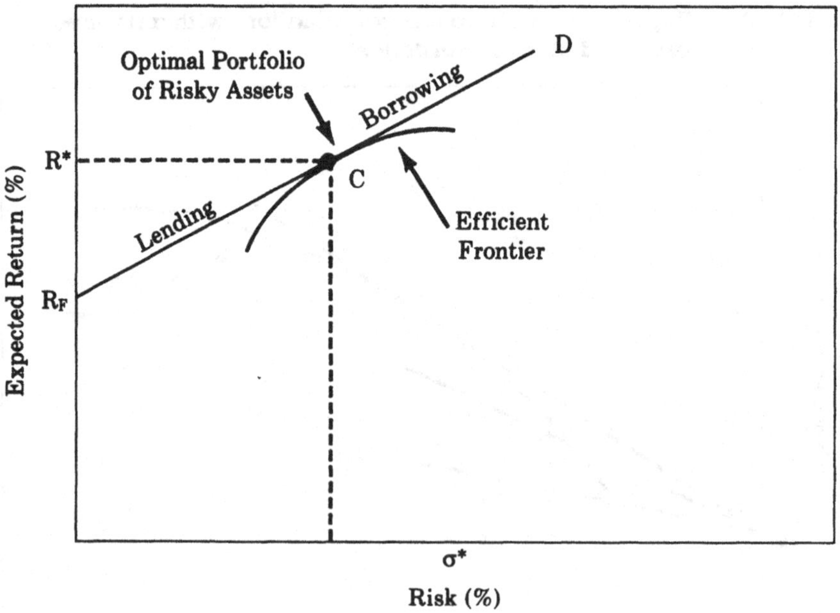

MANAGED FUTURES: EVIDENCE OF PORTFOLIO PERFORMANCE

A number of academic studies have investigated the investment performance of managed futures. The theoretical framework used in nearly all studies was Modern Portfolio Theory. As such, the objective of the studies was to test whether the addition of managed futures to well-diversified securities portfolios caused (ex-post) a positive shift in the efficient frontier. This type of shift is illustrated in Figure 2.6. Assume that the only difference between Efficient Frontier I and Efficient Frontier II is that investment in managed futures is allowed in the latter, but not the former. Since Efficient Frontier II dominates Efficient Frontier I, it can be said that investment in managed futures produced a favorable shift in expected return-risk tradeoffs. Also note that comparison of optimal portfolios A and B yields the same

FIGURE 2.6. A positive shift in the efficient frontier.

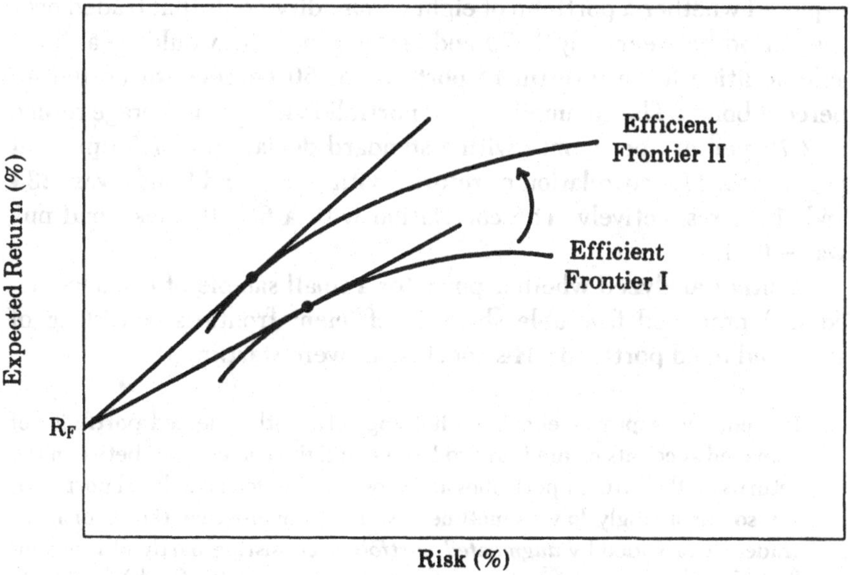

conclusion. That is, B dominates A because B has a higher expected return and lower risk.

Most academic studies have concentrated on one segment of the managed futures industry-public commodity pools. This is due to the availability of reliable return data for public pools over relatively long sample periods. However, as noted earlier, public commodity pools have a retail-level cost structure that is not likely to be relevant to institutional investors.

With this caution in mind, the next section examines academic studies of public commodity pool investment performance. Then, the costs of different managed futures investments will be examined and, finally, a review of a recent analysis relevant to institutional investors will be presented.

Investment Performance of Public Commodity Pools

Harvard Professor John Lintner was the first academic researcher to examine the investment performance of public commodity pools. He explored whether a portfolio of eight commodity pools that traded over the period between July 1979 and December 1982 would be a desirable addition to an investment portfolio of 60 percent stocks and 40 percent bonds. The commodity pool portfolio yielded an average return of 2.72 percent per month with a standard deviation of 7.35 percent per month. The correlation of returns with stocks and bonds was .234 and .151, respectively. The correlation with a 60:40 stock/bond mix was −.024.

Lintner analyzed whether pools (or a small sample of managed accounts) produced favorable shifts in efficient frontiers consisting of stock and bond portfolios. His conclusions were startling:

> Indeed, the improvements from holding efficiently selected portfolios of managed accounts or funds are so large—and the correlations between the returns on the futures-portfolios and those on the stock and bond portfolios are so surprisingly low (sometimes even negative)—that the return/risk tradeoffs provided by *augmented portfolios*, consisting partly of funds invested with appropriate groups of futures managers (or funds) combined

> with funds invested in portfolios of stocks alone (or in mixed portfolios of stocks and bonds), clearly dominate the tradeoffs available from portfolios of stocks (or from portfolios of stocks and bonds). Moreover, they do so by very considerable margins.

Lintner's research, and especially his conclusions, attracted considerable attention and stimulated additional research. Of particular concern to other researchers was the limited sample period considered by Lintner. Hence, researchers began gathering more comprehensive data on public commodity pool returns.

Irwin and Brorsen analyzed returns from 84 commodity pools that traded during the nine-year period of January 1975 through December 1983. The mean annual rate of return was 15.2 percent, with a corresponding annual standard deviation of 25.1 percent. Portfolio performance was studied by estimating efficient frontiers with and without investment in commodity pools. Irwin and Brorsen concluded that the addition of public commodity pools to a portfolio of Treasury-bills, bonds, and stocks increased the rate of return at all levels of risk. A concern with this study was that only five or fewer public pools traded during the first three years of the study period.

Murphy evaluated the performance of 11 commodity pools that traded over the five-year period May 1980 to April 1985. These pools used only technical trading systems. The 11 pools had a monthly arithmetic mean rate of return of 0.89 percent per month and a monthly geometric rate of return of 0.57 percent per month. The average standard deviation was 7.83 percent per month. After comparing the returns of the 11 pool market portfolio with stocks and stocks and bonds, Murphy concluded that technically traded pools performed adequately in a portfolio context, but there was no statistical evidence of abnormal returns above a naive buy-and-hold strategy.

Irwin and Landa updated the data base used by Irwin and Brorsen to include 1984 and 1985. As a result, their sample period covered the eleven-year period 1975 through 1985. They investigated the effects of adding real estate, buy-and-hold futures, public commodity pools, and gold to a traditional investment portfolio of stocks and bonds. Irwin and Landa concluded that commodity pools had a positive impact on expected return-risk tradeoffs of efficient stock and bond portfolios over the time period studied. Again, a concern with this study was that only five or fewer public pools traded during the first three years of the study period.

Elton, Gruber, and Rentzler studied the monthly returns of all public commodity pools active from July 1979 to June 1985. The data set ranged from 12 pools in the first year to 85 pools in the sixth year. Over the study period, commodity pools returned 0.73 percent per month for a monthly holding period, and −0.07 percent per month for an annual holding period. The standard deviation of returns was 11.3 percent per month. On average, commodity pools had a lower mean return and a higher standard deviation than common stocks, corporate bonds and Treasury-bills over both the six-year period and the previous 25-year period. Public commodity pool returns were found to have a small negative correlation with stock returns (−.121) and bond returns (−.003). In contrast to earlier studies, Elton, Gruber, and Rentzler found that the addition of public commodity pools did not produce a positive shift in the return-risk tradeoffs of stock and bond portfolios. Their conclusions were unequivocal:

> It is found that randomly selected funds offer neither an attractive alternative to bonds and stocks nor a profitable addition to a portfolio of stocks and bonds. Furthermore, past performance of these funds offers very little information about future performance.

Elton, Gruber, and Rentzler produced a second study in 1990 based on a longer sample period. In this study, public commodity pool returns from January 1980 through December 1988 were examined. They found no evidence that would reverse the conclusions stated in their previous paper.

The difference in results between the Elton, Gruber, and Rentzler studies and previous studies motivated further research by Irwin, Krukemyer, and Zulauf. They hypothesized that the difference in results may have been due to the variety of data periods investigated. In particular, studies that included data from the high return years of the late-1970s tended to find positive portfolio results (for example, Irwin and Brorsen, 1985). In contrast, studies that used samples solely from the 1980s reported negative portfolio results (Elton, Gruber, and Rentzler, 1990).

Irwin, Krukemyer, and Zulauf examined monthly return data for all public commodity pools active from January 1979 through December 1989. The sample was the most comprehensive used in a study of commodity pools. As hypothesized, public commodity pool returns were sensitive to the period examined. For a monthly holding period, pool returns averaged 1.125 percent per month over 1979 to 1989, but decreased to 0.599 percent per month over 1982 to 1989 and 0.751 percent per month over 1985 to 1989. Correlations between public commodity pool returns and stock and bond returns were near zero and were not highly sensitive to the sample period considered.

Not surprisingly, given the variation in public commodity pool returns over different time periods, the portfolio performance of commodity pools also was highly sensitive to the sample period considered. From 1979 to 1989, the addition of commodity pools produced a favorable shift in the return-risk tradeoffs of stock and bond portfolios. In contrast, over the 1982 to 1989 and 1985 to 1989 periods, public commodity pools did not generate a favorable shift.

These results confirmed Irwin, Krukemyer, and Zulauf's hypothesis that the difference in results of previous studies was due to the different sample periods investigated. Hence, their conclusion that additional years of observation are needed to confirm which period of analysis is consistent with long-term performance of public commodity pools.

In sum, the results of academic studies of public commodity pool performance have produced decidedly mixed results. The correlation of public commodity pool returns and stock and bond returns has been about zero, a beneficial level for producing diversification benefits. However, the level of public commodity pool returns has been so variable that a consistent shift in the return-risk tradeoff of stock and bond portfolios has not been observed.

Costs Charged to Managed Futures Investors

A number of researchers have attributed the performance problems of public commodity pools to high operating costs. Irwin and Brorsen produced the first estimates of the operating costs of public pools. They obtained cost data for 20 pools from audited prospectuses. At least one year of observations was gathered for each pool.

Two cost categories were formed by Irwin and Brorsen: commission costs; and management, incentive, and administrative costs. Each was expressed as a percent of average annual equity. Their results are reproduced in Table 2.2. Commission costs for the 20 public pools averaged 10.7 percent per year, with a range of 6.0 to 27.8 percent. They reported that the relatively high level of commission costs was due to the pools paying 70 to 80 percent of retail commission rates. Irwin ana Brorsen noted that the general partner for most pools is a brokerage firm, and that the same firm serves as the futures commission merchant

TABLE 2.2. Public commodity pool annual costs.

Public Commodity Pool	Average Annual Commission Cost (% of Average Equity)	Average Annual Management, Incentive, and Administrative Costs (% of Average Equity)	Total
1	27.8	3.6	31.4
2	7.0	4.1	11.1
3	18.7	5.9	24.6
4	12.1	10.1	22.2
5	10.7	8.4	19.1
6	6.0	23.8	29.8
7	6.9	15.5	20.4
8	6.3	10.1	16.4
9	10.3	11.4	21.7
10	13.3	0.7*	14.0
11	11.4	2.3*	13.7
12	7.7	13.3	21.0
13	9.6	7.7	17.3
14	8.5	4.4	12.9
15	9.6	9.2	18.8
16	11.9	6.1	18.0
17	11.8	5.4	17.2
18	7.2	11.9	19.1
19	8.9	4.2	13.1
20	8.4	12.6	21.0
Average	10.7	8.5	19.2

* Management and incentive fees were paid as a percent of commissions.

Source: Irwin and Brorsen (1985).

for the pool. Hence, given the trading volume generated by most public commodity pools, and thus the potential for reduced commission rates, general partners may be subject to conflict of interest.

Management, incentive and administrative costs averaged 8.5 percent of average annual equity in Irwin and Brorsen's sample, with a range of 0.7 percent to 23.8 percent. When reported separately, administrative costs were less than 2 percent per year. Trading advisors in 18 of the 20 pools were paid a fixed management fee 4 to 6 percent of average equity, with an incentive fee of 12 to 15 percent of gross trading profits.

Total cost averaged 19.2 percent per year, with a range of 11.1 percent to 31.4 percent. By comparison, investment costs of stock mutual funds are about one percent of annual equity. The comparison is even bleaker given the fact that Irwin and Brorsen's cost estimates do not account for initial sales commissions in the range of 8 to 10 percent of initial equity. Hence, public commodity pools face a major cost hurdle in generating competitive rates of return.

Two additional studies have examined the operating costs of public commodity pools. Murphy examined data which came from 11 technical public pools that traded from May 1980 through April 1985. He found that annual expenses as a percent of total equity ranged between 12.5 and 26.7 percent, with an average of 17.5 percent. Basso estimated the operating costs of 118 public commodity pools using 1988 data from the Commodity Futures Trading Commission. Total costs averaged 17.4 percent, with a range from 0.5 to 56.6 percent. Average commission charges were 9.3 percent of total equity. This ranged from 0.0 to 36.4 percent of equity.

The cost estimates produced in the three studies are highly consistent. Further, Irwin and Brorsen show that the costs imply that public commodity pools have generated substantial gross trading profits. Hence, portfolio performance on a net return basis could be markedly improved with a reduction in costs.

Cost reductions have in fact been a focus of institutional pension plans that have invested in managed futures programs. Institutions have negotiated much lower commission and management costs than those paid by public investors. A representative comparison of the costs paid by public and institutional investors in managed futures is presented in Table 2.3. Total costs for institutional investors are 10 to 12 percent of annual

TABLE 2.3. Annual managed futures investment costs.

	Management (% assets)	Incentive (% gross profits)	Commission (% assets)	Total (% assets)
Public Investors	5	20	9.3	17–18
Institutional Investors	2	25	2.5	10–11

Sources: Irwin and Brorsen (1985); Murphy (1986); Basso (1989); Hecht (1989).

equity, approximately eight percentage points less than costs for public commodity pools. The biggest cost reduction is in commissions, which are reduced from about 9 to 2 percent of annual equity. This reflects a much lower brokerage charge per trade.

Pro-Forma Managed Futures Performance

From the perspective of an institutional investor, a key issue is whether lower costs actually lead to a significant improvement in portfolio performance. This issue has been investigated by Irwin, Krukemyer, and Zulauf. Their analysis was conducted by adjusting monthly net returns of public commodity pools over 1979 to 1989 to reflect the lower costs paid by institutional investors.

The creation of the pro-forma managed futures return series required two steps. First, gross returns of public commodity pools were estimated. This entailed subtracting Treasury bill returns from net public pool returns and then adding back the public pool costs (assumed to be those listed in the first row of Table 2.3). Second, the net return to pro-forma managed futures was estimated by subtracting the costs of institutional investors from the estimated gross returns and adding back Treasury bill returns (institutional costs were assumed to be those listed in the second row of Table 2.3). Complete details of the procedure are reported in the Appendix of Irwin, Krukemyer, and Zulauf's paper.

Lowering costs did substantially impact portfolio performance. The addition of pro-forma managed futures produced a favorable shift in the return-risk tradeoff of stock and bond portfolios over each of the three sample periods considered (1979–1989, 1982–1989, 1985–1989). The improvement in the return-risk tradeoff of optimal portfolios over 1979 to 1989 was 27 percent. Smaller improvements, in the range of 1 to 5 percent, were reported for the two subperiods. Further, over 1979 to 1989, the optimal investment in pro-forma managed futures was 10 percent, the maximum level allowed in the analysis. Over the shorter samples, 1982 to 1989 and 1985 to 1989, proportions ranged from about 2 to 8 percent of optimal portfolios.

Irwin, Krukemyer, and Zulauf argued that the results provide strong evidence of the impact of costs on the investment performance of managed futures. First, the results suggested that cost reductions may be important for the future of public commodity pools as competitive investments. Second, the results suggest that institutional investors, through their ability to obtain lower costs than public investors, may benefit from investment in managed futures.

IMPLICATIONS FOR INSTITUTIONAL INVESTORS

In the introduction to this chapter, three basic questions regarding institutional investment in managed futures were asked:

1. Should managed futures be held in a securities portfolio?
2. What proportion of portfolios should be invested in managed futures?
3. How much will portfolio performance improve with the addition of managed futures?

Evidence from academic studies of managed futures investment performance based on MPT provides a reasonable basis for answering these questions. With regard to the first question, the answer depends crucially on the type of managed futures return series analyzed. If public commodity pool returns are examined, portfolio performance is mixed at best. On this evidence, most institutional investors would conclude that a conservative answer to the question is no.

However, if public commodity pool returns are adjusted for the lower costs institutional investors are charged, then a different picture emerges. With lower costs, portfolio performance improves to a level attractive to institutional investors. Perhaps the best conservative answer is that a managed futures program with carefully negotiated costs should not be dismissed easily.

If a managed futures investment program is initiated, the second question needs to be answered. Academic studies generally have limited the proportion of portfolios devoted to managed futures to no more than 10 percent. Investment in the range of 2 to 8 percent is likely to yield the return-risk benefits suggested by pro-forma analysis of commodity pool returns.

The third question is the bottom line: How much will overall portfolio performance improve with the addition of managed futures? First, it should be said that, given a relatively small investment in managed futures, miracles cannot be expected. Academic evidence suggests that a conservative estimate of the improvement in portfolio return-risk tradeoffs is in the range of 3 to 5 percent.

3 USING ALTERNATIVE INVESTMENT STRATEGIES AND MANAGED FUTURES ACCOUNTS IN PENSION PORTFOLIOS

Mike Dunmire

Plan sponsors are well aware of the need to diversify pension plan portfolios. However, until recently, plan sponsors could select from only a relatively small number of different management styles, all utilizing the same investment strategy, such as long stock positions. Considerable effort has been put into classifying conventional investment managers into styles such as growth, value, yield, rotation, which could be used by plan sponsors to diversify, and more importantly, reduce overall risk in a portfolio as measured by volatility.

Yet, while the underlying investment theory of diversification calls for using conventional managers who each utilize different investment styles (the multi-manager, multi-style approach) appears sound, in reality it has several restrictive shortcomings.

Figure 3.1 illustrates the risk/return characteristics of typical long stock portfolios for a five-year period. When return is calculated, it is expressed as the compounded annual return. Risk is measured by annual standard deviation of return.

FIGURE 3.1. The problem with "conventional" investment management approaches.

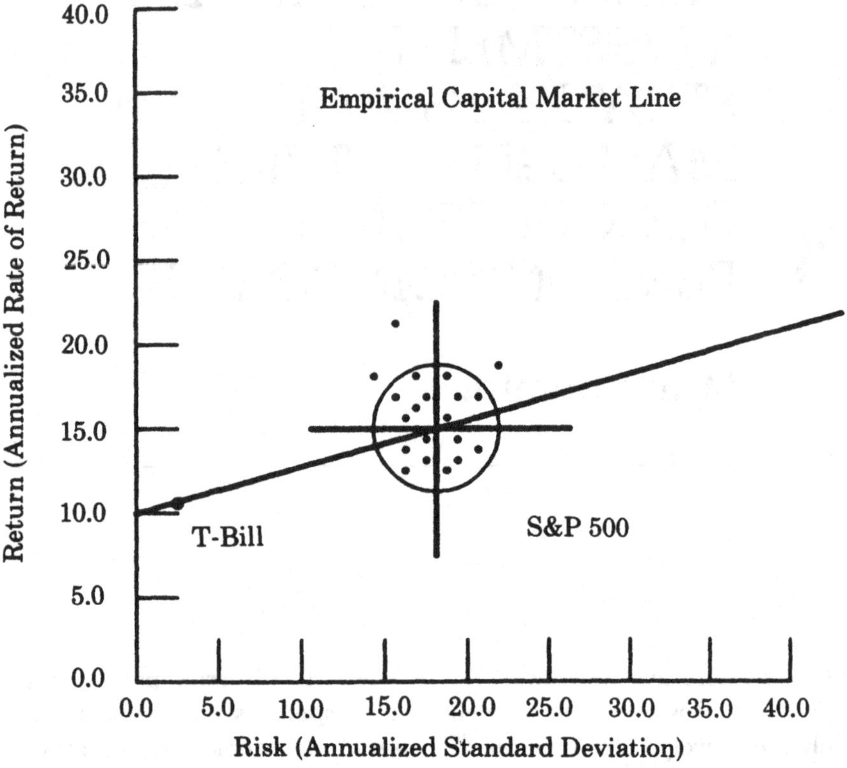

Source: Paradigm Partners, Inc.

The restrictive aspects of the theory are best illustrated by examining the *empirical capital market line.* Figure 3.1 is a standard risk return diagram displaying the empirical capital market line that existed between 1985 and 1989. The empirical capital market line is constructed by connecting the points representing the risk/return characteristics of the S&P 500 and lower-risk U.S. Treasury bills. The capital market line provides a framework to evaluate return and risk generated by different investment strategies and styles.

Points along the capital market line represent the returns of managers who are being appropriately compensated for the assumed risks measured by portfolio volatility; points below the line represent returns not being fully compensated for risk; points above the line are those managers who are being over-compensated for risk taken.

All too often investors focus on return without taking into consideration the risk being assumed by a particular manager or which is inherent in the investment strategy. Without an understanding of the risk/return tradeoff, it is difficult to evaluate an investment strategy effectively, construct a well-diversified portfolio or evaluate performance properly. All of these shortcomings usually lead to an unsatisfactory result.

There are many different ways (such as the Sharpe Ratio, drawdown) to gain insight into the risk/reward tradeoff of a manager or investment strategy. All of the methods have their own strengths and weaknesses. However, evaluating managers relative to the capital market line is particularly useful since it contains much more information than any single ratio.

In addition to clearly displaying absolute risk and return, this diagram also provides numerous measurements relative to the environment that existed during the time period being examined. It is comparatively easy to see how numerous managers stack up against each other and to identify standout managers. The diagram makes it easy to identify the strategy that produced the highest return for an acceptable level of risk; the strategy that produced an acceptable return with the lowest risk, or the strategy that had the highest risk adjusted excess return (Alpha).

No single measure can be regarded as a comprehensive manager evaluation tool. However, we find Alpha, or risk-adjusted excess return, an extremely powerful tool. Figure 3.1, the capital market line analysis, graphically displays Alpha. Alpha is the vertical distance, measured in percent, between the data point representing the risk/return characteristics of a manager and the capital market line. Over time a manager must be fully compensated for the investment risk assumed, otherwise returns will be subpar. (This assumes there is a reasonable spectrum of both high and low risk environments during the time period under study.) Depending on managers who don't produce a positive Alpha means the investor relies on luck or a favorable environment to produce superior returns.

The difficulty in diversifying using only conventional investment managers becomes readily apparent by examining Figure 3.1. For a meaningful time period, such as five years, the vast majority of manager's risk/return characteristics gravitate toward a broad market index such as the S&P 500. There are several reasons for this phenomenon. First, conventional managers tend to produce remarkably similar results regardless of their style. Second, conventional managers typically have the same focus of relative performance versus a major market index. The absolute level of return is relegated to a lower level of importance.

Table 3.1 makes the same point in a somewhat different way. Various style categories are listed. The results represent the annualized returns for 1985–1989 for essentially second quartile managers. As can be seen, in virtually every instance the high return and low return of second quartile managers bracket the return of the S&P 500. The narrow range of returns and the fact that these returns are gross of investment management fees, makes a very strong case that even if plan sponsors were successful at selecting only second quartile conventional managers, it would be exceedingly difficult to outperform a broad market index such as the S&P 500.

Figure 3.2 graphically depicts the phenomena occurring that make it difficult for a large plan sponsor to build a portfolio of conventional investment managers who are likely to produce superior returns.

This phenomena makes it very difficult for a large plan sponsor to build a portfolio of conventional investment managers who are likely to produce superior returns (Figure 3.2).

How Diversification Reduces Nonmarket Risk

As illustrated in Figure 3.2, when one purchases a stock there are three distinct risk components: Specific issue risk accounts for approximately 60 percent of the total, market segment or economic segment risk about 15 percent, and general market risk for approximately 25 percent. As Figure 3.2 shows, the risk changes considerably when one builds a portfolio of stocks, as opposed to owning an individual issue. When a portfolio is constructed, general market risk dominates and is approximately 94 percent of the total portfolio risk. Combining several conventional style managers, each with their own portfolio, increases general market risk to about 99 percent, while combining many managers ensures virtually 100 percent general market risk with virtually no specific stock risk or economic segment risk.

TABLE 3.1. Equity style performance. (before fees)

	Annualized Returns 1985–1989	
Style	1st Quartile Manager	Median Manager
Growth	21.0	19.7
Value	22.3	20.1
Yield	21.7	20.6
Rotation	21.2	19.0
S&P 500	20.3	

Source: SEI Corporation.

FIGURE 3.2. Shortcomings of the 1980s approach—how diversification reduces nonmarket risk.

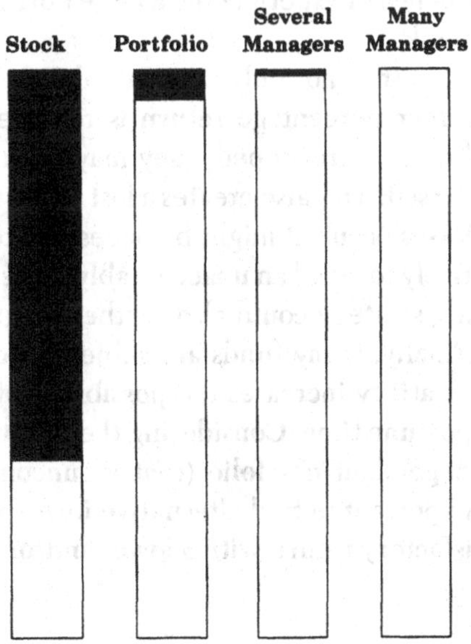

- Multiple Manager/Multiple Styles Approach Insures Little Specific Risk and High Market Risk
- Market Risk is Uncontrollable and Unpredictable

	Stock	Portfolio	Several Managers	Many Managers
• Specific Issue Risk	60%	4%	0.5%	0%
• Market Segment Risk	15	2	0.5	0
• General Market Risk	25	94	99	100

Source: Investment Policy, Charles D. Ellis.

While many large plan sponsors are forced to utilize numerous conventional managers as the only viable way of investing their large asset base, it creates one very serious problem. When "many" conventional managers are hired, the overall plan sponsor's portfolio risk becomes 100 percent market risk. Market risk is considered by most academics and professionals as uncontrollable and unpredictable. The implication of this phenomenon is that portfolio returns will be driven almost entirely by major market moves, *both* up and down. Reducing the portfolio's risk level also will be minimal while the high transaction fees will virtually ensure under-performance.

By having a portfolio that depends so much on overall market performance, the overall plan is exposed to the risk level inherent in the entire equities market. When the market is rising, the high level of market exposure is a benefit. Conversely, during market breaks (such as in October 1987), or more classic bear markets (1973–1974), the portfolio could be exposed to larger losses than might be desirable. The consequence of experiencing a large portfolio loss is higher than most managers think.

First, not only is asset value lost, but as the asset base contracts, a larger percentage return is required to recoup losses. Second, even if losses are recouped, they may occur after an extensive time period has passed. This also creates a lost opportunity cost. Third, when large abrupt losses occur, it might be necessary to invest the portfolio more conservatively to avoid an unacceptably larger loss. This more conservative investing strategy could also further lengthen the portfolio's recovery period. Finally, many funds are subject to unanticipated withdrawals. Portfolio volatility increases the possibility of assets being withdrawn at an inopportune time. Considering the negative repercussions of a highly market-dependent portfolio (that is, uncontrollable risk exposure), it becomes important to find alternative investment vehicles that will produce a satisfactory return with a lower and/or more controllable risk level.

ALTERNATIVE INVESTMENT STRATEGIES

Alternative investment strategies are defined as strategies that are different from those followed by conventional equity managers, such as a long stock strategy. These strategies use only liquid securities comprised of stocks, bonds, options, and futures that are priced daily. The important distinction between alternative investment strategies and a conventional long stock portfolio is that the risk-return profile can be altered dramatically from that of a conventional manager by using derivative securities and short positions to either amplify or reduce portfolio risk. Typical strategies would include hedged investments such as convertible bond hedges, short selling, various forms of arbitrage, and managed futures accounts.

Typically, these strategies are found in a limited partnership structure where the general partner invests his or her own capital and only receives a fee when performance is positive. Contrary to popular belief, avoiding a loss dominates the investment process of the vast majority of nontraditional managers. The primary reason is that the partnership structure provides some strong incentives. A loss on an annual basis would result in loss of both the limited partner's and general partner's capital, no incentive compensation for a 12-month period, and in many instances, the need to make up any loss prior to incentive compensation being paid in the future. (Separate account structures do not provide as strong an incentive to be conservative, but may offer other benefits.) These partnerships, and certainly separately managed accounts, tend to be small in asset size. This allows managers to act quickly on new information or take advantage of investment ideas that would be too limiting for conventional managers with much larger asset bases.

Using derivative securities and short selling allows the investment professional to create strategies that span the entire risk spectrum and are not clustered around the risk-return characteristics of the S&P 500. In most instances, these investment strategies have statistical characteristics that are markedly different from those of conventional managers. Importantly, the R^2, or coefficient of determination, of these strategies with the S&P 500 is normally .6 or lower, versus R^2s for conventional managers that range from .85 to 1.00. The importance of the low R^2 cannot be over emphasized when the investment objective is to reduce portfolio risk. Commingling investment approaches with low R^2s can significantly reduce risk. For this reason, these strategies should receive serious consideration from plan sponsors.

Alternative investment strategies have several characteristics that can be beneficial to a plan sponsor seeking lower risk and higher returns. These can be summarized as:

- High specific risk dominates alternative investment strategy portfolios.
- The low R^2 allows portfolio risk to be meaningfully reduced.
- Many strategies take advantage of market inefficiencies and, while limited by size to a niche category, offer some powerful statistical characteristics for the plan's sponsor's consideration.
- Alternative investment strategies in some instances have technical advantages that can often lead to an enhanced return.

ALTERNATIVE INVESTMENT STRATEGIES: CATEGORIES AND USE

There are numerous alternative investment strategies, the each distinct from one another. They span the entire risk spectrum, which makes it imperative to categorize these strategies so their statistical properties can be better defined. Categorizing alternative investment strategies can be done more precisely than categorization of conventional managers since the returns and the variability of returns tend to be strategy and not market-dependent. The returns of conventional managers are highly market-dependent as evidenced by the high R^2 to the general market. This is a key distinction because a manager can often have a much higher level of predictability when returns are driven by a strategy rather than market-driven. This is because the market remains unpredictable while a strategy can be applied consistently. By contrast, if you were trying to predict the returns of a conventional manager who is highly market-dependent, then to be successful one has to be able to predict both the market's direction and magnitude of change.

Categories

It is possible to categorize alternative investment strategies by statistical characteristics into five distinct categories. The five categories are:

low volatility strategies, market neutral/event-oriented strategies, high return/high volatility strategies, and negative correlation strategies. A fifth category, collateralized transactions, is used for those strategies where the ability to fund the strategy with assets other than cash is the dominant investment characteristic. Managed futures are a component of this last category.

Low Volatility Strategies

These strategies tend to have a volatility of returns less than one-half of the S&P 500. The volatility of the S&P 500, as measured by standard deviation, is typically around 18 percent per year. Low volatility strategies most often have standard deviations of 5 percent or 6 percent a year. The investment positions are often hedged and are very independent of the market's direction. An important statistical property of low volatility strategies is that the R^2s are typically low, often hovering around zero. Whether the Dow Jones Index goes up or down 100 points should not make much difference. Over a five-year time frame, most low volatility strategies generate returns that are commensurate with the market. However, they are achieved by assuming considerably less risk than the S&P 500.

Market—Neutral/Event-Oriented Strategies

The most typical example of a market-neutral/event-oriented strategy is risk arbitrage. For the vast majority of the time, returns from these strategies are not directly dependent upon the direction of market movements. Rather, the returns from these strategies are dependent upon an event either happening or not happening. For example, historically, more than 90 percent of all announced mergers and acquisitions are consummated and news drives the risk arbitrageur's return, not general market movement. Return patterns for this category typically have a volatility that is somewhat higher than the S&P 500 and returns that are commensurately higher. The R^2s range from .1 to .5 indicating that they can be a very powerful diversifying tool without necessarily sacrificing return.

High Return/High Volatility Strategies

The most typical strategy in this category is the "classic" hedge fund that is simultaneously long and short stocks. While the goal of these strategies is maximum capital appreciation, the returns are not driven solely by market direction. Rather, they are driven by the manager's ability to distinguish accurately between under-priced and over-priced investments. Returns and volatility both tend to be higher than the S&P 500. R^2s typically run from .5 to .8. While these coefficients of determination are high for alternative investment strategies, they are still very low when compared to conventional equity managers. Consequently, this category of strategy offers the ability to reduce risk substantially more than by using a mix of conventional equity managers.

Negative Correlation Strategies

Short selling is the most obvious negative correlation strategy. The returns have a negative correlation to the S&P 500 and often have a volatility that is 50 percent higher than the S&P 500. While the R^2s are typically about .6, it is important to realize that these are derived from a negative R value (coefficient of correlation). Consequently, negative correlation strategies can be a very powerful tool for plan sponsors seeking to reduce portfolio risk and market dependence.

Collateralized Transaction Strategies

Managed futures accounts are the most obvious collateralized transaction strategy. Returns and risk characteristics of managed futures accounts can vary considerably depending on the specific strategy employed. However, all managed futures accounts have one common element: All transactions can be initiated using collateral rather than cash.

These five categories of strategies are portfolio building blocks. Defined by their statistical and investment characteristics (as opposed to styles which have similar statistical and investment characteristics), they offer the plan sponsor the opportunity to construct some very creative portfolios.

Using Alternative Investment Strategies

Alternative investment strategies offer some unique advantages to the plan sponsor. For example, when one selects conventional managers, there is a lot of emphasis placed on picking the "best" manager. When the sponsor is unable to select the "best" manager, the conventional approach to building a portfolio collapses. Generating good investment results by building a portfolio of alternative investment strategies is not as heavily dependent upon selecting the best manager. This is because the strategies are so different, one need only select strategies that have powerful statistical characteristics which can be combined in a way to significantly reduce risk. Good results with much lower risk can be "levered up" to produce higher returns at perhaps an appropriately higher risk level.

As shown in Table 3.1 one must consistently select first quartile conventional managers in order to generate a *net* return that will better the broad market return. Since alternative investment strategies are very different, it is only slightly easier to select the "best" alternative investment manager. However, when using alternative investment strategies, it is less important to select the best manager. This is because combining several managers will not necessarily reduce the overall return to a market return (at a market risk level) minus fees and commissions as is the case with highly correlated conventional managers.

Research has indicated that using numerous alternative investment strategy managers with different strategies tends to reduce the overall portfolio risk or volatility without necessarily sacrificing return. This phenomenon is due to the fact that these managers and strategies not only have low correlations with the S&P 500, but also have low correlations among themselves. This low correlation makes it possible to reduce the portfolio risk without diminishing returns.

Still, a large pension portfolio faces some significant problems in constructing a portfolio using alternative investment strategies. First, none of these strategies are huge in terms of capacity. A partnership that is $200 million to $300 million is a large entity for alternative investment strategies. Consequently, it is often necessary to use a multi-manager approach in each category of strategy in order to create sufficient capacity. Using multiple managers in each of the five categories has the added advantage of each category having more stable statistical characteristics. In the low volatility category, for instance, we might select three or four managers. In the high volatility/high return category, perhaps 10 to 12 managers might be needed in order to capture the excess return phenomena and add stability and predictability to the return pattern. The five categories then can be combined to create some truly unique portfolios capable of generating a high absolute return and a high risk adjusted rate of return.

One additional advantage of alternative investment strategies impacts return potential rather than risk reduction. All strategies, regardless of category, have the ability to generate positive returns in virtually any market environment, up, down or flat. The ability to take long and/or short positions provides the capability of being aggressive, rather than simply defensive during hostile market climates.

ALTERNATIVE INVESTMENT STRATEGIES

As Table 3.2 shows, each strategy category has some very powerful and unique statistical properties. The uniqueness of these statistical properties allows plan sponsors to combine the five categories to produce portfolios with superior statistical characteristics.

TABLE 3.2. Alternative investment strategies.

Statistical Characteristics	Low Volatility	Market Neutral	High Return	Negative Correlation	Managed Futures	S&P 500
1985–1989						
Annualized Return	18.1	27.1	30.7	35.2	15.2	20.3
Standard Deviation	5.0	19.2	18.3	17.6	23.6	18.3
R^2	.27	.62	.83	.53	.07	1.00
Alpha	7.5	6.2	10.4	15.4	−8.9	0.0
Risk Adj T Stat	4.1	.7	1.1	1.6	−.72	0

Sources: Managed Account Returns, Paradigm Partners, Inc.

DIFFICULTIES IN EVALUATING FUTURES SPECULATION STRATEGIES

Like most investment strategies, futures speculation has its own advantages and disadvantages, some apparent and some real.

Disadvantages

- *Futures speculation is a zero sum investment.* The preceding statement is one that arouses considerable debate. Supporters of this point out that, unlike equity investments, futures speculation is a zero sum game, since every long futures position is offset by a short position. In total, the gains and losses must sum to zero. Proponents of managed futures accounts point out that many market participants' decisions are driven by forces other than maximizing return. Certainly, for a corn farmer or grain processor the desire to minimize overall business risk may take precedence over creating an offsetting futures position at the highest price. But two open issues remain: (1) to what extent does offsetting a business risk cause the sacrificing of returns and (2) are there enough instances for the speculator to get a significant edge to compensate for the increased risk taking?

  After reviewing the data on both sides, it appears there is some truth to each position. Hedgers exist and seek to maximize overall business return, although commodity hedging is only one component of this process. Hedging transactions, however, represent only a small fraction of all futures trades. Whatever inefficiency the hedger introduces into the market gets diffused as the number of speculative transactions increases. Consequently, the inefficiency introduced into the market by hedgers provides some (but our guess is not much) of an edge to the speculator. It appears unlikely that the inefficiencies introduced by the hedgers are sufficient to provide a strong underpinning to futures speculation for a significant number of market participants.
- *Frictional costs and management fees are high.* A lot of emphasis is placed on the abnormally high fees incorporated into brokerage house 20 percent retail products. Fees, in this instance, can often run 15 to 20 percent of assets per year, making it virtually impossible for

participants to produce a superior return. The sheer size of pension portfolios allows fees to be negotiated to reasonable levels that don't jeopardize manager performance. For large accounts, it is assumed that frictional fees can be reduced to levels that don't unduly penalize returns.

- *The predominant investment technique is technical trading.* There are several sound reasons why technical trading is the prominent investment technique used by futures traders.

  One could argue that from a fundamental perspective, supply/demand factors (as represented by price/volume changes) are more relevant to commodity prices than to stock prices. If technical trading is accepted as a valid equity trading investment technique, it should be at least equally embraced when applied to commodities.

  Perhaps the strongest arguments in support of technical analysis come from the nature of futures investments. Purchasing a futures contact allows investors to achieve significant financial leverage. More important, the investor need only put up "a good faith deposit" often representing 5 percent or less of the commodity's value. This figure is comparable to the 50 percent margin required for stocks. The reasoning behind the lower required investment is that futures positions are marked-to-market daily, consequently, positions are "squared up" by debiting or crediting cash to the account to reflect the day's changes. Therefore, the investor always has a good faith deposit adequate to cover any daily loss.

  Stock margin and a good faith deposit on a futures position differ in another important way. When an investor purchases a stock on margin (at 50 percent), he borrows the other 50 percent from the broker at the prevailing interest rate. When a futures investor makes a good faith deposit, no money is borrowed. In addition, rather than putting up cash, futures positions can be collateralized. This means the investor is actually earning interest on the collateral rather than paying interest to carry the position as is the case with stock bought on margin.

  This combination of high financial leverage and comparatively positive cost of carry gives the commodity investor the ability to establish very large investment positions relative to their equity capital.

Leveraged portfolios (where the assets controlled are greater than the account equity) generally produce more volatile returns and rapid, abrupt changes in account equity. It is this phenomenon that leads to the necessary use of technical analysis. Simply put, futures traders cannot adopt a buy and hold strategy as is the case with many equity investors. Consequently, virtually all futures speculators utilize technical analysis to a greater or lesser degree.

- *Returns are extremely volatile, often appearing somewhat random.* This point is a difficult one for many equity investors to accept. It is not unusual for a managed futures account to generate a return or loss in excess of 20 percent in any one month, even in a diversified portfolio. Critics would argue that excess returns generated over a multi-year period are often the result of several favorable month's returns. Consequently, it is difficult to be confident that returns in a managed futures account can be repeated.

  Highly volatile returns are the nature of leveraged transactions. This "randomness" is due to the leverage and low correlation to equity market returns. While this often raises false concerns, volatility can be controlled by managing the size, diversification, type of investments and investment strategy employed.

  The fact that high returns and large losses occur sporadically raises questions about the integrity of the data. Extreme volatility occurs when returns from a few time periods drive the overall performance result. This makes time dependence a bigger issue than might otherwise be the case. Simply put, determining if the record is repeatable, or determining if the specific time period was unique, becomes a more meaningful consideration. This is one major reason why using shorter time periods for analysis is preferable to using longer periods.

- *It is difficult to select futures speculators that will generate a positive alpha.* There are several reasons that prospective investors feel that identifying the better futures managers is as difficult as identifying a good conventional equity manager. First, investment records are relatively short and the assets being managed are often relatively small. As of the end of 1989, there were fewer than 50 commodity trading advisors with accounts of more than $5 million who had been in business more than five years. Second, investment records often are compiled using relatively small asset bases. It is questionable whether these records could be produced using asset bases that would be meaningful to any large pension fund.

When dealing with investment records that were established with relatively small asset bases, it is important to evaluate both dollar-weighted and time-weighted rates of return. Because of the rapid growth and the size of accounts, it is entirely possible that a manager whose time-weighted record indicates returns in excess of 50 percent actually wound up losing money for his clients in total. As with other successful investment vehicles, assets seem to roll in after a few good years of results have been produced. For the data during the time period selected (1985–1989), time-weighted returns from equally-weighted managers were used.

Risks of Futures Speculation Strategies

Many people quickly overlook the risks of using futures as an investment technique. Although they may never materialize as a problem, the risks remain.

The risks are a result of three factors: the highly leveraged nature of the investment (sometimes exceeding 20:1); the requirement to mark-to-market daily; and the possibility of abrupt changes in circumstances. This combination provides both the opportunity for quick gains as well as losses. An unanticipated negative change in events can create major losses for a portfolio that is highly leveraged, especially if investment positions are concentrated. For example, concentrated leverage of 5:1 would produce a 100 percent loss if a change of events caused a 20 percent change in the underlying investment. While such rapid changes are unusual, they do occur. The requirement to mark-to-market daily can produce an immediate realized loss.

Anyone investing in futures speculation strategies needs to be aware of the risks and adjust the strategy and exposure accordingly.

Advantages

- *Potentially high returns.* Undoubtedly, managed futures accounts have the potential of generating abnormally high returns, especially if leverage is employed. There is a small set of managed futures advisors who have been able to demonstrate superior returns over many years. The key question then becomes: Is it possible to identify these managers with foresight?

- *Low R^2s offer excellent diversification potential.* One of the more compelling advantages of futures investments is the loss correlation of determination. In general, managed futures accounts have R^2s of approximately zero, implying that they offer extremely powerful diversification benefits when incorporated in a 100 percent equity portfolio. Proponents often argue that managed futures accounts should be included in a well diversified pension portfolio, if only for diversification benefits.
- *Lower transactions costs.* Over time, transactions costs are a factor in total return. In this regard, futures investments have a decided advantage over equities when one compares commissions per dollar of investment position. Commissions vary widely within the futures industry and from a fiduciary perspective, it is important that commission levels be reasonable and fully justifiable. It is assumed that the size of pension accounts would enable the investor to achieve commission rates at the low end of the prevailing scale.
- *Highly liquid markets.* Most markets, and specifically the markets for financial futures instruments, are highly liquid and offer the investor the opportunity to move large volumes of assets quickly and inexpensively. Other markets are clearly too illiquid to accommodate vast volumes of pension dollars. We have assumed that investors will operate only in markets that offer no size problems which will enable them to take advantage of the liquid futures markets. Financial futures, such as stock indexes, bonds, currencies as well as oil, metals and the Nikkei Index would meet most liquidity needs at this time.
- *A collateralized transaction.* The most overwhelming advantage and uniqueness of managed futures accounts is that futures transactions are collateralized. Unlike investors who purchase common stock with cash, futures purchases can be collateralized by putting up Treasury bills or other adequate collateral. This allows the investor to earn a return on the collateral while at the same time seeking to generate an incremental return through investments in futures. One should not

minimize this advantage because it dramatically reduces the required return on the futures investment in order to make it a meaningful addition to a pension portfolio.

In summary, there are significant problems in effectively evaluating futures speculation strategies. Most revolve around the difficulty in dealing with unusually volatile return patterns and the need for the integrity of the data to be high.

EVALUATION OF FUTURES STRATEGIES

There are several decisions involved in evaluating any investment strategy. These include the following:

- *Timeframe.* The key factor here is choosing the longest timeframe relevant to the decision being made today. Too long a timeframe runs the risk of incorporating "ancient history" that is no longer relevant due to outdated circumstances. Selecting too short a timeframe runs the risk of having insufficient data to form conclusions. The data used in this study incorporated a five-year timeframe for evaluation because the rapid changes in financial markets, and futures markets make data much older than five years ancient history. The rapid growth both in assets and in new instruments appear to support this decision. Data going back 10 years was generated by managers with exceedingly small asset bases, focusing on almost exclusively nonfinancial instrument investments. Since five years spans a "typical" economic cycle, it should be sufficient time to experience both favorable and unfavorable environments.
- *Data.* For this analysis Managed Account Reports (MAR) data was used for the time period 1985 to 1989. The data was net of fees and commissions and was available on both a time-weighted and dollar-weighted basis.

  The data is for 25 managers who manage $30 million or more and represent approximately 80 percent of managed futures accounts. The data representing the larger futures managers was important when evaluating the feasibility of managed futures accounts for pension funds, which most typically have large assets to deploy.

The major shortcoming in the data series is the level of fees and commissions extracted from the returns. It is extremely difficult, if not impossible, to accurately adjust fees and commissions to levels more in line with the lower fee schedules major institutions would command. Some high fee managers would be willing to adjust fees schedules, others would not. Our best guess, and it is little more than that, is that annual returns could be enhanced by 2 to 7 percent per year given lower fees and commission rates. This adjustment is enough to make returns competitive with equities before adjusting for risk. While rates of return and alpha might be increased 2 to 6 percent per year due to more favorable fee and commission structures, other key statistical measures such as standard deviation, R^2 and T statistics would show little change.

Table 3.2 has all the relevant data one needs to evaluate futures strategies as an alternative or adjunct to conventional or alternative equity strategies.

ALTERNATIVE INVESTMENT STRATEGIES

Annualized Return

Annualized return is the annual compounded rate of return over a five-year period, 1985 to 1989. When the 15.2 percent per year return for managed futures accounts is adjusted for the lower fee and commission structures large pension accounts would command, it is likely that returns would be competitive with equity returns of 20.3 percent during the five-year period under observation. We believe this to be a realistic assumption given our conversations with futures managers.

While many would argue these return statistics understate what futures managers can deliver, we would argue that selecting superior futures managers in advance is exceedingly difficult due to the myriad of problems previously discussed. It is not that superior managers do not exist, certainly they do. Rather, data integrity, timeframe, size considerations and the uniqueness of the time period analyzed make the analysis difficult. On a nonrisk adjusted basis, it appears futures speculation could produce returns that are competitive with stocks. Depending on the uniqueness of the time period they could be higher or lower in the aggregate.

Standard Deviation of Returns

Standard deviation is a measure of variability around the mean return. In this chapter, quarterly data was annualized and used to generate statistics for the five-year timeframe.

The standard deviation for futures returns is 23.6 percent per year versus 18.3 percent for the S&P 500. While higher than the S&P 500 or a well-diversified portfolio, it is comparable to the volatility experienced by more aggressive equity investors focusing on more volatile small capitalization stocks.

The higher standard deviation means that risk adjusted returns will be reduced as discussed in the comments on Alpha. R^2 is the coefficient of determination, a measure of the correlation of the return pattern to the equity market. The R^2 of .07 indicates virtually no correlation to the equity market implying that an investment in futures could provide some diversifying benefit to an equity portfolio. This is a strong benefit of futures investing. However, the benefit would be somewhat diminished if futures investments were made exclusively in financial markets, S&P 500 futures in particular. Nonetheless, the ability of futures managers to be either long or short would help this beneficial characteristic.

Alpha

Alpha is risk-adjusted excess return. Put simply, it is the return premium an investment generates given the risk being assumed. An Alpha of −8.9 indicates the return is 8.9 percent less than it should be given the risk being taken (as measured by standard deviation of returns). We have already discussed that the futures returns in our data are probably understated by 2 to 6 percent due to higher fee and commission structures incorporated into the data. Making an adjustment for lower fee structures still would result in a negative Alpha. A negative Alpha is not a desirable characteristic over the long term given a sampling of favorable and unfavorable investing environments.

Risk-Adjusted T Statistic

Many statistical tests assume a normal distribution which means that it is accurately described by its mean and standard deviation. For data of small sample sizes (less than 30 observations), the assumption of a normal distribution is often not valid. The T statistic is used to adjust data to account for the fact that the distribution may not be normal, but rather that the distribution is likely to have a higher probability of larger deviations or more variability. Such a distribution is flatter and more spread out than a normal distribution.

Calculation of a T statistic is a way of gaining confidence that returns were not generated by chance. It is a function of three variables: (1) the return, (2) the standard deviation, and (3) the number of observations. In essence, we are trying to determine if returns are chance events or generated by skill or a superior investment technique.

By calculating a risk-adjusted T statistic, we are asking the question: "Given the risk assumed, what is the likelihood that the returns are generated by chance?" A T statistic of 2.0 or more would give us confidence that we were not dealing with chance observations, but rather that either superior skill or a superior investment technique was the overriding factor in generating a return.

A high level of return and a small standard deviation could combine to produce a T statistic greater than 2.0, as is the case with a low volatility investment, even with a small sample size (20 quarters of data).

As can be seen from the data, there is no indication that returns for managed futures accounts is anything more than chance observations. There is no reason to believe that superior skill or superior investment technique exists that will lead to above-average returns.

Our analysis of futures speculation returns indicates that they are volatile investments that generate equity-like returns. After adjusting for risk, futures speculation strategies are likely to produce sub-par returns. The major attraction appears to be limited to the low R^2 and its diversification impact. In our view, there is no strong evidence to support the thesis that futures speculation strategies should be incorporated into a pension portfolio in lieu of equity investments since the diversification benefits are likely to be minimal in a large well-diversified pension portfolio. However, there may be a role for futures strategies in a pension portfolio if two criteria can be met. The criteria are:

1. Futures strategies that have a lower variability of returns
2. Take advantage of the collateralized nature of futures investing.

HOW MANAGED FUTURES CAN BE EFFECTIVELY UTILIZED BY PENSION FUNDS

Perhaps the most quoted study involving managed futures accounts was made in 1983 by Harvard Professor John Lintner. Lintner addressed the question of what combination of managed futures accounts and conventional equity portfolios would produce the most efficient (highest return per unit of risk) portfolio. It is important to realize that Lintner's study addressed only the equity portion of the portfolio, not a more modern pension portfolio with many diversifying asset classes.

For this reason, Lintner's conclusion that 30 percent of an equity portfolio could be invested in managed futures and still provide a benefit is probably too high for a better-diversified portfolio. Practically speaking, considering the unresolved issues regarding managed futures accounts, such a high percentage would appeal only to a few plan sponsors. Other asset classes, with the exception of equities and fixed income investments, usually represent 10 percent or less of diversified portfolios.

The data supporting the case for the inclusion of futures speculating as a separate asset class with a goal of producing high risk-adjusted rates of return is, in our view, inconclusive. More reliable data spanning a much longer time period would go a long way toward increasing potential investors' confidence levels.

Collateralized Futures Positions

While the arguments revolving around managed futures account returns, statistical characteristics, and stability of statistical characteristics may rage on for the next decade, there is a more pragmatic approach to utilizing managed futures accounts that should offer beneficial results.

As mentioned previously, the collateralized nature of futures transactions is a powerful and unique characteristic which significantly changes the evaluation procedure. The ability to collateralize a transaction significantly lowers the return requirements of a managed futures account. This feature can be very beneficial to a pension portfolio.

Being able to collateralize futures positions with return-generating assets means that managed futures accounts can be looked at as generating an incremental return on top of the return that would already be generated by the existing collateral. In essence, it offers the ability to make additional investments without increasing the asset base. Viewing managed futures accounts in this context has an important ramification.

Less aggressive strategies with lower return characteristics, but a higher probability of achievement can be considered to provide an "incremental" return to the overall portfolio. This can be done in lieu of focusing on investments whose role is to seek the highest level return by assuming commensurately higher risks.

In order to take this approach, the prospective investor must believe that it is possible to identify futures strategies that will produce a positive trading return (net of all expenses) since every dollar return produced is incremental. This is a substantially easier evaluation process than trying to select the next Commodity Trading Advisor (CTA) superstar.

The key question then becomes: Is it possible to predict those managers capable of executing strategies where the primary focus is to produce a positive net trading return? There are two areas that appear to make sense under the revised requirements: (1) Equity surrogate strategies, and (2) hedged trading strategies. Both areas provide significant advantages that increase the probability of adding incremental benefit.

Examples of Equity Surrogate Strategies

- Unleveraged equity index portfolios
- Highly leveraged equity index portfolios.

Examples of Hedging Strategies

- Bull Call Spread
- Bull Put Spread
- Bear Call Spread
- Neutral Calendar Spread
- Vertical Butterfly Spread
- Ratio Call Spread
- Ratio Put Spread
- Long Straddle
- Short Straddle
- Synthetic Long Call
- Synthetic Long Futures.

The hedging strategies are considered low risk and are employed by futures traders in more liquid futures contracts such as U.S. Treasury bond futures. They employ extensive use of options on futures and should provide adequate liquidity for major investors.

SUMMARY

The specific strategy employed is not as important as the overall objective of producing a more precisely defined profit/risk profile that has a higher probability of a favorable outcome, even though at a lower level of return. In other words, what are often regarded as highly speculative investment vehicles (options on futures, for example) can be converted into a much more conservative investment by using unconventional investment techniques.

The result of utilizing collateralized hedged futures strategies can provide equal or greater benefit than investing directly in futures speculation strategies. For example, consider a pension plan that has $100 million of assets, 50 percent of which is invested in common stocks, 40 percent of which is invested in fixed income securities, and 10 percent in cash equivalents.

If the cash portion of the portfolio were utilized to collateralize futures transactions in less aggressive strategies (where frictional costs and commissions have been reduced to acceptable levels), it is not unlikely that highly predictable, consistent trading returns of 10 percent or so could be generated. This incremental return of 10 percent would increase the return on the $100 million portfolio by one full percentage point, while at the same time, serving to reduce the overall risk level of the portfolio. The amount of risk reduction would depend on which specific strategy was utilized. In all likelihood there would only be a small amount of risk reduction in a well-diversified pension portfolio.

By way of contrast, if 10 percent of the assets were allocated to futures speculation, the return of the investment would have to be the portfolio return plus 10 percent to raise the entire portfolio return by one full percentage point. However, it should be noted that in this case, the futures speculator would have the interest on the collateral added to the overall return.

By viewing managed futures accounts as a collateralized transaction with the role of producing an incremental return, the prospective investor has changed the investment process in a way that significantly improves the probability of increasing overall portfolio return.

Taking an incremental return approach allows the plan sponsor to get involved with futures by using more conservative strategies that can add benefit to the overall portfolio. Over time, as experience is gained, strategies can be adjusted to higher risk profiles.

4 Multi-Manager Commodity Portfolios: A Risk/Return Analysis

Thomas Schneeweis
Uttama Savanayana
David McCarthy

In recent years, there has been an increase in the number of new alternative commodity trading products that can invest in the commodities and financial markets. While academic research has addressed the importance of publicly traded commodity funds in overall asset management (see Chapter 2), these usually high-cost investment vehicles may not reflect the performance of alternative commodity trading products (such as individually managed commodity trading accounts) available for institutional investors.

In this chapter, we analyze the performance of individually managed multi-manager portfolios compared to the performance of an average

The authors would like to thank the helpful comments of Edwin Elton and Bob Jaeger. An earlier version of this paper was presented at the Fifth Canadian International Futures Research Seminar.

individual commodity trading advisor (CTA) and the performance of a multi-manager portfolio compared to traditional stock, bond, and commodity indices. There are several reasons why it is important to analyze the performance of multi-manager portfolios. First, some academic analyses of public commodity fund data may not reflect risk/return opportunities from alternative commodity products, such as individually managed commodity trading accounts, which are often available for large individual and institutional investors. Second, the large management fees charged by certain public commodity funds often do not reflect the negotiated fees applicable to large investors or portfolio managers.

This means public commodity fund data may not reflect the representative cost structure for large individual investors or institutional investors. Last, publicly-traded commodity funds are often managed by only one or two CTAs. On an individual basis, these publicly-traded commodity funds may not provide sufficient risk diversification in contrast to a larger portfolio of CTAs.

THE MULTIMANAGER PORTFOLIO

In searching for the benefits of portfolio diversification, a growing number of investors have sought to create multi-manager commodity trading advisor portfolios (multi-manager portfolio). Firms with expertise in investment manager evaluation can select from the universe of professional commodity trading advisors (CTAs) a limited set of traders who meet predetermined criteria. This final group constitutes a multi-manager commodity portfolio.

For instance, a multi-manager portfolio could include a number of individual CTAs who would be expected to outperform a universe of CTAs or a randomly selected group of CTAs by at least the cost of the manager search. Even if the multi-manager portfolio is unable to outperform a randomly selected group of individual CTA accounts (or investments in individual funds or pools) of similar size, the advantages of a centrally managed portfolio may prove economically advantageous to the investor.

The results from this analysis show that a diversified multi-manager portfolio can be constructed that provides superior or additional risk/return opportunities to a portfolio of bonds or stocks as well as other commodity trading vehicles. In addition, this analysis shows that superior risk/return opportunities are available from using simple trading rules to select the advisors for the multi-advisor portfolios. The ability of investment manager selection firms to screen the CTA universe for superior performing CTAs and bargain for fee reductions from individual CTAs may more than offset the cost of the investment management selection firm's search and management services.

DATA AND METHODOLOGY

The data employed in our risk-return analysis is the composite monthly rates of return of 14 CTAs with full data over the time period January 1982–October 1987. These composite rates of return include performance managing individual accounts, publicly-traded commodity funds, and privately organized pools. The rates of return are net of all commission costs and fees. These CTAs can invest in a wide range of futures contracts, including financial and equity futures, as well as futures and options contracts on more traditional commodities, such as gold and other metals.

In order to make comparisons with alternative investments, indices of monthly rates of return on several other types of investments were used. Monthly returns on the MAR indices of CTA-Equal Weighted, CTA-Dollar Weighted, Pool Index, Fund Index, and Ibbotson and Sinquefield stock (S&P 500) and long-term government bond indices (Bond) are used for comparisons with alternative investment vehicles.

The decision on whether a commodity portfolio is used with an existing portfolio of stocks and bonds is based on the methodology presented in the work done by Elton, Gruber and Rentzler, and John Lintner. In their approach, a commodity portfolio should be added to an existing portfolio if its return exceeds the "break-even return" required to shift the efficient frontier. This approach tests for the inclusion of the commodity trading vehicle relative to an existing portfolio only. A more rigorous analysis would involve a comparison of the commodity trading vehicle with portfolios on an existing efficient frontier.

Several caveats are necessary when working with composite CTA data. First, return measures offered by the CTAs are monthly rates of return and do not indicate the effects of possible intramonth drawdowns. As a result, intramonth returns may differ dramatically from reported monthly returns. Second, the composite CTA rate of return (for the period analyzed) includes only customer funds. The performance of the personal account of the CTA may differ from the overall performance of the CTA customer account. Under current CFTC regulations, funds managed by the CTA for their personal account are held in a separate account and may be traded differently from customer funds (for example, on a more leveraged basis). Last, the use of the CFTC approved Net Asset Value approach to return measurement may bias results because intramonth cash flows produce incremental return over funds held from the beginning of the month.

The above caveats on CTA return measurement should have little effect on the results of this analysis. First, in this study we assume that the investor is continually invested for the period of analysis. Second, the CTA indices correctly reflect only customer accounts and do not include funds held for a CTA's personal account. Last, most CTAs analyzed generally hold incoming funds until month-end before integrating them into their trading. It is also important to note that the risk/return performance analysis in this study assumes equal weighing among CTAs and does not indicate the benefits of running mean return/variance-based optimization programs on individual CTAs.

PERFORMANCE COMMODITY TRADING ADVISORS (CTAs)

In order to analyze the risk/return performance of a pre-selected set of 14 CTAs (the multi-manager portfolio), three commonly used trading rules on the full set of 14 CTAs were chosen. The trading rules were:

1. Best 10 CTAs in terms of absolute returns in year t-1 invested in year t (Best 10).

2. The 10 CTAs with lowest correlation in year t-1 invested in year t (Low Correlated 10).
3. Worst 5 CTAs in terms of absolute returns in year t-1 invested in year t (Worst 5).

The use of the Best 10 criteria tests the ability of managers to consistently outperform a set of comparison managers on a consistent basis. The use of the Worst 5 criteria tests the contrarian strategy; that is, CTAs underperforming in one year will outperform a comparison set of CTAs in the following year. The use of Low Correlated 10 tests for the effect of lowering the overall variance of an equally weighted portfolio.

The most striking result from Table 4.1 is the significant difference between the average standard deviation of the 14 individual CTAs and the standard deviation of the multi-manager portfolio. For the period analyzed (1983-October 1987), the standard deviation of the multi-manager portfolio (5.23) is approximately 40 percent less than the average standard deviation of the 14 individual CTAs (8.67). Moreover, the percentage reduction in risk from using the multi-manager portfolio in contrast to the average is consistent over all years analyzed. Given that the average returns of the multi-manager portfolio and the average return of the individual CTAs are equal, the lower standard deviation of the individual CTAs indicates that significant gains in return/risk relationships are possible from diversifying among CTAs.

Since standard deviation may not be the sole determinant of risk for some investors, the minimum return, maximum return, and skewness are also reported in Table 4.1 for the multi-manager portfolio and the average CTA. The lower minimum value for the average CTA indicates the greater chance of a lower monthly return; however, the higher maximum return also indicates the possibility of choosing a CTA with a high monthly return. While the maximum monthly return in any one year for the multi-manager portfolio was less than the maximum of the average CTA, the multi-manager CTA portfolio minimum monthly return was less negative than the minimum value of the average CTA.

Moreover, even if the multi-manager portfolio and the average CTA had equal return and variance, the greater positive skewness of the multi-manager portfolio would be indicative of a greater probability of a higher return level for the multi-manager portfolio. While an

TABLE 4.1. Risk and return data for commodity trading advisors.

	Multi-Manager CTA Portfolio					Average of Individual CTAs				
Year	Mean	Standard Deviation	Min	Max	Skew	Mean	Standard Deviation	Min	Max	Skew
1983	1.134%	4.817	−5.0	11.95	.89	1.134%	7.929	−13.67	14.79	.04
1984	1.986%	6.625	−5.6	17.21	1.3	1.986%	9.370	−10.66	21.40	.80
1985	1.962%	5.243	−5.3	9.97	.01	1.962%	8.788	−8.74	16.30	−.16
1986	1.176%	5.022	−3.6	11.35	1.0	1.176%	7.838	−10.90	16.27	.40
1987	2.412%	5.771	−3.5	15.92	1.8	2.412%	8.746	−11.15	19.20	.51
1983–1987	1.712%	5.235	−5.6	17.21	.95	1.712%	8.668	−20.67	24.15	.44

* Using standard F test, the variance of the multi-manager CTA portfolios is significantly lower (level of significance of .01) than the average variance of the individual CTA in each of the years analyzed.

individual CTA may provide a maximum return in excess of that of the multi-manager portfolio, when risk performance is measured by maximum to minimum return, skewness or standard deviation, a risk-averse investor (as well as a risk-seeking individual) may desire to invest in the multi-manager portfolio.

The results in Table 4.1 indicate that a multi-manager portfolio may outperform the average CTA in terms of return versus risk (for example, standard deviation, skewness, and maximum to minimum return ratio). However, the multi-manager portfolio should also be compared against a larger sample of CTAs representing managed commodity portfolios, as well as other commodity trading products and traditional equity and bond investments, in order to assess relative performance attributes. From Table 4.2, results show:

1. The average monthly return of the multi-manager CTA portfolio (1.71 percent) for the five-year period was greater than the S&P 500 average monthly return of (1.34 percent) with almost identical standard deviations of 5.23 for multi-manager portfolio and 5.20 for the S&P 500;
2. The multi-manager portfolio had an average monthly return (1.71 percent) greater than the Bond Index (1.019 percent), but with a significantly higher standard deviation, 5.23 for the multi-manager portfolio and 3.70 for the Bond Index;
3. The minimum monthly return of the multi-manager portfolio (−5.67 percent) was significantly less negative than the minimum S&P 500 return (−24.23 percent) and was similar to the minimum of the Bond minimum return (−5.32 percent);
4. The maximum monthly return for the multi-manager portfolio, (17.21 percent) exceeded that of the S&P 500 (12.60 percent) and Bond Index (10.84 percent);
5. The multi-manager portfolio has positive skewness (.95) over the five-year period while the S&P 500 experienced negative skewness (−1.958) and the Bond Index showed little evidence of positive or negative skewness (.23).

Thus, for the overall period, the multi-manager portfolio had a greater average return than either the S&P 500 or the Bond Index. Moreover,

TABLE 4.2. Risk and return data for alternative asset classes. (1983–10/1987)

	Mean Return	Standard Deviation	Min	Max	Skewness	Difference
S&P 500	1.340	5.198	−24.233	12.602	−1.958	.372
Funds	.313	6.423	−12.897	17.033	.519	1.399
Bond Index	1.019	3.704	−5.319	10.841	.228	.693
CTA–Equal Weighted	1.303	6.900	−11.541	22.298	.751	.409
CTA–Dollar Weighted	1.202	6.282	−11.732	20.740	.669	.510
Pool Index	.920	6.241	−11.856	16.729	.617	.792
Worst 5	1.213	5.460	−8.927	17.530	.447	.499
Best 10	2.304	5.053	−9.102	15.229	.788	−.592
Low Correlation 10	2.321	4.976	−7.203	17.706	.993	−.609
Multi-Manager CTA	1.712	5.235	−5.669	17.210	.950	—

* Standard T-Tests and F-Tests for differences in means and variances are given in Appendix II.

** Difference equals difference between the mean returns of the multi-manager CTA portfolio and alternative asset class.

while the multi-manager portfolio had similar standard deviation to the S&P 500 and greater standard deviation than the Bond Index, it had a comparatively greater maximum return to minimum return ratio as well as greater positive skewness. For this period examined, as a stand-alone investment vehicle, the multi-manager portfolio appears to offer an attractive alternative to either of the comparison asset (S&P 500 and Bond Index) groups.

The multi-manager portfolio, however, is only a subset of the universe of CTAs, as well as only one possible commodity investment vehicle. The ability of the multi-manager portfolio to outperform the CTA–Equal Weighted, CTA–Dollar Weighted, Pool Index, and Fund Index further indicates the possible benefits to a selection process compared to a naive selection of other representative commodity investments. Other benefits of the multi-manager portfolio (based on the results from Table 4.2) show:

1. The multi-manager portfolio had an average return (1.7 percent) superior to the alternative commodity investment CTA–Equal Weighted (1.30 percent), CTA–Dollar Weighted (1.20 percent), Pool Index (.92 percent) and Fund Index (3 percent) respectively;
2. The multi-manager portfolio had a lower standard deviation (5.23) over the entire period (1983 to October 1987) than the CTA–Equal Weighted (6.90), CTA–Dollar Weighted (6.28), Pool Index (6.24), and Fund Index (6.42), however, the differences are significant only at a relatively low level of (a = 90);
3. The multi-manager portfolio had a higher minimum return (−5.67 percent) than the CTA–Equal Weighted (−11.54 percent), CTA–Dollar Weighted, (−11.73 percent), Pool Index (−11.86 percent), or Fund Index (−12.90 percent);
4. The multi-manager portfolio maximum return (17.21 percent) was above that of the Pool Index (16.73 percent) and Fund Index (17.03 percent) but below that of the CTA–Equal Weighted (22.30 percent) and CTA–Dollar Weighted (20.74 percent);
5. The multi-manager portfolio had higher positive skewness (.95) than any of the comparison commodity assets; CTA–Equal Weighted (.75), CTA–Dollar Weighted (.67), Pool Index (.62), and Fund Index (.52).

The multi-manager portfolio offers both higher return and lower risk in terms of standard deviation and absolute maximum/minimum return ratio than any of the comparison commodity investments. Moreover, the multi-manager portfolio had higher positive skewness than the reported commodity trader indices. These results indicate the possible advantage of multi-manager selection as a means of outperforming alternative "index based passive" commodity investment vehicles.

ALTERNATIVE APPROACHES

While the results in Tables 4.1 and 4.2 indicate that the multi-manager portfolio could be viewed as a possible alternative investment to either the comparison stock, bond or commodity indices, the results are reflective of a rather limited manager search process. Alternative multi-manager portfolios could be obtained using even more simplified trading rules. The trading rule-based alternative multi-manager portfolios should outperform the multi-manager portfolio (14 CTAs) by at least the cost of the trading rule selection and monitoring process. The following results are observable from Table 4.2:

1. The Best 10 and Low Correlated 10 had higher average monthly returns (2.30 percent, 2.32 percent, respectively) than the multi-manager portfolio (1.71 percent).
2. The average monthly standard deviations for the multi-manager portfolio, Best 10 and Low Correlated 10 were similar (5.23, 5.05 and 4.98, respectively).
3. The multi-manager portfolio had a higher return than the Worst 5 over the five-year period (1.71 percent and 1.21 percent, respectively), while the standard deviation of monthly returns were approximately equal (5.23 and 5.46, respectively).
4. The multi-manager portfolio, Best 10, Low Correlated 10 and positive skewness (.95, .79, .99, respectively) almost twice that of the Worst 5 (.45).

These results indicate that on an individual comparison level, simple trading rules may create subsets of the multi-manager portfolio. This in turn may offer improved return/risk performance or at least remove a subset (Worst 5) which, on average, would lessen the performance of the multi-manager portfolio.

The results in Tables 4.1 and 4.2 are reported over a five-year period with no direct adjustment for differential expenses in creating the different investment alternatives. While the level of annual expenses for CTA manager selection is dependent on the manager selection source, quoted fees range from 1 percent per annum for manager selection to 5 percent per annum for a full service firm.

In this study, we assume a split between the two fees and use a 3 percent annual fee. As shown in Table 4.2, even with the assumption of an annual CTA portfolio management cost of approximately 0.25 percent monthly (3 percent annual), relative to management cost of the S&P 500, Bond Index, and commodity indices, the multi-manager portfolio had a return that exceeded that of S&P 500, Bond Index, CTA–Equal Weighted, CTA–Dollar Weighted, Pool Index, and Fund Index by at least the differential expenses (0.37 percent/S&P 500; 0.69 percent/Bond Index; 0.41 percent/CTA–Equal Weighted; 0.5 percent/CTA–Dollar Weighted; 0.79 percent/Pool Index; 1.45 percent/Fund Index).

These results confirm our previous suggestions that in an efficient market, returns of comparable risky assets (for example, a CTA portfolio and the S&P 500) should differ at most by the differential management costs. The results also show that the trading rule-based CTA portfolios (Best 10 and Low Correlated 10) provided excess returns above the multi-manager portfolio of about 0.60 percent. With all else equal, the Best 10 and Low Correlated 10 would provide an excess return relative to the multi-manager CTA portfolio as long as the expense ratio was less than 0.6 percent monthly.

Last, while the principal concern of this study is the relative performance of CTAs, the large differential return between the multi-manager portfolio and the Fund Index raises questions as to the risk/return performance of public commodity funds relative to other assets. These results also tend to support the conclusions of Elton et al. on the value of public commodity funds, and also support the possible benefits of alternative commodity vehicles such as a portfolio of individual CTA accounts and pools.

Of equal importance to the overall usefulness of CTA portfolios in asset management is the degree to which the results are consistent over time; that is, did the asset class that had a high-performance measure in one period tend to have high-performance value in the subsequent periods?

Results in Table 4.3 confirm earlier discussions on the benefits of multi-manager portfolios compared to commodity investments reflecting the cited indices. In terms of returns (such as the Sharpe Ratio, maximum/minimum return ratio, and positive skewness), the multi-manager portfolio was ranked highest or next-to-highest in four of the five years when compared to the rankings of the CTA–Equal Weighted, CTA–Dollar Weighted, Pool Index, and Fund Index. The results in Table 4.3 confirm earlier discussions on the benefits of multi-manager portfolios compared to an investment in commodity trading reflecting the cited stock and bond indices.

Results in Table 4.4 show that the CTA portfolio created by simple trading rules (for example, the Best 10 and Low Correlated 10) generally outperformed the S&P 500, the Bond Index, and the multi-manager portfolio in terms of return, Sharpe Ratio, maximum/minimum return ratio, and the highest positive skewness. In terms of returns, the Best 10 and the Low Correlated 10 outperformed the S&P 500, Bond Index, the multi-manager portfolio, and Worst 5 in all five years. Likewise, in terms of positive skewness the Best 10 and Low Correlated 10 had the highest or second and third highest skewness in four of the five years. In terms of the Sharpe Ratio, the Low Correlated 10 had either the highest or second highest in four of the five years examined.

In contrast, the Worst 5 portfolio had the lowest return in three of the five years examined, the lowest or next to lowest positive skewness in four of the five years examined, as well as the worst Sharpe Ratio in three of the five years examined. Thus, for the trading rule-based commodity portfolios, relative performance remained consistent over the yearly holding periods of the time period examined.

However, when the multi-manager portfolio is compared to the stock and bond indices, results are not as consistent as when the results for the multi-manager portfolio are compared to either the alternative commodity indices or the trading rule-based CTA portfolios (for example, Best 10, Low Correlated 10, and Worst 5). While the multi-manager portfolio outperformed the S&P 500 and the Bond Index in terms of highest return, Sharpe Ratio, and positive skewness over the entire period (1983 to October 1987), for individual years the results

TABLE 4.3. Performance ranking: Multi-manager CTA portfolio and popular commodity indices.

Ranking by Returns

Investment Portfolio	1983	1984	1985	1986	1987	AVG	Rank
Multi-Manager CTA	1	1	1	1	4	1.6	1
CTA—Equal Weighted	2	2	2	3	3	2.4	2
CTA—Dollar Weighted	4	3	3	4	1	3.0	3
Pool Index	3	5	5	2	2	3.4	4
Fund Index	5	4	4	5	5	4.6	5

Ranking by Standard Deviation

Investment Portfolio	1983	1984	1985	1986	1987	AVG	Rank
Multi-Manager CTA	4	5	3	4	3	3.8	4
CTA—Equal Weighted	2	1	1	1	1	1.2	1
CTA—Dollar Weighted	5	2	5	3	5	4.0	5
Pool Index	1	3	4	5	4	3.4	3
Fund Index	3	4	2	2	2	2.6	2

Ranking by Sharpe Ratio

Investment Portfolio	1983	1984	1985	1986	1987	AVG	Rank
Multi-Manager CTA	1	1	1	1	3	1.4	1
CTA—Equal Weighted	2	3	3	3	4	3.0	3
CTA—Dollar Weighted	5	2	2	4	1	2.8	2
Pool Index	3	5	5	2	2	3.2	4
Fund Index	4	4	5	5	5	4.6	5

Ranking of Skewness

Investment Portfolio	1983	1984	1985	1986	1987	AVG	Rank
Multi-Manager CTA	1	2	1	3	1	1.6	1
CTA—Equal Weighted	3	1	5	2	4	3	3
CTA—Dollar Weighted	4	3	4	4	5	4	4
Pool Index	2	4	2	1	2	2.2	2
Fund Index	5	5	3	5	3	4.2	5

Ranking by Absolute Value of Max/Min Return Ratio

Fund	1983	1984	1985	1986	1987	AVG	Rank
Multi-Manager CTA	1	1	1	2	4	1.8	1
CTA—Equal Weighted	3	2	4	3	2	2.8	3
CTA—Dollar Weighted	4	3	5	4	3	3.8	4
Pool Index	2	4	2	1	1	2.0	2
Fund Index	5	5	3	5	5	4.6	5

Highest = 1
Lowest = 5

TABLE 4.4. Performance ranking: multi-manager CTA portfolio, trading rules, and stocks and bonds.

			Ranking by Returns				
Investment Portfolio	**1983**	**1984**	**1985**	**1986**	**1987**	**AVG**	**Rank**
Multi-Manager CTA	4	4	4	5	3	4	3
Low Correlation	1	1	3	1	2	1.6	1
Best 10	2	2	1	2	1	1.6	2
Worst 5	6	3	6	6	4	5	6
S&P 500	4	6	3	3	5	3.8	4
Bond Index	5	5	5	4	6	5	5

High = 1			Ranking by Standard Deviation				
Investment Portfolio	**1983**	**1984**	**1985**	**1986**	**1987**	**AVG**	**Rank**
Multi-Manager CTA	3	2	2	5	2	2.8	3
Low Correlation 10	2	3	4	3	4	3.20	4
Best 10	1	4	1	2	5	2.6	2
Worst 5	4	1	3	1	3	2.4	1
S&P 500	5	5	5	4	1	4	5
Bond Index	6	6	6	6	6	6	6

High = 1			Ranking by Sharpe Ratio				
Investment Portfolio	**1983**	**1984**	**1985**	**1986**	**1987**	**AVG**	**Rank**
Multi-Manager CTA	4	5	5	5	3	4.4	5
Low Correlation 10	2	2	4	2	2	2.4	2
Best 10	3	1	3	3	1	2.2	1
Worst 5	6	4	6	6	4	5.2	6
S&P 500	1	6	2	4	5	3.6	4
Bond Index	5	3	1	1	6	3.2	3

High = 1 Positive			Ranking of Skewness				
Investment Portfolio	**1983**	**1984**	**1985**	**1986**	**1987**	**AVG**	**Rank**
Multi-Manager CTA	3	4	2	3	3	3	3
Low Correlation 10	2	3	6	1	1	2.6	2
Best 10	1	1	3	2	2	1.8	1
Worst 5	6	5	5	4	5	5	6
S&P 500	4	2	1	6	6	3.8	4
Bond Index	5	6	4	5	4	4.8	5

		Ranking by Absolute Value of Max/Min Return Ratio					
Investment Portfolio	**1983**	**1984**	**1985**	**1986**	**1987**	**AVG**	**Rank**
Multi-Manager CTA	3	3	2	3	2	2.6	2
Low Correlation 10	2	2	5	1	3	2.6	2
Best 10	1	1	3	2	1	1.6	1
Worst 5	5	4	6	5	5	5.0	6
S&P 500	4	5	1	6	6	4.4	4
Bond Index	6	6	4	4	4	4.8	5

Highest = 1
Lowest = 6

are not consistent in terms of rankings. While the multi-manager portfolio ranked higher in return than the Bond Index in four of the five years, it outranked the S&P 500 in only two of the five years. Likewise in terms of strict rankings of the Sharpe Ratio, the multi-manager portfolio outperformed the S&P 500 in only two of the five years (1984 and 1987) and the Bond Index in only two of the five years 1983 and 1987).

Strict comparisons on the basis of the Sharpe Ratio may, however, not provide a proper measure of the value of the multi-manager portfolio in asset management. First, as shown in Table 4.4 in terms of positive skewness, the multi-manager portfolio outranked the S&P 500 in three of the five years (1983, 1986, and 1987) and outranked the Bond Index in all five years. In addition, in terms of the maximum/minimum return ratio, the multi-manager CTA portfolio outperformed the S&P 500 or the Bond Index in four of the five years.

More importantly, the multi-manager portfolio should not necessarily be compared directly with the S&P 500 or the Bond Index in terms of absolute performance. Modern Portfolio Theory has shown that while an individual security may not outperform an alternative asset or portfolio on a stand-alone basis, if the assets considered are not perfectly correlated, the security may offer a return/risk benefit in terms of an enlarged investment opportunity set and could be added to the comparison portfolio.

COMMODITY PORTFOLIOS IN OVERALL PORTFOLIO MANAGEMENT

In the previous section, we analyzed the risk and return performance of the multi-manager portfolio in comparison to commodity portfolios obtained under various trading rules and other traditional investment alternatives (that is, stocks and bonds and commodity indices). The question now arises as to whether a portfolio of CTAs (multi-manager portfolio) selected from a universe of CTAs should be added to a portfolio of existing stocks or bonds. Whether the commodity portfolio enters an existing portfolio depends on the relative means and standard deviations of the commodity portfolio and of the comparison portfolio, as well as the correlation between the commodity portfolio and the comparison portfolio.

As seen in Table 4.5, the maximum correlation between the S&P 500 and the multi-manager portfolio is 0.44 for 1985. The correlation coefficients for the S&P 500 and the multi-manager portfolio are negative in 1984 and positive in all other years. The correlation coefficients between the multi-manager portfolio and Bond Index indicates negative

TABLE 4.5. Correlation coefficients.

	Multi-Manager CTA Portfolio with Other Investments				
Year	S&P 500	Bond Index	Worst 5	LC 10	Best 10
1983	.1626	−.6823	0.9301	0.9321	0.979
1984	−.3982	.3387	0.9387	0.9702	0.9107
1985	.4389	−.2043	0.9286	0.9517	0.9298
1986	.3552	.7076	0.7692	0.8112	0.8881
1987	.1421	−.3360	0.6606	0.8545	0.8788
1983–87	.0787	.0423	0.8691	0.9313	0.9438

	Multi-Manager CTA Portfolio			
Year	CTA-Equal Wt.	CTA-Dollar Wt.	Pool Index	Fund Index
1983	.9197	.8911	.7947	.8910
1984	.9679	.9609	.9505	.9746
1985	.9245	.9090	.9627	.9363
1986	.9621	.9088	.8843	.8829
1987	.9669	.9296	.9175	.9781
1983–87	9391	.9003	.8615	.9219

	Average of the Individual CTAS Correlation Coefficients with Other Investments					
Year	S&P 500	Bond Index	CTA-Equal Weighted In.	CTA-Dollar Weighted In.	Pool Index	Fund Index
1983	−.1143	−.4245	.5483	.5637	.4994	.5511
1984	−.1804	.2179	.5371	.5418	.5358	.5428
1985	.2662	−.1011	.5194	.5277	.5448	.5326
1986	.1909	.4352	.5577	.5889	.5302	.5345
1987	.1257	−.1669	.5684	.5745	.5426	.5867
1983–87	.0526	.0253	.5069	.5261	.4855	.5196
1983–87σ^2	.1204	.1213	.2373	.2340	.2323	.2255

correlation in three years (1983, 1985, and 1987) and positive correlation in two years (1984 and 1986). Overall, the correlations of the entire period (1983 to October 1987) for the multi-manager portfolio with S&P 500 and the multi-manager portfolio with Bond Index are similar and close to zero (0.08 and 0.04, respectively). Correlation coefficients between the multi-manager portfolio, commodity indices, and commodity portfolios determined using trading rules (that is, Worst 5, Low Correlated 10, and Best 10) indicate that the returns on these trading rules and commodity indices are positively and highly correlated with those of the multi-manager portfolio. The correlation between the returns of the trading rule portfolios or commodity indices and that of the multi-manager portfolio never fall below 0.60 during the period studied. For the whole period (1983 to October 1987) the correlation between the CTA portfolios determined using trading rules and commodity indices and the multi-manager portfolio never fall below 0.86.

In Table 4.6, results show that for the entire period from January 1983 to October 1987, the multi-manager portfolio must earn a return of about 7 percent per year (exclusive of management fees) in order to represent an attractive addition to the comparison stock portfolio (S&P 500), and a return of about 6 percent per year in order to represent an attractive addition to the bond portfolio (Bond Index).

It is also important to point out that break-even results are dependent upon assumptions about the risk-free rate and correlation coefficient. For instance, in our analysis for the whole period we used positive correlation coefficients of 0.078 (multi-manager portfolio and S&P 500) and 0.042 (multi-manager portfolio and Bond Index). In individual years, the correlations coefficient with stocks (S&P 500) ranged

TABLE 4.6. Multi-manager CTA break-even performance level for inclusion in comparison portfolio.

	1983	1984	1985	1986	1987	1983–87
Multi-Manager CTA vs. S&P 500	.4296	.9583	1.7655	.8135	.4626	.6690
Multi-Manager CTA vs. Bond Index	1.3581	1.0428	.1204	1.4632	1.0041	.6353

from as low as −0.39 to as high as 0.43, and for bonds from a low of 0.68 to a high of 0.70. As noted, a negative correlation coefficient would reduce the required break-even rate.

In fact, given a negative correlation, the higher the standard deviation of the multi-manager portfolio the lower the break-even rate. Moreover, the break-even rate in Table 4.6 is also a direct function of the assumed risk-free rate. For assets with low correlation, the risk-free rate may well dominate the determination of the break-even rate. For instance, in our analysis the average risk-free rate for the period 1983 to October 1987 was approximately 6 percent per year and our break-even ratios are also approximately 6 percent. For an assumed correlation of zero the break-even rate would equal the risk-free rate.

As mentioned earlier, the monthly rate of return data used in this analysis are net of all fees and costs to the investor except, in our analysis, the cost to search out, construct, and monitor a portfolio of 14 CTAs.

The additional costs from this activity ("manager of managers" function) is estimated to be approximately 3 percent per annum (some of this in the form of incentive fee payment.) Results from Table 4.1 indicate that for the five-year period (1983-1987) the annual return of a commodity portfolio was 20.5 percent. In Table 4.7, we report on the differential between the actual return relative to the break-even rate. To the degree that the differential between the actual return and break-even rate is above its additional management fees (for example, the range of 3 percent per annum), it can be assumed that even with these additional fees the asset is an attractive alternative. For instance, with an annual expense of 3 percent (0.25 percent monthly), the multi-manager CTA portfolio is an attractive addition to a portfolio of stocks in all years except 1985 and to bonds in all years except 1983 and 1986.

TABLE 4.7. Multi-manager CTA differential break-even performance (actual return—break-even return).

	1983	1984	1985	1986	1987	1983–87
Multi-Manager CTA vs. S&P 500	.7044	1.0337	.1965	.3625	1.9494	1.0430
Multi-Manager CTA vs. Bond Index	−.2241	.9492	1.8416	−.2872	1.4079	1.0764

The results for the overall period (1983 to October 1987) reflect the results given in the individual years. With an expense rate of 3 percent per year, the multi-manager portfolio provided a positive differential break-even return relative to the S&P 500 and the Bond Index. As important, the differential break-even returns in Table 4.7 for the multi-manager portfolio relative to the S&P 500 and Bond Index (1.04 and 1.07, respectively) are higher than the absolute differential results reported in Table 4.2 for the multi-manager portfolio relative to the S&P 500 and Bond Index (0.372 and 0.693, respectively). This indicates the benefit of comparing the multi-manager CTA portfolio as an addition to a portfolio versus a direct single asset comparison.

RESULTS OF THE ANALYSIS

- An investment policy based on the purchase of investment portfolios with widely differing subsets of securities (multi-portfolios) is gaining acceptance.
- In addition to diversifying across investment classes, investors may wish to diversify within an asset class across managers, (the multi-manager approach).
- The existence of a multi-manager portfolio provides both diversification by style (utilizing managers employing a variety of trading approaches) and diversification of judgment (several managers analyzing the same subset of securities).
- Multi-advisor portfolios significantly outperform the average individual CTA and alternative commodity investment vehicles such as pools and publicly traded funds.
- Multi-manager CTA portfolios outperformed (exclusive of selection and management fees) traditional investments (Ibbotson and Sinquefield stock and bond indices) on an individual basis for the entire period, and also provided a positive addition to the portfolio of stocks and bonds for the entire period.
- Publicly traded commodity funds show relatively poor performance as stand-alone investments and as additions to portfolios of stocks and bonds.

APPENDIX I. Comparison of CTA indices to other indices.

In order to compare the construction of the CTA indices to other popular investment indexes, the Table 4.A is provided for reference.

Index Name	Percent of Universe	Number of Entities in Index	Value Wt'd or Equal Wt'd	Price or Total Ret Index	Indexing Method	Description
Dow Jones Industrial	25% of NYSE	30	Equal	Price	Arithmetic	Top Industrials
S&P 500 Index	75% of NYSE 58% US Stk $	500	Value	Both	Ratio of $	500 Top Mkt Value
NYSE Index	All NYSE 77% US Stk $	2000 Active	Value	Tot Ret	Ratio of $	All Common Stocks
Salomon Bond Indices	All Above $25 Million	Varies	Value	Tot Ret	Value Wt'd Return Avg	Index By Type
MAR CTA Indexes	79% of $ Under Management	25	Value & Equal	Tot Ret Commis & All Fees	Value Wt'd Equal Wt'd Monthly Ret	All CTAS in Top 25% of CTAS Based on $ Under Management
MAR Pool	All Domestic	Active	Equal	Tot Ret Commis & All Fees	Equal Wt'd Monthly Ret	All Domestic Private Pools
MAR Fund	All Domestic	Active	Equal	Tot Ret Commis & All Fees	Equal Wt'd Monthly Ret	All Domestic Public Funds

- Both the multi-manager portfolio and the average CTA would have offered diversification benefits relative to comparison of stock and bond indices.
- The multi-manager portfolio offers similar return at a lower risk than the average CTA of the subsample or the CTA index.
- Multi-manager portfolios may offer a superior risk/return tradeoff to stock and bond indices. Plus, using simple trading rules may allow the selection of CTAs so their return performance can be enhanced with little or no increase in risk.

BIBLIOGRAPHY

Bodie, Zvi and Victor Rosansky, "Risk and Return in Commodity Futures," *Financial Analysts Journal* 36 (May–June, 1980), 3–14.

Brorsen, B. Wade and Louis P. Pukac, "Optimal Portfolios for Commodity Futures Funds," *Journal of Futures Markets* Vol. 10, No. 3 (1990). 247–258.

Brorsen, B. Wade and S. Irwin, "Examination of Commodity Funds Performance," *Review of Research in Futures Markets,* Vol. 4, (1985), 84–94.

Commodity Futures as an Asset Class, New York Futures Exchange, Report by Powers Research Associates (January, 1990).

Cornew, Ronald. "Commodity Pool Operators and Their Pools: Expenses and Profitability," *Journal of Futures Markets,* Vol. 8, No. 5 (1988), 617–637.

Edwards, F. and Andy C. Ma, "Commodity Pool Performance: Is the Information Contained in Pool Prospectuses Useful," *Journal of Futures Markets,* Vol. 8, No. 5 (1988), 589–616.

Elton, E. J., M. J. Gruber, and J. C. Rentzler, "Professionally Managed, Publicly Traded Commodity Funds," *Journal of Business* (April, 1987), 177–199.

Elton, E. J., M. Gruber, and J. C. Rentzler, "New Public Offerings, Information, and Investor Rationality: The Case of Publicly Offered Commodity Funds," *Journal of Business,* Vol. 6, No. 1 (1988) 1–15.

Elton, E. J., M. Gruber, and J. C. Rentzler, "The Performance of Publicly Offered Commodity Futures," *Financial Analysts Journal* (July/August, 1990), 23–30.

Howard, C. T. and L. J. D'Antonio, "A Risk/Return Measure of Hedging Effectiveness," *Journal of Finance and Quantitative Analysis* (March, 1984), 101–112.

Irwin, S. H. and B. W. Brorsen, "Public Futures Funds," *Journal of Futures Markets* (Fall, 1985), 463–485.

Irwin, S. H. and D. Landa, "Real Estate, Futures, and Gold as Portfolio Assets," *Journal of Portfolio Management* (Fall, 1987), 29–34.

Lintner, J. "The Potential Role of Managed Commodity-Financial Futures Accounts (and/or funds) in Portfolios of Stocks and Bonds." Paper presented at the Annual Conference of the Financial Analyst Federation, Toronto, Canada, May, 1983.

Lukac, Louis, B. W. Brorsen, and S. H. Irwin, "Similarity of Computer Guided Technical Trading Systems," *Journal of Futures Markets* (February, 1988), 1–14.

Levy, H. "Futures, Spots, Stocks and Bonds: Multi-Asset Portfolio Analysis, *Journal of Futures Markets,* No. 4 (1987), 383–395.

Schneeweis, T., U. Savanayana, and D. McCarthy, "Alternative Commodity Trading Vehicles: A Performance Analysis," *Journal of Futures Markets* (1991).

Sharpe, William. *Investments,* Prentice Hall, 1984.

Szala, G. "In Search of the Right Commodity Trading Advisor," *Futures Magazine* (September, 1987), 46–47.

Szala, G. "Reading A Performance Table: Not an Easy Task!," *Futures Magazine* (September, 1987).

Yau, Jot, U. Savanayana, and T. Schneeweis, "Alternative Performance Models in Interest Rate Futures," in B. Goss, Ed. *A Review and Analysis in Rational Expectations and Efficiency in Futures Markets* (Methuen, 1990).

PART TWO

APPLICATIONS OF MANAGED FUTURES INVESTING

5 EVALUATING COMMODITY TRADING ADVISORS

Laleen Collins Doerrer

Performance evaluation is part science and part art. The science aspect lies in measuring performance; current computer technology and the ready availability of security data make this so. The art aspect lies in assessing the performance number; the multiplicity of factors involved in managing a portfolio necessitates a blending of both qualitative and quantitative judgments to reach a conclusion regarding the acceptability of performance. New creative evaluation techniques will continue to be introduced . . .

Ron Sturz
in *Portfolio and Investent Management*

Investment markets and specifically futures markets, have become increasingly complex, volatile, and interconnected. The trading volume and new uses for futures contracts have grown to dimensions rarely imagined 20 years ago. Today, contracts exist for hedging risk in the classic commodities, such as agricultural products and metals contracts, and also for most aspects of legal international trade, including currencies and financial instruments.

The investors in the futures markets have also changed. For years, large consortiums and individual speculators dominated the markets. Today's clients include financial trading firms, international corporations, and banks. In particular, the presence of foreign investors in U.S. futures markets have changed many of the characteristics of futures trading. Trends in markets appear to be shorter in duration. Liquidity in various markets has dramatically shifted. Liquidity in financial futures and currencies continues to increase, while liquidity in markets such as copper, lumber, cocoa, sugar, and livestock is diminishing. At the same time, risk-reward ratios of 2:1 seem to be harder to find.

Many managers will be hard-pressed to produce high rates of return during the upcoming decade. On the other hand, today's complexity offers tremendous opportunities to those who are ready to address it and are willing to add managed futures to their total portfolios.

Managed futures has been one of the fastest growing areas of opportunity in investment markets. The trade newsletter *Managed Account Reports,* estimated that in 1990 at least $20 billion had been committed to managed futures products. The managed futures industry has been growing at a substantial rate of 35 percent compounded annually.

Managed futures is now a recognized means for enhancing portfolio growth and diversification. Academic research in the area of Modern Portfolio Theory has generally given greater credibility to managed futures. Many researchers who use measures of portfolio rewards in terms of risk, have concluded that managed futures are capable of enhancing the performance of most standard portfolios.

Commodity Trading Advisors (CTAs) are professional futures traders. Most investment managers, pool operators, and Futures Commission Merchants (FCMS or brokers) use CTAs to invest in futures for profit. CTAs are very similar to equity managers. However, due to the lack of valid long-term data, the trading performance of CTAs is more difficult to evaluate than equity managers using standard quantitative techniques. Most of today's best CTAs have less than five years of performance data. A recent study, conducted by Mitchell Rock and Joseph Rosen, evaluated the performance history of 90 CTAs over a 54-month period, from January 1985 to June 1989. During this period, the study showed that capital invested jumped from $577 million in 1985 to $4.2 billion in 1989.

PROBLEMS IN EVALUATING COMMODITY TRADING ADVISORS (CTAs)

The first observation on formulating an evaluation method for CTAs is that it is difficult to design a rigorous objective method that will work well for all advisors. The growth explosion in the managed futures industry has brought a variety of advisors to the marketplace who do not resemble the older established advisors.

Successful advisors with more than five years of trading performance and over $10 million under management are most likely to use technical analysis and rely on some form of trend-following system. Technical analysis is defined as the study of charting price formations as opposed to fundamental analysis which relies on information relative to the commodity, such as anticipated supply and demand. Technical analysis often includes a study of the actual daily, weekly, and monthly price, averages, volume and open interest data, utilizing charts or computers for analysis.

The result of using this type of trading technique is that rates of return are generally uneven. Annual rates of return usually range from negative returns to over 100 percent. Figure 5.1 and Table 5.1 show that standard deviations and rates of returns are likely to be much higher among most of the older established advisors than equities and fixed income investments measured during the same period.

As the managed futures industry has grown, so has the universe of CTAs. According to the National Futures Association (NFA), there were over 2500 CTAs registered with the Commodity Futures Trading Commission (CFTC). Out of the available pool, less than 20 Advisors have public track records of at least 10 years or longer. Many of the most profitable advisors with sustainable track records are unavailable for new accounts.

Availability is a difficult problem in selecting advisors. The pool of available CTAs with long credible track records is smaller than the registration numbers indicate. Some of these advisors no longer accept new equity and are actually distributing profits to investors. Other advisors have established requirements to purposely slow expansion, such as only accepting equity through private limited partnerships or raising minimum deposits to very large amounts.

FIGURE 5.1. Comparison of investments.

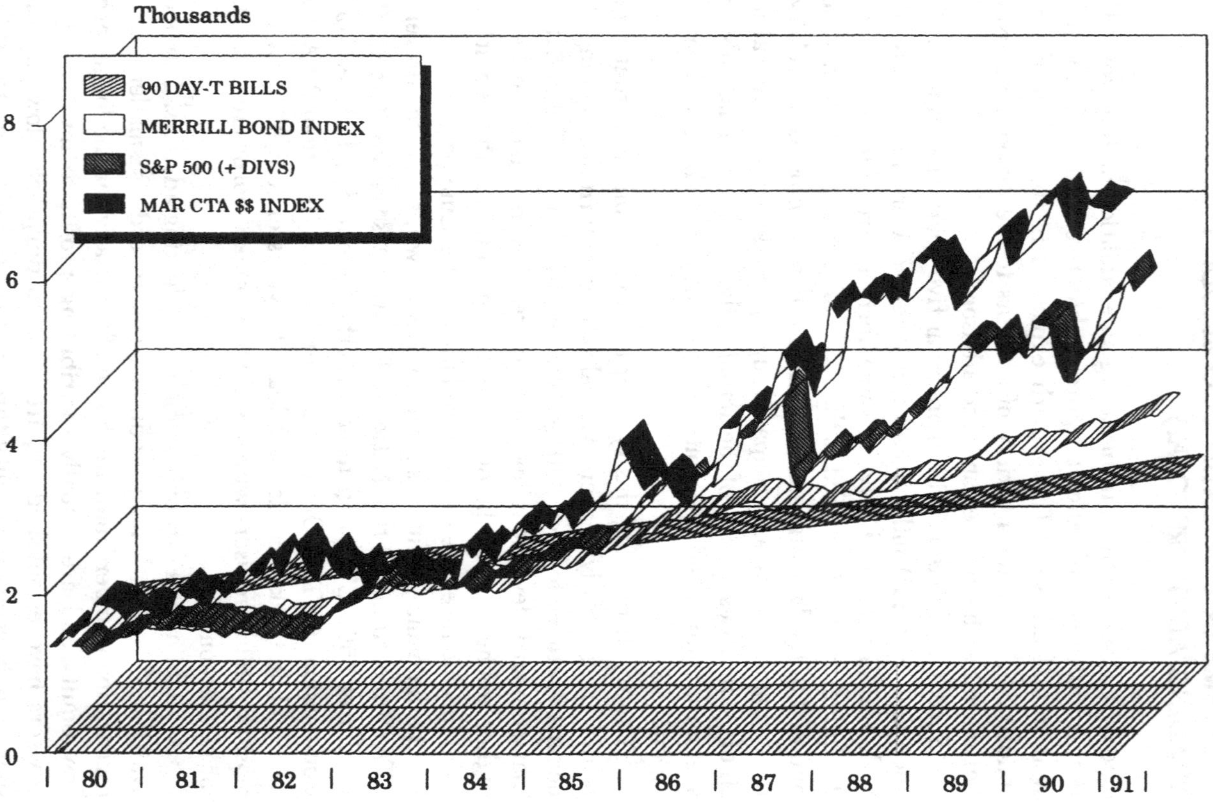

TABLE 5.1. MAR EQU. CTA, S&P 500, and Merrill Bond Indices.

Name of Index	Average Annual Return	Average Standard Deviation
MAR Weighted CTA	25%	31%
S&P 500 (Adjusted)	17%	20%
Merrill Bonds	13%	11%

These efforts have been adopted by advisors because their size can restrict their effectiveness in the futures markets. They may face liquidity problems in several markets, especially in the agriculture and soft commodity markets, (for example, cocoa, cotton, and sugar.) Position limitations, as defined by the CFTC, may be another problem in several markets. They may also want to restrict the number of orders entering the markets at the same time. In situations where a CTA has several different broker groups executing orders, a CTA may enter the orders consecutively and cause the broker groups to compete with each other. This situation can greatly increase the price of execution in some of the less liquid futures contracts.

A fast-growing CTA with a small administrative staff is often unprepared to face the administrative difficulties of order entry problems and administration as they are selected to trade for new FCMs. Each FCM or wirehouse may use an entirely different procedure for order entry, price allocation, and so on, which the CTA must incorporate into their operation. This problem is very common among CTAs with less than five years of experience.

The problem with having so few advisors with longer track records equates to a simple quantitative dilemma, namely, established quantitative procedures require a basic timeframe of data to be statistically significant. Frankly, there are few available CTAs with enough history to make their performance statistically reliable for predictive analysis.

Compounding these difficulties in evaluation methods is the fact that the 1988 and 1989 futures markets were especially volatile, especially in the short-term. Such reversals accounted for poor performance results among the group of advisors who used long-term trend following techniques. By contrast, 1990 provided this same group of advisors with strong trending markets.

To better understand some of the difficulties facing public futures funds, a study was conducted among public funds with five years or more of trading histories. Most of these funds were single advisor funds. The following are case examples of some typical difficulties found in evaluating CTAs.

Problem 1. Standard Risk-Reward Ratios Overlook Advisors

One of the biggest impediments to objective quantitative analysis is that futures advisors often change their trading methods over time, particularly after experiencing a large loss. The performance record may show desirable rates of return despite large losses.

An example of this situation is the trading advisor who made significant changes in trading methodology after a very bad year. Table 5.2 depicts the performance data for such an advisor. The total performance record for this advisor could have been rejected in most objective evaluations using quantitative analysis. For instance, the risk associated (as measured by standard deviation) is derived from the entire performance record and can be twice the possible average return. Most common methodologies, such as the use of the Sharpe-Markowitz allocation model, would have rejected such an advisor for an allocation. Yet, such an advisor could easily be a top performer and produce an annual rate of return in excess of 30 percent.

Problem 2. Equity Incapacitating the System

An advisor's performance can be affected by significant changes in equity. Advisors who perform extraordinarily well with small amounts of equity may or may not perform evenly as equity increases or decreases.

This problem is very common. The amount of equity under management seems to have a slightly negative impact on overall performance, especially if the CTA is a discretionary trader and primarily relies on fundamental analysis. Table 5.3 presents the performance data for an

TABLE 5.2. Individual CTA performance.

Performance Statistics						B-1					80/1 - 90/12		
Yr	1	2	3	4	5	6	7	8	9	10	11	12	Year
81	12.88	−4.09	−17.34	19.24	4.90	21.44	5.46	12.17	−13.37	−28.21	36.52	−16.14	14.49
82	7.99	−9.81	14.67	−1.69	−2.04	29.30	−7.89	21.51	24.69	−6.55	−15.22	−17.95	26.16
83	25.62	13.03	8.45	3.65	3.68	−19.57	11.06	15.00	2.32	11.25	−7.51	−14.15	53.64
84	−2.30	3.89	0.96	−10.28	6.88	−13.50	34.26	−8.95	−7.95	−4.28	−8.47	11.94	−6.20
85	2.62	0.38	8.93	6.69	−3.13	−4.76	17.12	−5.98	−20.20	9.84	−5.32	5.26	6.24
86	8.90	5.59	10.97	−10.31	6.62	2.68	−1.20	10.51	−2.51	−19.73	1.41	−9.16	−1.38
87	4.90	−1.64	11.40	40.05	−23.75	−3.64	2.93	−10.62	11.74	−0.70	17.50	6.88	51.63
88	5.99	−3.64	0.59	−13.14	11.73	33.23	−23.29	−19.52	3.01	9.11	−3.95	2.30	−9.43
89	7.28	−2.32	8.86	−2.05	16.93	2.40	−6.14	−1.59	14.55	−13.96	1.67	1.96	26.26
90	13.59	−6.71	1.81	10.16	−2.72	−1.35	3.25	18.98	−1.76	11.35	0.15	4.28	60.07

TABLE 5.3. Individual CTA performance.

Performance Statistics						B-2					85/1 - 90/12		
Yr	1	2	3	4	5	6	7	8	9	10	11	12	Year
85	70.00	−30.50	32.50	−41.00	22.50	6.20	21.70	−14.00	36.20	4.20	34.80	16.10	179.3
86	−21.90	41.30	30.00	0.50	−15.60	−5.40	−41.50	24.80	−20.80	17.80	−8.30	3.10	−25.87
87	8.70	39.80	12.90	21.40	0.50	4.70	11.00	11.10	20.40	−9.80	−2.80	−1.40	181.3
88	3.20	4.70	−3.90	−0.80	0.01	1.60	0.30	1.00	−1.90	−3.30	0.50	0.10	1.19
89	0.90	4.50	4.50	2.20	0.10	0.70	9.20	5.70	1.50	4.30	5.30	0.30	46.49
90	0.20	−0.10	0.30	0.20	0.40	0.30	2.10	−2.30	0.01	0.30	0.30	0.30	1.98

advisor with the classic inverse relationship between equity and performance. This effect could be due to a variety of factors, including the mind-set of the trader. It has been suggested that a trader becomes more "risk-averse" as equity increases.

Others believe a trader is likely to change trading styles as his or her lifestyle changes. There are several examples of smaller CTAs that employ one discretionary trader who has a diminishing track record. One should monitor any significant lifestyle changes with discretionary traders, such as building a new house or moving offices, as these changes are likely to affect overall performance as time and attention are diverted from trading.

Problem 3. Changing Markets and Static Systems

Another impediment to using quantitative analysis exclusively is that CTAs who fail to incorporate some form of heuristic methodology in a trading program may experience higher risk and volatility as the overall markets change, particularly in the soft commodities, grains, and meat contracts.

There are several examples of older, established advisors who did not change their trading styles or methods as the markets changed. Their track records often reveal diminishing margins of return with higher levels of risk associated with more recent trading performance. Table 5.4 presents the performance data of an advisor who had not adjusted the trading system through it's tenure. One of the simple ways to examine this is to use a simple correlation of time versus a risk-reward measurement.

Careful scrutiny to both heuristic methodology and characteristics of various markets used in the trading system should be considered in evaluations.

Another example of the same problem can be found in advisors who rely on certain technical systems such as moving averages and stochastics. Unless adjustments to historical data are periodically made, changing market characteristics will undermine the integrity of the system. Some even claim that the markets have become more volatile as huge orders are simultaneously executed when large numbers of advisors use the same technical systems.

TABLE 5.4. Individual CTA performance.

Performance Statistics							B-3				80/1 - 90/12		
Yr	1	2	3	4	5	6	7	8	9	10	11	12	Year
80	45.20	19.90	4.20	1.10									83.40
81	5.90	31.70	6.00	−9.70									33.50
82	22.80	13.80	−7.30	−19.70									4.02
83	7.70	−2.20	15.50	7.30									30.54
84	1.40	17.60	10.70	−10.40									18.28
85	4.70	−26.40	14.00	33.70									17.45
86	−9.50	5.60	−17.40	1.60									−19.80
87	28.92	10.35	0.41	32.69									89.55
88	−18.79	30.89	−10.95	5.22									−0.40
89	−3.12	−8.33	−8.06	25.42									2.41

TABLE 5.5. Individual CTA performance.

Performance Statistics							B-4				80/1 - 90/12		
Yr	1	2	3	4	5	6	7	8	9	10	11	12	Year
87	10.41	8.21	7.82	4.78	1.05	4.37	10.97	−2.35	2.45	19.58	19.18	6.41	139.7
88	−9.47	−0.47	1.34	0.49	12.07	15.39	0.45	0.61	−0.97	−2.16	0.26	0.55	17.14
89	1.04	0.49	1.81	−3.80	7.46	3.04	0.10	−0.27	−1.61	−1.80	−0.98	−3.36	1.63
90	−1.73	−1.22	2.68	3.17	−0.41	−3.09	2.92	−4.15	4.20	14.46	0.90	−2.58	14.78

Problem 4. Diminishing Margins of Return and Growth

In some cases, advisors may change trading techniques and contracts as equity increases. For example, several large advisors have quit trading markets, well-known for their poor liquidity, and moved to the cash or foreign exchange markets.

Most successful advisors with experience managing over $100 million have completely changed their trading methodology and markets. Table 5.5 presents a record built on trading in pork-bellies and cocoa. As the advisor experienced market limitations and liquidity difficulties, the advisor began trading the cash foreign exchange and cash commodity markets. This is one main reason why large established advisors often have diminishing margins of return in their records.

Although equity has an inverse relationship with performance, equity generally has a positive relationship with diminishing risk. While many advisors produce lower returns as equity increases, they usually experience lower risk, thus maintaining an approximately similar risk-reward ratio.

A similar problem occurs when equity increases and the advisor experiences liquidity problems. In such a situation, the advisor often adds other markets to the trading system and experiences a natural diversification of the total trading. The net result is usually lower rates of return and less volatility.

These are just a few examples of the numerous complications that arise in evaluating CTAs and their performance data. Each complication makes a purely quantitative evaluation inaccurate. Moreover, a five-year or longer requirement may eliminate some of the most desirable advisors in the industry. Finally, an attractive long-term record may not be an accurate indication for potential future returns.

Due to the shortcomings of purely quantitative and comparative approaches, an increasing number of experienced managers have opted for a multidimensional approach to CTA evaluation. The most significant feature of this approach is the incorporation of a characteristic evaluation into the total process.

Since single evaluation techniques may lack the capability to handle the large variety of performance issues that exist in the managed futures industry, the use of a multiformat evaluation is desirable.

THE MULTIDIMENSIONAL APPROACH TO EVALUATION

The formal advisor evaluation process usually starts with an examination of the advisor's performance data, trading systems, and business profile. This information is found in the CTA's Disclosure Document. This document is filed with the CFTC on a semi-annual basis.

The Disclosure Document gives a general description of the fund, its advisor, principals, the trading system and its methodology. The advisor is also required to maintain tables of historical performance that are set up as composites of all managed accounts and hence, are an average, rather than an actual account. For a variety of reasons, Disclosure Documents are often revised and thus require continual review. Since one of the most common charges is in the performance composite tables, it is important to track an advisor's performance relative to these tables.

Most managers take the information presented in a Disclosure Document's performance composites and use it for a preliminary statistical evaluation. In the case where a CTA's Disclosure Document breaks data into several tables, the table that most likely represents what a client is likely to "buy" is used for evaluation. For example, if the actual record used a low or high commission rate, such as $10 or $100 dollars per round turn, (a round-turn commission is both the buy and sell cost of executing a futures trade) and the CTA also provides a "pro-forma" table, such as $45 per round turn, the pro-forma table will be used for evaluation.

Pro-forma tables can be extremely useful in an evaluation. However, one should note that these tables are hypothetical. Extreme care should be exercised when a CTA has a losing record, yet presents a pro-forma table based on completely hypothetical assumptions, such as different commission and fee schedules or trading systems. In some instances, such presentations may demonstrate that the advisor has a poor understanding of the trading system and has exercised poor judgment in conducting business.

The manager should request that the CTA provide a current Disclosure Document and copies of all pertinent NFA filings, such as the 7R and amendments and 8Rs and amendments for the CTA and its principals. These combined documents should give a clear description of the advisor's trading philosophy, methodology, and track record of performance, as well as brief biographical information on the principals.

A manager should also request that the CTA provide a copy of at least one year of monthly statements on their most representative account. By comparing the account statements with the performance tables in the Disclosure Document, one can insure that the reported performance is not being skewed by a large account that has more favorable fees and conditions associated with it. The second advantage of obtaining actual account statements is that one can become familiar with the advisor's trading.

This information should be sufficient to provide a full understanding of the CTA as a business and how the CTA trades. Depending upon the duration of the record, one may obtain an idea about how profitable the advisor is likely to be based on past performance. The next step is to take this information into an interactive evaluation format to capture enough information to formulate an opinion on the probability of profitable trading in the future.

A multidimension evaluation is the most useful approach to understanding CTAs and interpreting their probability for future success. This format contains at least three evaluation approaches: quantitative, qualitative, and comparative.

Quantitative Evaluation

A quantitative evaluation should be conducted before any other procedure. The reasoning is simple: An investor should determine if the risk and returns are within their investment parameters. Further, a simple look at return exclusive of risk may be hazardous. This is because some CTAs have extraordinarily high rates of return and equally high risk profiles.

The performance record should be analyzed from a complete quantitative perspective. Depending upon the criteria of the investor, the most useful information is the average annual rate of return and annual standard deviation. Generally, a desirable advisor will have an annual rate of return and annual standard deviation that are approximately equal. This 1:1 ratio is as likely to pinpoint a desirable advisor as most other statistical methods.

The two most important measurements used in evaluation are Expected Rate of Return and Standard Deviation. The Rate of Return measures the prospects of an advisor. Generally, the higher the Rate of Return, the more desirable the advisor. The actual Rate of Return does not completely summarize the desirability of an investment and some measure of risk is needed. One of the most common measures of risk is Standard Deviation.

The methods of obtaining measurements of Rates of Return vary due to the treatment of equity that is added or withdrawn and the inclusion of interest in the final return. As long as the methodology is known, this should not matter. There are problems with relying totally upon an advisor's performance data.

The following measurements are commonly used in the futures industry. With the exception of the Sharpe Ratio, it is important to keep in mind that many of the common measures in the futures industry lack reliable data and scholarly study to support their usefulness as a predictive measure.

- **Monthly Rate of Return**: Monthly measurements of Rate of Return are made by taking the difference between beginning equity and ending equity and dividing the difference by beginning equity. This value is then multiplied by 100 to put it in a percentage value.

  In some instances, the Monthly Rate of Return is adjusted to account for large additions or withdrawals. If we are using beginning and ending equity to obtain a return, additions and withdrawals can substantially skew results.
- **1-Year Average Rate of Return**: A twelve-month frequency is used to define a one year average. Each month of return is compounded. We then take the geometric mean of the compounded growth factor.

$$\begin{array}{c}\text{Geometric Mean}\\ \text{(1-Year Average ROR)}\end{array} = \frac{\dfrac{(1+R1)}{100}\ \dfrac{(1+R2)}{100}\ \dfrac{(1+R3)}{100}}{3}\ \ldots -1$$

- **Expected Annual Rate of Return**: A log-normal distribution approach is used for calculating the projected annual rate of return. This approach considers both the compounding and the natural volatility of the monthly returns. Each monthly compounded return has the log of the underlying growth factor included. This approach forms a statistical expected return and standard deviation.

Note that the log-normal annual rate of return (expected annual rate of return) will usually be slightly larger than the geometric mean (one year average rate of return).

Measures of Risk and Risk Reward

- **Standard Deviation**: Standard Deviation is the square root of variance. It is commonly used as a measurement of relative dispersion, that is, the likely divergence of an actual return from expected return. In a sense, it summarizes the spread of the probability distribution. Since it is based on deviations of the observations from the mean, it is termed in the same units as the observation. The standard deviation of monthly return is annualized by multiplication by the square root of 12.
- **Sharpe Ratio**: The Sharpe Ratio is a conservative estimate of risk-to-reward. The ratio is calculated by subtracting a risk-free ratio from the average annual return and dividing the difference by the annual standard deviation of monthly returns.

  A Sharpe Ratio of 1.0 indicates that the investment is as desirable as a riskless return. There are very few futures investments that have Sharpe Ratios approximating 1.0. One of the reasons for this is that many *futures programs have higher volatility on the upside*. Since this also affects the Standard Deviation, it may make the Sharpe Ratio less meaningful. A Sharpe Ratio of 0.6 or higher is considered very desirable in managed futures and places the advisor in the top quartile of the industry. Lower Sharpe Ratios are acceptable if the Average Annual Rate of Return is very high and the CTA is placed in a multiple advisor allocation to reduce overall portfolio volatility.

  Compared to the overall industry, the Dollar Weighted Index of Futures Managers (an index comprised of the largest and generally highest performing registered advisors in the futures industry compiled by the industry newsletter, Managed Accounts Reports), has an overall Sharpe Ratio average during the last five years of only .55.

- **Sterling Ratio**: The Sterling Ratio is another risk-to-reward ratio. It is calculated by dividing the average annual return of the last three calendar years by the average of the worst drawdowns in each of those years plus 10 percent. The Sterling Ratio is especially well-suited to futures because the ratio relies on only three years of data.

  Generally, a Sterling Ratio of 1.0 or higher is very desirable. The median of the most recent range of reported Sterling Ratios was .55. Research on the Sterling indicates that nearly 92.5 percent of the time, being in the top-half of the Sterling range is a reasonable predictor of staying in the top-half of the range in the future.
- **Maximum Drawdown**: The Maximum Drawdown measures the maximum rate of a decline in returns. This loss is usually measured in consecutive periods. The purpose of isolating such a losing period is that some regard this measurement as an investment's empirical risk and thus may conclude this is most likely risk for the future.

  While there is little evidence to verify this conclusion, common sense dictates that if the record is significantly long, that is, approximately five years, the advisor has experienced enough market conditions to indicate a probable worst-case scenario. Maximum Drawdown is much less informative on short-term records.
- **Peak to Valley**: This is another term for the Maximum Drawdown. It is considered an answer to the question: "What is the worst possible loss an investor could have incurred had he or she entered and exited the advisor's management program at the worst possible time?"

  Again, the same reservations noted in Maximum Drawdown should be emphasized here. Unless a long-term track record is being presented, a Peak to Valley measurement may not be a useful measurement of risk.
- **Recovery Time**: The amount of time, usually measured in months, taken for the portfolio to recover from the maximum drawdown.
- **Risk**: Risk is defined as the relationship between average return and divergence from the defined return. There are two components to risk: nonsystematic risk and systematic risk.
- **Semi-Deviation**: Several managers observe the downside variance from the average and present this divergence as a risk measurement.

There is a lack of evidence to indicate that the semi-deviation measurement is a more accurate measurement of risk than a standard deviation.

- **Nonsystematic Risk**: This type of risk is particular to the specific investment program being considered. An example of such risk is when a major strike adversely impacts the value of a particular company. A well-diversified managed futures portfolio should dissipate most nonsystematic risk.
- **Systematic Risk**: This type of risk is held in common by all investments in an asset class or portfolio. For example, all stocks, bonds, and holdings in properties would be adversely affected by a major worldwide recession. These factors impact an entire portfolio and thus are common to all its securities. One way to quantify systematic risk is with a Beta measurement of the investment relative to the market or index for the investment.
- **Risk of Ruin**: Risk of Ruin is a probability measurement that an investment will lose X percent of equity at any point. The probability is calculated with a normal probability distribution of possible outcomes with an objective probability of each occurring. One common calculation is based on a .98 probability; there is a 2 percent margin of error.

These are some of the more common measurements in the managed futures industry. However, some managers use more complicated measurements. For example, one manager claims to use 90 different performance variables. Regretfully, many of these measurements are often "pseudo-statistics" rather than reliable measurements with valid substantiation. Another common misapplication of quantitative analysis, especially in the use of probability statistics, is that they are sometimes applied to advisors with less than two years of monthly performance data. In such cases, statistical significance is closer to random chance than purposeful probability.

The managed futures industry is new and rapidly changing so there is a lack of inclusive data and scholarly study. One of the real challenges to the managed futures industry during the next five years will be to fully test these measurements and determine what "really works."

Several software packages are commercially available to compute many of these performance statistics. Some of the systems also offer data with subscriptions to the software.

The decision to subscribe to a database should be carefully evaluated. In particular, the CTA selection process and procedures for checking reliability for the database should be fully understood. For a variety of reasons, the data may not be completely reliable.

Another issue that may arise with a purchased database is selectivity bias. In some cases, the database may only include advisors who have other business dealings with the vendor. In other cases, the database only includes advisors with high minimums or ten-year records, a generally unavailable group of advisors. Finally, some databases may have no procedures established for periodically checking the reliability of data.

ISSUES FOR QUALITATIVE EVALUATION

A purely quantitative approach may be insufficient for evaluating CTAs. Figure 5.2 more clearly explains why this is so. In Figure 5.2, three independent CTAs have been graphically depicted. Based on average annual rates of return and standard deviations, these advisors appear to be statistically similar. Each has a maximum loss (drawdown) of approximately 11 percent and has average returns of approximately 32 percent. Each CTA trades completely differently and has significantly different correlations with the MAR CTA Index:

- CTA 1 is a discretionary trading advisor with a tendency to use some trend-following techniques in his trading system. The CTA employs only two individuals, the trader and his wife who performs most administrative duties. The CTA has recently raised more than $10 million dollars. Further, from 1988 through 1990, the trader went through a series of significant personal changes. Most of the advisor's record is based on an incentive-based fee structure that averages about 22 percent.
- CTA 2 is a discretionary trading advisor who trades only one commodity based on fundamental information. The advisor uses an

FIGURE 5.2. Sample of three advisors with similar statistics.

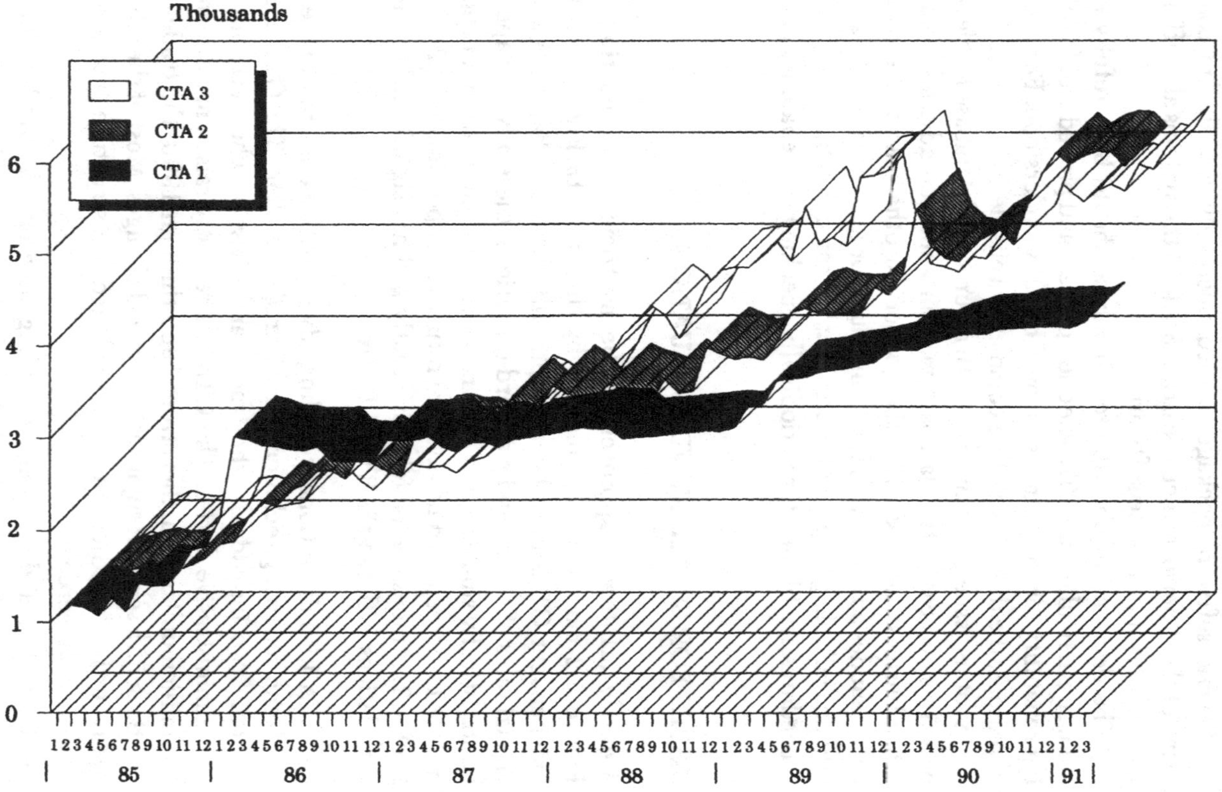

arbitrage-style of trading. In 1990, the advisor quadrupled equity under management. Personnel also was increased. The advisor has significantly restricted access and the manager believes they have reached capacity in the markets currently being traded. The traders are considering adding a new trading program in foreign exchange. The record has an average fee structure of a 2 percent management fee and a 15 percent incentive fee. The advisor is currently asking for 4 percent management fee and 20 percent incentive fee.

- CTA 3 is a systems trader who uses trend-following techniques. This program trades markets which are well-known for their trending characteristics and liquidity (financial and selected metals.) The advisor has had little personnel turn-over for nearly four years and has increased equity at a rate of approximately 20 percent per year. The advisor has a fee structure of 3 percent management fee and a 15 percent incentive fee. The advisor is currently charging a 4 percent management fee and a 20 percent incentive fee.

These cases are presented to highlight the problems with exclusive use of quantitative evaluations. All three advisors have low correlations to the MAR CTA Dollar Weight Index and have similar ranges of returns, standard deviations, and risk-reward ratios. However, only one of these CTAs is truly capable of accepting new equity with little risk of experiencing significantly different returns than historical performance might indicate.

Though the risks are difficult to quantify, a qualitative evaluation and characteristic review can significantly reduce the chance of selecting an unsuitable advisor. With this understanding, a qualitative evaluation can be a helpful selection tool.

QUALITATIVE EVALUATION AND CHARACTERISTIC REVIEW

One should not assume that all advisors are similar. Understanding the specific characteristics of advisors is essential in analyzing performance data. One obvious reason in understanding the advisors' characteristics is that the performance data may not be a sufficient indicator of potential performance. However, if one understands what the advisor does and how their business operates, one may have a better understanding of potential risks.

The major difference between characteristics and statistical review is that the former requires subjective analysis. When CTAs are placed in categories, each one has a tendency to produce certain types of risk-reward profiles. However, these tendencies should be considered in the context of the individual advisors and categorization may not always be appropriate.

Part of a manager's characteristic review should cover fees and commissions. CTA fee requirements can sometimes be an issue that will eliminate the advisor from a portfolio, especially if the portfolio consists of pension funds that may have limitations on fees. CTAs usually charge management and incentive fees, though some may opt to charge only one of these. The majority of advisors charge a management and incentive fee in the range of 2 percent and 15 percent, respectively. There is usually a 1 percent management fee trade-off for every 5 percent of incentive fee. Established advisors may charge more.

Commissions are another sensitive issue that should be covered in the evaluation. One must determine the "commission sensitivity" of the advisor. Generally, the larger the number of trades per unit of investment, the more commission sensitive the advisor will be. Commissions range from $8 per round turn up to $100. The advisor must acknowledge in the Disclosure Document if the advisor or principals of the advisor receive any portion of the commission from the clearing merchant. Such a situation can present a clear conflict of interest.

The size and maturity of an advisor may also hold many measurable characteristics. Generally, the performance of a CTA is analogous to the performance of other companies. Larger established CTAs (CTAs with over five years of experience and over $40 million under management) seem to perform similarly to mature companies. Both also have flattening growth curves and produce consistent rates of return.

The emerging group of CTAs (CTAs with three to five years of experience and less than $20 million under management) tend to emulate growth companies. Equity under management grows quickly. The company grows in volatile spurts and produces revenues that reflect this pattern of growth. Investments in emerging CTAs may hold unquantifiable risk, but can be an extremely lucrative part of the CTA industry because fees are generally lower and equity has not started to affect trading.

Finally, new CTAs (CTAs with less than three years of experience and less than $3 million under management) are similar to start-up companies. Data is insufficient to make any type of quantitative forecast, so attention should be paid to management and trading practices. Generally with new CTAs, the risks and rewards are unknown.

The following definitions should prove useful in categorizing CTA trading styles and practices. The definitions are based on observations of approximately 500 advisors over a one-and-a-half year period.

System vs. Discretionary

This category relates to how the manager executes a trading decision.

- **System**: If the advisor executes a trade based on a system signal (usually generated by a computer system), the advisor is defined as a systems manager. To a certain degree, the advisor has eliminated discretion from trading decisions. On balance, if the system is working properly, it will have a tendency to produce consistent risk-reward ratios over time.

  The system should be as completely evaluated as the CTA will allow. CTAs rarely allow an investor to view software and criteria for trading decisions. However, CTAs will provide general information, such as, if they use moving averages, market sentiment data, and risk-reward parameters.
- **Discretionary**: The discretionary CTA makes trading decisions with the use of human input and emotions. This type of manager often uses personal experiences to make and execute trading decisions, but may also use some sort of computer system as well. The key in this case is that the advisor may or may not, with almost equal probability, follow the signals being generated by the "system." Discretionary CTAs have a tendency to produce inconsistent risk-reward ratios over time.
- **System/Discretionary**: Some advisors primarily rely on a system, but traders who periodically override the system's signals are

defined as S/D. It should be noted that advisors who elect to not exit a trade after such a signal are usually over time, riskier traders. This may or may not be apparent in the performance data.

This category of trader has been growing during the last three years. As markets have become less predictable, advisors are using both methods of decision making. Discretionary advisors are discovering they need more consistent decision-making procedures, particularly as they have greater amounts of equity under management. Systems advisors are discovering they can eliminate some risk by using a small amount of discretion over certain parts of their system.

Technical vs. Fundamental

These descriptions relate to how a trading advisor makes trading decisions, that is, what things are important to the CTA's decision-making process.

- **Technical Analysis:** Technical analysis is based on the study of price patterns in order to provide a means of anticipating future prices. Technical analysis often includes a study of the actual daily, weekly, and monthly price volume and open interest data and price patterns. Charts and computers are often used for the analysis. Sentiment indicators, such as call-to-put ratios, or relative strength are also technical analysis instruments.
- **Fundamental Analysis:** Fundamental analysis looks at the external factors that affect the supply and demand of a particular commodity in order to predict future prices. Items such as government actions, the release of information concerning weather conditions and statistical information are fundamental events which can result in actual price movements.

  Generally, there are two types of fundamentalists. Fundamentalists who trade on the basis of short-term disparities between markets, such as cash vs. futures; and long-term fundamentalists who trade on the basis of macro-economic information. Short-term fundamentalists tend to experience lower risk-reward ratios and long-term fundamentalists tend to experience high risk-reward ratios.

- **Technical/Fundamental**: Many CTAs use a combination of technical and fundamental analysis. These CTAs usually use fundamental analysis to determine the general direction of a given commodity and then use technical analysis to determine entry and exit points.

Diversified vs. Specialized

This category relates to which futures contracts advisors will trade.

- **Diversified**: Indicates that the CTA may trade a wide variety of futures contracts. For the most part, this type of advisor will purposely diversify a portfolio of futures contracts and options to reduce nonsystematic risk. In most cases, an advisor who indicates they are diversified relies primarily on technical analysis.

  Generally, a fully-diversified advisor will experience moderate risk-reward ratios. The MAR CTA Indexes represent a good benchmark of diversified trend followers.
- **Specialized**: This category indicates that the advisor will trade a narrow group of futures contracts. CTAs in this category are most often arbitrage or tactical managers. Their futures management programs often involve some sort of arbitrage technique.

Limited Capacity

Many advisors find their trading system or methods are only effective up to a certain equity level. One of the best pieces of information an investor can obtain is to know whether the advisor has a limited capacity.

Equity Volatility Correlation

This category indicates the advisor may experience performance volatility as equity is increased.

Duration of Trades

This refers to how long most trades are held. Duration can have significant bearing on risk-reward ratios.

- **Short-Term:** Advisors who usually place trades that last between one day and one week are considered short-term traders. Generally, these advisors are commission sensitive and are likely to require very low commission rates, ranging from industry lows of $8.00 to $20.00. Trading usually ranges from 5,000 to 10,000 trades (round turns) per million dollars of equity.

  Short-term advisors tend to assume lower risk. Rates of return can significantly vary. Commitment of equity to margin requirements usually averages around 10 percent of total equity.
- **Intermediate-Term:** Advisors who usually placc tradcs that last from one week to one month are considered intermediate term. Generally, these advisors are slightly commission sensitive. They also are most likely to use technical analysis and discretion. Trading usually ranges from 1,800 to 3,000 trades per million dollars of equity.

  Intermediate-term advisors are the most difficult group to determine their general risk-reward ratios. The advisor usually commits less than 30 percent of total equity to trade margins.
- **Long-Term:** Advisors who usually place trades that last more than two weeks to several months are considered long-term. Generally, these advisors are not commission sensitive. They are likely to use both systems and discretion. They often use fundamental analysis, although a large minority of long-term advisors use some of the more "esoteric" forms of technical analysis such as Gann analysis, Fibonacci sequences, and Elliot Wave analysis. These advisors usually trade between 500 and 1,200 trades per million dollars of equity.

  Long-term advisors usually have high risk-reward ratios. It is a logical outcome of keeping trades in place through long periods. Many advisors in this category establish important risk-reward parameters before entering trades, such as 3:1. They usually will not place stop orders though they may have some concept of limits elsewhere.

A great deal of this qualitative information can be obtained through the filing and disclosure documents previously described. The disclosure documents contain pertinent information about a CTA's principals. Since a CTA does not have to disclose personal information about a trader (if the trader is not a principal of the firm), one should ascertain who is trading for the CTA and has authority to execute trades.

A disclosure document is often used as a marketing piece for the advisor and thus may not provide a fully detailed description of each principal. The registration documents (7Rs and 8Rs) can be used to find more specific details about the principals and the advisor. The 7R document requires ten years of personal employment history and education information.

During the qualitative review, a CTA should be contacted several times and asked a variety of questions. If at all possible, a personal visit to the CTA's office should be made. A visit or periodic calls can reveal much about how the CTA conducts business. One should look for professionalism and established procedure. Office logistics should be examined to assure that trading orders can be placed easily and access to someone representing the CTA is always possible.

Among the most desirable characteristics for the principals and traders is demonstrated success and endurance. These characteristics seem to have as much predictive ability for successful advisors as actual experience in managed futures. There are numerous examples of successful established CTAs who were employed in other occupations, ranging from social worker to engineer to physician.

In particular, the principals of systems CTAs were often employed in other occupations which required strong quantitative and systems skills. These skills were obviously incorporated into the CTA's trading methods. These principals are not required to be present; the system provides signals for trades. Often, this type of CTA has another principal who monitors the system and maintains contact with investors.

Other types of CTAs are less likely to have principals involved in other endeavors. The more a trader for the CTA uses discretion, the more necessary it is for the trader to be present for the execution of trades. Again, specific procedures and assurance of access must be present. This is especially true if the CTA's office is located in a home. The trading/office area should be clearly segregated from the rest of the home.

Logistics and procedures need to be established, otherwise an investor cannot be assured that the trader or advisor is carefully watching their investments. In the situation where an advisor does not seem to have easy access to incoming and outgoing calls, the advisor must use specific risk management techniques, such as placing stop-orders or employ a full-time trading assistant with authority to place orders.

Since CTAs are actually businesses, they should be evaluated as such. A good trader may not be a good office administrator. A CTA should have enough personnel to conduct trading and administration of accounts. CTAs that have only one principal who trades and manages all aspects of the business are usually unprepared to handle growth.

By contrast, large CTAs may have several employees with vague employment duties. In these cases, a specific person should be identified for client contact. Further, the evaluation should focus on traders and administrators (including the office manager and accountant/bookkeeper).

One should be concerned about all aspects of a CTA's record. It is reasonable to ask questions pertaining to management of the business, why certain statistical anomalies have occurred in a track record, specific questions about trading methods, and how the CTA's business administration is planned and managed. Advisors who are not prepared to answer these questions may lack the ability to maintain profitability as business grows.

Continual monitoring of the advisor is recommended even after an advisor has passed both a quantitative and qualitative evaluation. Newer and less established CTAs have many of the same characteristics as growth stocks. If they have successful traders, their companies often grow much faster and larger than planned and hence, are often exposed to "growing pains." A brilliant trader may not be a good business administrator.

The other reasons for continually monitoring the advisor is to ensure that they are adhering to their trading methods, especially their prescribed risk management. One should periodically review positions, turnover and margin-to-equity ratios. Margin-to-equity ratios, in particular, are useful to evaluate potential risk. For example, if margins have suddenly increased from 10 percent of equity to 50 percent of equity, the trader may be in trouble. Often this is a sign that the portfolio is being exposed to extreme risk. A good rule to follow is that: *Anytime a pattern or rule changes, an inquiry should be made to the CTA.*

COMPARATIVE ANALYSIS IN EVALUATIONS

In comparative analysis, evaluations tend to exclusively use indexes. In the futures industry, some trading managers and publications have created composites of CTA performance that are often substituted for an industry benchmark. These composites should be used with caution, because individual CTAs may be extremely different than the CTAs most commonly used in the so-called "CTA Indexes." At this writing, the managed futures industry is dominated by long-term trend followers. Unless the advisor is primarily a trend follower, they are not very likely to have much in common with the more popular CTA indexes.

Another common criticism is that most "CTA Indexes" have a self-selection bias built into them. In situations with nonaffiliated reporting systems, the advisors may choose whether or not to report their performance. In cases in which an organization tracks performance, criteria for inclusion is likely to make the index spurious. In both of these cases, critics argue, the performance results are probably overstated. In the former case, poor performing advisors merely quit reporting their performance. In the latter case, the organization may choose to drop the poor performing advisors from the index. Further, the nature of these indexes has not been verified in a rigorous and scholarly manner. In most cases, one must simply assume they have log-normal characteristics.

Further, if an advisor has a short-term performance record, as most do, or if an advisor changes methodologies and contracts, comparative analysis may not prove to be particularly helpful in evaluating the advisor. Also, many advisors have unique characteristics which are more appropriately compared to other indexes. For example, a CTA which trades an S&P 500 Stock Index futures program is more appropriately compared to the S&P 500 Index than to a MAR CTA index.

A final approach to comparative evaluation is to place the advisor's performance in the context of alternative investments. In this context, one can simply treat managed futures as a separate investment vehicle and compare returns and standard deviations to a variety of other investment vehicles, such as the S&P 500, the Russell 2000, the Merrill Lynch Municipal Bond Index, or 90-Day Treasury bill rates.

This approach is reasonable since an appropriate benchmark does not currently exist in the managed futures industry and is not likely to be created for some time. Until some time as an industry benchmark develops, one should judge success of their portfolio in terms of what the best available investments were at any particular time.

COVARIANCE ANALYSIS AS PART OF THE EVALUATION

Covariance analysis, or the procedure for comparing multi-manager performance, is a recommended part of the evaluation process for CTAs. One process which is particularly useful is to compare similar advisors with each other and other asset classes. The process involves creating a universe of advisors with similar characteristics and then measuring central tendency. One can create a hypothetical table of monthly performance statistics by averaging all of the returns.

This analysis relies on both the quantitative and qualitative evaluations for building a substantial database with enough reliable data to make characteristic conversions and correlation ranking statistically meaningful. With this process, one may be able to more specifically assign risk levels to the advisor on the basis of the characteristic and qualitative evaluation, despite a lack of information for any individual CTA.

After the database has been established and risk variables are assigned for each characteristic, the individual advisor being considered is then compared to an "appropriate universe" to determine desirability. First, a comparison of annual rates of return and standard deviation should be made. Then, a simple regression analysis can be used to obtain specific quantitative dimensions relative to the universe.

This process is extremely productive when applied to multiple advisor pools. The pool of selected CTAs is generated through the characteristic matrix and covariance. Provided they have attractive rates of returns individually, a combination of noncorrelated CTAs can be combined to create a very attractive investment.

The other approach is to generate a list of CTAs who have low to negative correlation coefficients to other investment categories, most notably: the OTC, the S&P 500 Index, bonds, metals, and foreign equities. Low correlation coefficients between selected advisors should offer better performance than comparative assets.

There are several benefits to using either form of correlation analysis in CTA evaluation. First, since most manager's analysis is portfolio generated, performance records of CTAs are compared to assess both variability and returns for specific portfolios. This approach offers an understanding of CTA performance relative to risks which might be inherent in a class of investments or the portfolio in general.

The use of covariance analysis also eliminates some problems which might be encountered with a simple comparative process. For example, one popular approach is to emphasize covariance rather than just simple comparative performance of CTAs. This process allows evaluation with or without regard to subjective bias.

The formula for the correlation coefficient, denoted by r is:

$$r = \frac{n(\Sigma xy) - (\Sigma x)(\Sigma y)}{n(\Sigma x^2) - (\Sigma x)^2 n(\Sigma y^2) - (\Sigma y)^2}$$

A lack of subjective bias can be both useful and problematic. One advantage to this approach is that the process eliminates consideration of all unquantifiable variables and may increase the number of possible portfolio allocations. By reducing predetermined bias, more opportunities can be examined. Indeed, many CTAs and multiple advisor pools can offer substantial reward relative to risk, when compared to alternative advisors and investments.

The disadvantage with this approach is that important characteristics which may affect portfolio selection are excluded from the process. For example, an advisor's capacity constraints will not be addressed through this approach.

It is recommended that covariance analysis be used with a qualitative format despite the lack of objectivity. We usually obtain correlation coefficients for each CTA in a portfolio and run the data through the Sharpe-Markowitz model to obtain a theoretical allocation for the portfolio. After obtaining these measures, the portfolio is then recreated with subjective constraints.

CONCLUSIONS

The difficulties in applying standard evaluation techniques to CTAs will not be reconciled without substantially more time and data. While some managers and portfolio analysts are waiting for more data, many individual CTAs continue to outperform most other asset categories. Significant research in Modern Portfolio Theory has verified that the use of managed futures can enhance a portfolio. Further, the huge growth in managed futures indicates some astute portfolio managers are not going to wait for standard evaluation techniques to prove this investment category is worthwhile.

Through the use of multidimensional evaluation, which uses quantitative, qualitative, and comparative analysis, one may find an array of attractive CTAs to enhance a portfolio. Placing performance in context requires attention to qualitative characteristics, as well as performance data. The primary objective is to gauge performance in light of what risks were taken to achieve the result and in light of what alternatives were present at the time.

Since good advisors change their methods and characteristics over time, it is imperative that CTAs be evaluated continually. Further, since changes may occur which will not be noted within a quantitative format, actual dialogue must take place with the advisor to maintain a clear idea of how business is being conducted. Depending upon the trading methods employed by the advisor, certain business characteristics will have more bearing on performance than others.

Through the use of more sophisticated evaluation techniques, the futures industry, and especially CTAs, will manage a larger share of institutional assets because the rates of return relative to risk are too attractive to ignore. Further, continuous monitoring and diligent evaluation of CTAs currently in the "under five years of experience" category may identify trading advisors that portfolio managers should incorporate into their investment strategies.

Covariance analysis can be used to further refine CTA selection. First, covariance can be used within a contextual approach, such as measuring an advisor against the appropriate universe of advisors. This approach will help to select complimentary advisors for a multiple advisor allocation. Similarly, covariance analysis can be used in a comparative approach, such as selecting advisors on the basis of covariance with alternative investment classes. This use of covariance will help isolate a managed futures investment which will enhance a larger portfolio.

In many respects, this approach is contrarian and may help uncover the few truly significant advisors who possess unique characteristics and are most likely to generate profits in a variety of economic climates, that is, those advisors who perform better than average in their universe and have a low or negative correlation to the universe and other asset classes.

The advisor selection process is very similar to selecting a great piece of art. Just as significant pieces of art are not easily replicated, the advisors who "stand out" against their universe and alternative assets classes are the most desirable.

6 A GUIDE TO ORGANIZING A COMMODITY POOL

Mark H. Mitchell
David M. Kozak

Commodity pools are entities formed to trade in commodity interests such as futures and options contracts. Since 1980, the number of both public and private commodity pools has grown rapidly. According to a 1991 estimate, pool assets are now about $7 billion. The reason for this dramatic increase is that pools are relatively simple in concept and structure. They are similar to mutual funds in that they combine investors' contributions to create a pool for investment.

Commodity pools offer investors many advantages generally unavailable to an individual who engages in futures transactions directly. Unlike a direct investment in futures contracts, a commodity pool limits the liability of an investor to the amount of the original investment plus any profits earned. A pool participant cannot be held personally liable for margin calls over and above the original investment. Commodity pools also allow unsophisticated investors to benefit from the advice and experience of a professional trading advisor, often increasing the likelihood of a profitable return.

Further, commodity pools offer opportunities for diversification to investors who are reluctant to spend substantial time or resources in trading futures directly. A commodity pool's potential profit may not depend on favorable economic conditions, and may achieve profits even during economic conditions that normally would adversely affect an investment in stocks, bonds, or real estate. In addition to diversifying a portfolio, commodity pools allow investors to diversify among contracts to a greater extent than if they were trading directly in the futures markets.

Typically, pools are organized under state law as limited partnerships and investors are admitted into the partnership as limited partners. Under this structure, the general partner has exclusive administrative authority over the pool's activities, relieving the investors of any administrative responsibilities and, at the same time, achieving limited liability. Further, as a limited partnership, a commodity pool avoids double taxation since there is no tax at the partnership level; only the investor's profits are taxed.

The Internal Revenue Service (IRS) requires that a general partner of a limited partnership maintain a substantial net worth. The IRS has issued statements indicating that a general partner may meet this requirement by maintaining a net worth equal to at least 10 to 15 percent of total capital contributions to the limited partnership. The IRS also requires a general partner to have a general partner's interest of at least 1 percent of the total capital contributions.

Commodity pools are governed by both commodity and securities laws. The interests that are traded by pools are commodities, but the pool interests offered to investors are considered securities. Each pool sponsor must consider not only federal statutes and the rules adopted by two federal agencies—the Commodity Futures Trading Commission (CFTC) and the Securities and Exchange Commission (SEC)—but also state securities laws and the rules of two self-regulatory organizations, the National Futures Association (NFA) and the National Association of Securities Dealers, Inc. (NASD). These agencies and organizations provide the general framework of securities and commodity law regulating pools.

SECURITIES LAW

A participant's interest in a commodity pool is regarded as a security and must meet the registration requirements of the federal and state securities laws unless an exemption exists. Generally, registration requirements distinguish between two types of offerings—public pools registered with the SEC (and the states) and private pools which may be exempt from registration with the SEC (and the states) pursuant to Regulation D and comparable state rules.

Public Pools

The major advantage of offering a public pool is that marketing strategies may be employed that are not available to private pools. For example, a public pool may advertise and solicit an unlimited number of investors, whereas a private pool may not advertise the offering and is restricted in the number and type of investors it solicits. Two major types of registration for public pools are available—Form S-1 and Form S-18.

Form S-1 and Form S-18

Form S-1 is the traditional and most common registration form used. It may be used in any offering, but is generally used for offerings of more than $7.5 million. Form S-1 requires complete disclosure in the form of a prospectus and registration statement that must be filed with the SEC at its headquarters in Washington, DC. On the other hand, Form S-18 is designed for public offerings by smaller pools offering no more than $7.5 million within a one-year period and may be filed with the SEC in any of its regional offices or in Washington. For offerings of less than $7.5 million, Form S-18 may be more cost effective, decreasing the time and complexity of the registration process.

A public offering cannot begin until the SEC (and the states in which the offering is to be made) have declared the registration statement effective. SEC and state staff members may have comments on the adequacy of disclosure in the registration statement, which can require revision of that document before an offering begins.

Reporting Requirements

The Securities Exchange Act of 1934 requires pools registered under Form S-1 or Form S-18 to file annual, quarterly, and other periodic reports with the SEC. In order to satisfy the annual and quarterly reports the pool must file with the SEC Forms 10-K and 10-Q, respectively, and must file a Form 8-K whenever any material event occurs.

State Regulation of Public Pools

Public pools must register at the state level as well as with the SEC. Most states allow a public pool to be registered by coordination, that is, concurrently with effectiveness of registration with the SEC. However, some states have adopted substantive registration guidelines for public pools which go beyond the disclosure requirements established under the federal securities laws. These state requirements are usually based on North American Securities Administrators Association (NASAA) Guidelines. For example, the Guidelines establish permissible compensation arrangements, suitability requirements, and experience requirements for pool operators.

As a result, public pools are forced to tailor their offering documents to satisfy the various state requirements in which the pools are to be offered. Presently, NASAA has proposed changes in its Guidelines. Counsel should be contacted to assure compliance with the various state requirements, which may also involve negotiation on a state-by-state basis to obtain registration.

Private Pools

In 1982, the SEC adopted Regulation D, Rules 501 et. seq., which provides a private offering exemption from registration. Private pools are attractive alternatives to public pools since they are less costly.

However, private pools face certain restrictions. Private pools may offer pool interests to only a limited number of persons, and the pools' initial investors are subject to restrictions on the redistribution of their interests. A pool may also only solicit investors through direct communications to persons known to satisfy certain investment qualification standards. No general advertising, general seminars or mass mailings are permitted.

Rules 504–506 provide private offering exemptions under Regulation D. In claiming an exemption from registration pursuant to Rule 504, a pool operator may offer or sell no more than $1 million in interests. Under Rule 504 there are no special qualification standards an investor must satisfy in order to be offered or sold an interest in the pool and the number of investors the private offering can solicit is not limited, but the offering is subject to state registration requirements which must be considered carefully in conjunction with Rule 504.

In claiming an exemption pursuant to Rule 505, a pool operator may offer or sell no more than $5 million in interests in any twelve-month period. No more than 35 investors, excluding accredited investors, may participate in the offering. Under Rule 505, the pool must satisfy all Rule 502 requirements. Rule 502 outlines terms which must be disclosed in the offering.

In claiming an exemption pursuant to Rule 506, a pool operator may make sales only to persons the operator believes have sufficient knowledge and experience in business matters to evaluate the merits and risks of the investment, and there may not be more than 35 purchasers, excluding accredited investors. There is no dollar limit on sales.

Regulation D defines the term "accredited investor" to include, among others, (1) any person who has a net worth (or joint net worth with spouse) of $1 million or more or (2) any person whose income was in excess of $200,000 during the two most recent years and reasonably expects to maintain such a level in the current year, or (3) any person whose joint income with spouse was in excess of $300,000 during the two most recent years and reasonably expects to maintain such a level in the current year.

A filing is required to be made with the SEC on all Regulation D offerings.

Other Considerations in Connection with Private Offerings

The states do not uniformly follow Regulation D. In many instances, state securities laws tend to be more restrictive. For example, the number of permitted pool investors is often more limited than under Regulation D.

Lack of compliance with the rules relating to the private offering of pools may result in a loss of the exemption. Pools that fail to satisfy the requirements for exemption may face litigation from investors demanding the return of their original capital contributions, based on the theory that the interests were unlawfully offered. Further, unlawfully offering pool interests may result in both federal and state enforcement actions by government agencies.

In addition, persons engaged in the business of selling pool interests are required to register as broker-dealers under both federal and state securities laws unless the sales staff members qualify for an exemption. Rule 3a4-1 under the Securities Exchange Act of 1934 provides one exemption from broker-dealer registration. It provides for exemption from registration under specified conditions. The person who solicits pool interests must not be associated with any securities broker-dealer and should not have participated in the offering of interests more than once every twelve months. Moreover, no sales commission may be received by such persons.

With respect to state securities laws, some states exclude persons from the definition of a broker-dealer if they only effect transactions pursuant to a limited offering exemption. If a state does not contain a specific exemption, then the determination of whether the person is engaged in the business of offering securities is generally a question of fact.

A pool sponsor may not offer on a continuous basis an unlimited series of private pools. The securities law concept of "integration" refers to the treatment of a series of substantially similar pools as though they were one larger offering. For instance, a pool sponsor might organize a series of related pools, claiming a private placement exemption for each pool. However, under certain circumstances, they may be judged to be merely parts of a single offering requiring registration, resulting in the loss of an exemption.

COMMODITY LAWS

The Commodity Exchange Act constitutes the other major source of regulation for pools. While securities law concerns itself mainly with regulation of the offering of pool interests, commodity law concerns itself with both the organizational and the ongoing operational aspects of a pool. The major focus of the Commodity Exchange Act, as implemented through the Commodity Futures Trading Commission (CFTC) and its regulations, is on the pool operator or sponsor.

Registration Requirements

The Commodity Exchange Act and the rules and regulations it promulgated make is unlawful for any person to act as a commodity pool operator unless he is registered with the CFTC, is a member of the National Futures Association or is exempt from the registration requirements. The CFTC defines a commodity pool operator to include any person who operates or solicits funds for a commodity pool, that is, an enterprise in which a number of persons contribute funds for the purpose of trading commodity interests. Each commodity pool operator must file a Form 7-R with the NFA. Each of the pool operator's principals must also file a Form 8-R that must be accompanied by the principal's fingerprint card. Any person acting as an associated person (basically a sales representative) of the pool operator must register in that capacity and pass the National Commodity Futures Examination (Series 3), subject to certain limited exceptions.

The CFTC provides exemptions from the pool operator registration requirements for small or private commodity pools. Commodity pools operators are not required to register if the total capital contributions of all pools managed by them does not exceed $200,000 and none of their pools have more than 15 participants. Alternatively, pool operators need not register if they are not otherwise required to register with the CFTC and are not affiliated with a registrant, do not solicit participants and are not compensated for their services.

Disclosure Requirements

Every registered commodity pool operator must provide each potential pool participant with a disclosure document at the time of or prior to solicitation. The disclosure document is very similar to the prospectus or private offering memorandum required under securities law, in that they are both designed to provide prospective clients with material information so that they may make informed investment decisions. As a result, there is no need to prepare two documents: a single document will generally serve both purposes.

CFTC rules set forth a host of disclosure requirements that must be included in the disclosure document. A disclosure document must contain, among other information, a description of any actual or potential conflicts of interests among any entity involved with the pool, the types of commodity interests the pool intends to trade, certain risk disclosure statements, and the actual performance record of all accounts managed by the pool operator and trading advisor. Generally, the document must contain any material information that would influence a customer's decision to invest. Although there is no specific format in which disclosure must be made, the CFTC does in certain instances require information to be disclosed in a specified format (that is, performance tables and certain risk disclosure statements).

Each pool must file two copies of the disclosure document with the CFTC and one copy with the NFA at least 21 days prior to soliciting customers. During this period, the CFTC may review the disclosure document. Once the document has been reviewed and necessary changes made, the pool may begin soliciting and accepting customer's funds.

Reporting and Recordkeeping Requirements

Every registered pool operator must maintain in accessible form for a period of five years information relating to the transactions, financial condition, performance, and disclosure document of the pool. Each month, pools that have assets greater than $500,000 must provide the pools' investors with an account statement. Smaller pools are required to produce such statements on a quarterly basis. Furthermore, the pool sponsor must provide a copy of the pool's annual report to each investor and three copies to the CFTC every year.

CONCLUSION

The regulation of commodity pools is a rapidly changing area of the law. Each year, new requirements are imposed by law or regulation. It is this chapter's goal to outline the major issues facing the organizer of a commodity pool. It suggests some important factors that should be considered when organizing a commodity pool. However, no single chapter can attempt to cover all the legal issues relating to the formation and operation of a commodity pool, nor can it provide a complete description of each requirement that has been mentioned. In view of the number of bodies of law that can affect a commodity pool offering and the variations in pool structure, it is essential to consult with experienced commodity pool counsel at an early stage in the development of an offering.

7 FIDUCIARY SELECTION AND PROHIBITED TRANSACTIONS UNDER ERISA

Joseph P. Collins
Diane V. Dygert

The growth of private pension plans in the 1960s and through the early 1970s was unprecedented. In 1960, these pension plans covered 18.7 million persons and held assets of $52 billion. By 1975, these figures had increased to 30.3 million covered persons and $217 billion of assets. This 62 percent increase in coverage was double the growth of the labor force. These massive increases came at the time when much criticism was being levied against perceived defects in the private pension system. The publicity surrounding these factors led to a movement in Congress to enact a comprehensive scheme of regulation, the outcome of which was the Employee Retirement Income Security Act of 1974 (ERISA).

ERISA did not slow the growth of pension plan assets. From 1950 to 1987, these assets grew at six times the total financial assets of the economy. As of 1990, $2 *trillion* was held by private pension plans and 60 million participants were covered. With so much money at stake, ERISA plans have become a highly sought-after source of investment capital. ERISA plans themselves are seeking new and better ways to invest their assets. Thus, familiarity with ERISA is an important concern for persons involved with the investment of plan assets.

Before the enactment of ERISA, the regulation and taxation of employee benefits were governed through piecemeal provisions of the Internal Revenue Code (the "Code") and the Welfare and Pension Plans Disclosure Act. ERISA attempted to set out the first single scheme for regulating pension plans. ERISA addressed the failings of the previous system by imposing minimum participation requirements, vesting and funding standards, plan termination insurance, reporting and disclosure requirements, and fiduciary standards. ERISA also revised the Code's plan qualification requirements for favorable employer and employee tax treatment. Furthermore, ERISA divided responsibility for administering its provisions between two existing government agencies (the Treasury Department and the Department of Labor) and created an entirely new agency (the Pension Benefit Guaranty Corporation).

ERISA is divided into four sections—Titles I through IV. Title I covers reporting, disclosure, and fiduciary responsibility, and is dealt with at length here. Title I provisions are administered by the Department of Labor. Title II amended the Internal Revenue Code and is administered by the Treasury Department. Title IV created the Pension Benefit Guaranty Corporation, which acts as an insurer for certain pension benefits. Liabilities for plan terminations and withdrawals are also imposed by Title IV. Title III apportions responsibilities among the various agencies. ERISA coverage applies in general to private pension plans maintained by an employer for the benefit of its employees. ERISA does not apply to government plans, church plans, and individual retirement accounts.

TITLE I OF ERISA

Fiduciary Status

Among the many complex rules of ERISA, the fiduciary standards found in Title I are of the most relevance to futures managers. The fiduciary rules of ERISA impose strict standards on those who deal with plan assets. These provisions, found in ERISA Sections 401 through 414, apply to fiduciaries of both pension and welfare benefit plans. However, the fiduciary standards of Title I of ERISA do not cover Keogh plans that benefit only self-employed individuals and their spouses. A Keogh plan that covers both self-employed individuals and other employees is subject to the fiduciary standards of Title I.

To understand the applicability of the fiduciary rules, it is necessary to determine who falls within the definition of a fiduciary. A party can become an ERISA fiduciary either by being named as such in the plan documents ("named fiduciary") or by virtue of a relationship to the plan. In the latter case, a fiduciary is defined in ERISA Section 3(21)(A) as someone who:

> (i) exercises any discretionary authority or discretionary control over plan management or any authority or control over management or disposition of plan assets;
> (ii) renders investment advice with respect to plan assets for any direct or indirect compensation, or has any authority or responsibility to do so; or
> (iii) has any discretionary authority or responsibility in the plan administration.

Every plan must have a named fiduciary; typically, plan administrators and trustees are named fiduciaries under the plan documents. Investment managers, who by definition are plan fiduciaries, may also be named in the plan documents. Any other person or entity could be considered a fiduciary if its actions, authority, or responsibility fall within the definition contained in ERISA Section 3(21)(A). Determination of fiduciary status under ERISA Section 3(21)(A) requires a factual analysis on a case-by-case basis.

Some general observations can be made about a few entities that are often involved with employee benefit plans. Almost every plan uses a broker to execute trades for the plan. In general, broker-dealers are not ERISA fiduciaries. They can avoid fiduciary status by fitting within these guidelines issued by the Department of Labor:

> A person who is a broker-dealer registered under the Securities Exchange Act of 1934 . . . shall not be deemed to be a fiduciary, within

> the meaning of Section 3(21)(A) of [ERISA], with respect to any employee benefit plan solely because such person executes transactions for the purchase or sale of securities on behalf of such plan in the ordinary course of its business as a broker [or] dealer . . . , pursuant to instructions of a fiduciary with respect to such plan, if: (i) Neither the fiduciary nor any affiliate of such fiduciary is such broker [or] dealer; and (ii) The instructions specify (A) the security to be purchased or sold, (B) a price range within which such security is to be purchased or sold . . . , (C) a time span during which such security may be purchased or sold (not to exceed five business days), and (D) the minimum or maximum quantity of such security which may be purchased or sold within such price range. . . . [29 C.F.R. § 2510.3-21(d)]

If a broker executes orders within these guidelines, such execution will not make the broker a fiduciary. If a broker's activities fall outside of the regulations, the question of fiduciary status needs to be analyzed under ERISA Section 3(21)(A). The question is very fact-specific and depends on the other actions of the broker and the relationship of the broker to the plan. Two recent cases illustrate the varying results that can be reached.

In *Farm King Supply v. Edward D. Jones & Co.*, the plan and plan trustees alleged that the broker should be held liable as a fiduciary for rendering investment advice to the plan. The Seventh Circuit found that the broker was not a fiduciary, even though the plan had purchased a majority of securities recommended by the broker. In reaching this conclusion, the court examined the Department of Labor regulations that elaborate on the meaning of investment advice. These regulations state that:

> (1) A person shall be deemed to be rendering "investment advice" to an employee benefit plan, within the meaning of Section 3(21)(A)(ii) of [ERISA] and this paragraph, only if:
>
> (i) such person renders advice to the plan as to the value of securities or other property, or makes recommendations as to the advisability of investing in, purchasing, or selling securities or other property; and
>
> (ii) such person either directly or indirectly . . .
>
> (A) has discretionary authority or control, whether or not pursuant to agreement, arrangement, or understanding with

respect to purchasing or selling securities or other property for the plan; or

(B) renders any advice described in paragraph (c)(1)(i) . . . on a regular basis to the plan pursuant to a mutual agreement, arrangement, or understanding, written or otherwise, between such person and the plan or a fiduciary with respect to the plan, that such services will serve as a primary basis for investment decisions with respect to plan assets, and that such person will render individualized investment advice to the plan based on the particular needs of the plan regarding such matters as, among other things, investment policies or strategy, overall portfolio composition, or diversification of plan investments. [29 C.F.R. § 2510.3-20(c)]

The court found that, while the broker was rendering advice to the plan as to the advisability of investing in various securities, it had no discretion with respect to the disposition of any plan assets. The plan made independent decisions as to which securities to purchase, from among those recommended by the broker. The court also found that no mutual agreement existed that the advice rendered would be the primary basis for investment decisions.

In contrast, a broker was found to be a plan fiduciary in *Stanton v. Shearson Lehman/American Express*. Although no express agreement existed in *Stanton,* the court found that the broker exercised authority or control over the disposition of plan assets by executing trades for the plan pursuant to instructions that were based on the broker's own specific unsolicited recommendations, which were consistently followed by the plan. This pattern, combined with the court's finding that the plan was dependent on and relied on the broker's special expertise, led to the conclusion that the broker had acquired fiduciary status:

> Even though a client may have the final word on how his or her assets will be traded and is, thus, technically in control of the assets, it is the stock broker who is *effectively* and *realistically* in control of the assets when, for whatever reason, the client merely "rubber stamps"—follows automatically or without consideration—the investment recommendations of the broker.

Another group that should be concerned about its status as ERISA fiduciaries is the managers of pooled investment vehicles. By broadly defining plan assets in a way that "looks through" to the underlying assets of an investment vehicle in which an employee benefit plan invests, the Department of Labor has subjected managers of the vehicle to ERISA fiduciary status. By nature of this "look-through rule," the assets of the investment vehicle become assets of the plan. Accordingly, the manager of the vehicle would become a fiduciary of the employee benefit plan investors, unless the vehicle meets one of four exceptions set forth in the regulations.

The most straightforward of these exceptions is insignificant participation by employee benefit plan investors. If investments by such plans are no more than 25 percent of the value of any class of equity interest, such investments are not significant and the look-through rule will not apply.

Nonequity interests held by employee benefit plans are excluded for purposes of the look-through rule; equity interests are defined as any interests in an entity, other than those that are treated as indebtedness under local law and have no substantial equity features. A profit interest in a partnership, for example, is expressly considered an equity interest.

Investments in publicly offered securities or in securities issued by an investment company registered under the Investment Company Act of 1940 are also not subject to the look-through rule. An interest in an entity whose securities are widely held, freely transferable, and registered under the Securities Act of 1933 is deemed to be a publicly offered security.

Finally, investments in entities that are "operating companies" are not subject to the look-through rule. An operating company is an entity that is primarily engaged, directly or through a majority-owned subsidiary, in the production or sale of a product or service other than the investment of capital. The term operating company includes a real estate operating company and a venture capital operating company. A real estate operating company must invest at least 50 percent of its assets, valued at cost, in real estate that the entity has the right to substantially manage or develop, and must, in the ordinary course of its business, be engaged directly in real estate management or development activities. A venture capital operating company must invest at least 50 percent of its assets (other than assets invested in short-term investments pending long-term commitment or distribution to investors), valued at cost, in "venture capital investments," and must, in the ordinary course of its business, actually exercise management rights with respect to at least one of the operating companies in which it invests.

An important exception to the definition of a fiduciary is stated in ERISA Section 404(c): if a plan is an individual account plan and if it permits a participant or beneficiary to exercise control over the assets in his or her individual account, then the exercise of this control does not make the participant or beneficiary a fiduciary for purposes of ERISA. Furthermore, no fiduciary of the plan will be liable for a loss or a breach of duty resulting from any investment decision or similar action the participant or beneficiary takes. Plans containing a cash or deferred arrangement under Code Section 401(k) often are structured to meet the requirements of ERISA Section 404(c).

The Proposed Regulations

On September 3, 1987, the Department of Labor issued proposed regulations ("the 1987 proposed regulations") regarding participant-directed individual account plans under ERISA Section 404(c). These regulations were extremely broad in their scope and were met with strong criticism from the investment community. The Department of Labor formally withdrew them and published new proposed regulations on March 14, 1991 ("the proposed regulations"). Their most salient features are discussed below.

A plan is considered an individual account plan under the proposed regulations if it permits a participant to exercise control over the assets in an individual account by making an independent choice, from a broad range of investment alternatives, regarding the manner in which any portion of the assets in the individual account is invested.

The proposed regulations also provide guidance on what is meant by allowing a participant or beneficiary to exercise control over the assets in the account. A plan meets this requirement if a participant or beneficiary has a reasonable opportunity to give written investment instructions—or oral instructions followed by written confirmation—to an identified plan fiduciary who is obligated to comply with such instructions. A plan may impose reasonable restrictions on the frequency with which the participant may give such investment instructions, charge the participant's account for the reasonable expenses of carrying out the instructions (provided that the participant is informed of this), or permit a fiduciary to decline to implement participant instructions if they would result in a prohibited transaction, generate taxable income for the plan, create a potential loss in excess of the account balance, or otherwise violate ERISA or the governing plan documents.

A specific concern among users of managed futures is the Department of Labor's discussion of the "reasonable restrictions on frequency of investment instructions." In general, a participant must be permitted to give investment instructions with a frequency that is appropriate, in light of the market volatility to which the investment may reasonably be expected to be subject. In the commentary to the 1987 proposed regulations, the Department of Labor cited the "highly volatile market of commodities futures"; this example survives in the proposed regulations. If an option to invest in the futures market is offered by a plan, the plan "may need to provide [a participant] the opportunity to give investment instructions at any time during which such futures are traded in order to assure reasonable opportunity to exercise control over the assets in his account." Numerous commentators have expressed concern over this requirement, stating that the proposed regulations seem to require more opportunities to give investment instructions than are necessary. In response, the Department of Labor retained its general rule with regard to investment instructions being judged in relation to the volatility of the investment. However, the Department attempted to relieve some of the commentators' concern by providing a framework that assigns a *minimum* frequency of quarterly investment instruction opportunities to at least three investment categories made available by a plan. Therefore, other investment categories that are not very volatile may have less frequent periods for investment instructions.

One caveat affects investment opportunities in futures: a plan must provide the opportunity to transfer account assets to or from the least volatile category of investments with the same frequency with which participants are permitted to make transfers to or from the most volatile investment option available under the plan. Therefore, if a futures investment option under the plan is the most volatile investment under such plan, the frequency with which participants are permitted to transfer to and from such investment will control the frequency with which participants may transfer to and from the least volatile investment under the plan.

The exercise of control by the participant or beneficiary must also be independent. The proposed regulations state that whether or not independent control has been exercised is dependent on the facts and circumstances. However, three circumstances are listed where control would *not* be independent:

1. The participant or beneficiary is subjected to improper influence by a plan fiduciary or the plan sponsor with respect to the transaction
2. A plan fiduciary has concealed material nonpublic facts regarding the transaction from the participant or beneficiary (unless the disclosure of such facts would violate securities or banking laws)
3. The participant or beneficiary is legally incompetent and the responsible plan fiduciary accepts the instructions of the participant or beneficiary knowing him or her to be legally incompetent.

The proposed regulations also discuss what is meant by a broad range of investment alternatives. A plan offers such a broad range only if the available alternatives are sufficient to provide the participant or beneficiary with a reasonable opportunity to:

(i) materially affect the potential return on amounts in his individual account with respect to which he is permitted to exercise control and the degree of risk to which such amounts are subject;

(ii) choose from at least three diversified groups of investments:

(a) each of which has materially different risk and return characteristics;

(b) which in the aggregate enable the participant by choosing among them to achieve a portfolio with aggregate risk and return characteristics at any point within the range normally appropriate for the participants; and

(c) each of which when combined with investments in either of the other categories tends to minimize the risk of a participant's portfolio at any given level of expected return; and

(iii) diversify the investments of that portion of his individual account with respect to which he is permitted to exercise control so as to minimize the risk of large losses, taking into account the nature of the plan and the size of the participants' accounts.

In determining whether a plan provides a participant with a reasonable opportunity to diversify the investments, the nature of the investment options offered and the size of the participant's account must be taken into account. Where the account of any participant is of such limited size that investment in a look-through investment vehicle is the only prudent means to assure appropriate diversification, a plan may satisfy the diversification requirements only by offering look-through investment vehicles. If look-through investment vehicles are available as plan options, the underlying investments of such fund will be considered in determining whether the plan is sufficiently diversified.

Special rules apply if an investment choice is a look-through investment vehicle or if the participant is allowed to select an investment manager. A plan providing look-through investment vehicles as an alternative meets the requirements of the proposed regulations only if an independent fiduciary designates a diversified group of available look-through investment vehicles. Similarly, if a plan offers the right to appoint a designated investment manager, then the plan must provide that an independent fiduciary will designate the particular investment managers from which the participant or beneficiary may choose.

If the conditions of the proposed regulations are not met, the plan does not necessarily violate the fiduciary responsibility provisions of ERISA, but the safe harbor relief from such fiduciary obligations is not available.

Fiduciary Rules

If a person or entity acquires fiduciary status under any of the above rule, the fiduciary duties of ERISA will apply to the person or entity and its conduct. Therefore, an understanding of these rules is an important prerequisite for management of ERISA funds. Many of the ERISA duties follow common trust law fiduciary duties. In fact, ERISA was drafted to apply many such common-law duties to plan fiduciaries, but ERISA also tailored them to take into consideration the special character and nature of employee benefit plans.

ERISA Section 404 sets out several requirements that have collectively come to be known as the Prudence Rule. Under ERISA Section 404, a fiduciary must discharge the fiduciary duties solely in the interest of the participants and beneficiaries of the plan and for the exclusive purpose of providing benefits to them and defraying reasonable expenses of administering the plan. These duties must be carried out "with the care, skill, prudence and diligence under the circumstances then prevailing that a prudent man acting in a like capacity and familiar with such matters would use in the conduct of an enterprise of a like character and with like aims." This phraseology has led some people to proffer the conclusion that ERISA has not just reiterated the traditional prudent man standard, but instead has set forth a prudent expert standard. Indeed, the ERISA Prudence Rule is a flexible standard requiring varying degrees of expertise, depending on the nature and needs of the plan.

ERISA Section 404 also provides that a fiduciary must diversify the investments of the plan to minimize the risk of large losses, unless it is clearly prudent not to do so.

Moreover, a fiduciary must carry out fiduciary duties in accordance with the plan documents insofar as they are consistent with ERISA. This point was emphasized in *Dardaganis v. Grace Capital, Inc.*, where the investment manager was held liable for violating plan documents that called for no more than 50 percent of the plan assets to be invested in equity securities. Grace Capital, Inc. ("GCI") had exceeded this limit for over 15 months, at one point reaching almost an 80 percent level of investments in equity securities. GCI raised two defenses—that the trustees had waived this limitation by allowing the investment mix to continue, and that the limitation was merely meant as a benchmark consistent with industry practice. Both of these arguments were struck down by the court, which stated that trustees cannot waive the right of participants and beneficiaries to have fiduciaries comply with the plan documents. The court also found that the investment management agreement required "strict conformity with the investment guidelines." Because GCI had exceeded the 50 percent mark by such a large margin, the court did not consider whether this language required a finding of liability for even small deviations. Accordingly, the issue of industry practice as a defense was not reached.

A plan fiduciary may be liable not only for its own acts, but also for the acts of its cofiduciaries. Such a liability will exist if:

1. The fiduciary knowingly participates in, or knowingly undertakes to conceal, an act or omission of another fiduciary when such act is known to be a breach.
2. The fiduciary enables the breaching fiduciary to commit the breach by failing to comply with his or her own fiduciary duties.
3. The fiduciary has knowledge of a breach by the breaching fiduciary and does not make reasonable efforts under the circumstances to remedy the breach.

The Department of Labor has interpreted reasonable efforts to mean that a fiduciary must take all reasonable and legal steps to prevent the breach of the cofiduciary. Such steps might include court injunction, notification to the Department of Labor, or publication of the action. Mere resignation of the fiduciary will not suffice to avoid this liability.

Delegation of Duties

ERISA Section 403(a) sets forth who has the authority and discretion to manage and control plan assets. The trustee of the plan generally has the exclusive authority in this regard, except to the extent that the named fiduciary has retained the authority and directs the trustee to carry out its decisions in this regard. In other words, the plan administrator could retain investment authority. The named fiduciary also may delegate the authority to manage, acquire, or dispose of assets to one or more investment managers. ERISA Section 402(c)(3) provides that a named fiduciary may appoint an investment manager or managers to manage the assets of the plan. Such appointment must be made prudently, in accordance with the fiduciary's Section 404 duties. ERISA Section 405(d) provides that if an investment manager has been appointed, then no trustee shall be liable for the acts or omissions of such investment manager or be under an obligation to manage the plan assets that are subject to the management of the investment manager. An investment manager, under ERISA Section 3(38), is a plan fiduciary that has the power to manage, acquire, or dispose of any plan asset; is registered as an investment adviser under the Investment Advisers Act of 1940, or is a bank or an insurance company qualified to perform plan asset management services under the laws of more than one state; and has acknowledged in writing that it is a fiduciary to the plan.

The legislative history of ERISA clarifies that a plan may permit a fiduciary to employ investment (and other) advisers to assist in carrying out the fiduciary duties. However, the fiduciary cannot be relieved of investment responsibilities unless the adviser employed is an investment manager. The Department of Labor, reaffirming that position in an Advisory Opinion in 1982, stated that the plan's trustees had requested an opinion that the appointment of an investment committee to manage the assets of the plan would not violate ERISA. The investment committee was not a named fiduciary under the plan nor an investment manager; thus, the appointment did not meet the provisions of ERISA Section 403(a). The requestor acknowledged that the appointment would not relieve the trustees of any liability under the fiduciary provisions of ERISA. The Department of Labor ruled that the appointment of the investment committee would not, in itself, contravene ERISA Section 403(a), as long as the trustees continued to maintain exclusive authority and discretion to manage plan assets within the Section's meaning. The ruling further noted that members of the committee would also be fiduciaries and subject to liability as such.

ERISA Section 405(c) provides that other fiduciary duties may be allocated among named fiduciaries and that named fiduciaries may designate other persons to carry out their fiduciary responsibilities, *other than investment responsibilities*. If such duties are allocated, then the named fiduciary will not be liable for any act or omission of the appointed person, unless the action of making the appointment was imprudent. Any such appointed person would, in turn, become a fiduciary of the plan.

Fiduciaries should keep in mind that providing investment management and other services in the corporate form may not shield the principals of the corporation from liability as a fiduciary. In *Dardaganis* (*supra*), the court found H. David Grace, president and chief executive officer of GCI, personally liable to the plan as a fiduciary for losses caused by a breach of his fiduciary duty. The court found Grace to be a fiduciary in his individual capacity, based on language in the investment management agreement stating that Grace would "personally supervise and manage the Account" and his admission that he was solely responsible for all investment decisions made on behalf of the plan account. As a fiduciary, Grace was personally liable under ERISA Section 409 for the losses suffered by the account.

Because a fiduciary must act prudently when selecting an investment manager, a number of considerations should be taken in account. When appointing an investment manager, a named fiduciary should have a written agreement executed by both the investment manager and the named fiduciary. The investment manager must accept the investment duties being delegated under the agreement and should affirmatively declare that the standards for an investment manager under ERISA have been met, including acknowledgment that the investment manager is a fiduciary to the employee benefit plan and has a duty to act in accordance with the Prudence Rule. The agreement also should contain a number of other items. The plan assets placed under management should be specifically described. The investment focus of the investment manager should be understood by the named fiduciary, reconciled with the investment philosophy of the plan, and clearly spelled out in the agreement.

Likewise, any specific investment guidelines of the plan must be documented. Because the liquidity needs of the plan are always a concern, there should be an obligation to provide the investment manager with ongoing information regarding these needs. The matter of obtaining a bond as required under ERISA should be dealt with, as well as any liability and indemnification provisions. Fee arrangements should be discussed and disclosed, along with brokerage selection. Finally, a mechanism for terminating the agreement on reasonably short notice should be addressed. Other specific matters of concern to a particular plan can be made part of any agreement.

Although not held responsible for the investment decisions made by a duly appointed investment manager, the named fiduciary retains the continuing duty to monitor such manager's performance. In this regard, the named fiduciary should review transaction summaries and—in the case of a discretionary brokerage arrangement—commission statements, to ensure that the agreed-on investment focus is being maintained and that there is compliance with any specific guidelines. The overall performance of the investment manager should be monitored to ensure a favorable return for the plan. If the named fiduciary feels the investment manager is not fulfilling the duties required for the plan or is not performing as expected for any significant period of time, the named fiduciary should appoint a replacement manager for the plan.

Prohibited Transactions

There are certain transactions that a fiduciary of an employee benefit plan is not allowed to engage in. These "prohibited transactions," contained in ERISA Section 406, can be divided into two groups for discussion purposes. In the first group are specific technical prohibitions that a fiduciary shall not cause the plan to engage in with a party-in-interest:

- A sale, exchange, or leasing of any property
- The lending of money or other extension of credit
- The furnishing of goods, services, or facilities
- The transfer to, or use by or for the benefit of, a party-in-interest of any assets of the plan
- The acquisition of any employer security or real property in violation of ERISA Section 407(a).

The second group of prohibited transactions attempts to address self-dealing and conflict-of-interest issues. A fiduciary may not:

- Deal with the assets of a plan in his or her own interest or for his or her own account
- Act in a transaction involving a plan on behalf of a party whose interests are adverse to the plan or its participants or beneficiaries
- Receive any consideration for a personal account from a third party, for a transaction involving the assets of the plan.

Because most of these transactions only become prohibited when parties-in-interest are involved, it is important to identify those within such a group. In general, a party-in-interest would be a fiduciary and any person providing services to a plan. A party-in-interest specifically includes:

- Any fiduciary, counsel, or employee of a plan
- A person providing services to a plan

- An employer whose employees are covered by the plan
- An employee organization whose members are covered by the plan
- Others with an ownership interest in the employer or the plan sponsor, or a familial relationship to a party-in-interest.

(Brokers are not generally fiduciaries of plans, but they are considered parties-in-interest when providing services to a plan.)

There are three types of exemptions from these prohibitions: statutory, class, and individual. ERISA Section 408 contains the statutory exemptions. For example, plan loans to participants and beneficiaries are exempted if they are made in accordance with other provisions of ERISA. Furthermore, goods and services may be provided to a plan by a party-in-interest if they are provided under a reasonable arrangement, they are necessary for the establishment or operation of the plan, and no more than reasonable compensation is paid. Class exemptions may be granted by the Department of Labor to specific groups of persons regarding designated types of transactions with employee benefit plans, after hearings are held on the matter. The class exemption is generally applicable whenever a member of the class engages in such a transaction. About 30 class exemptions have been granted. Individual exemptions are granted on a case-by-case basis, if the Secretary of Labor makes a determination that the proposed transaction is administratively feasible, is in the interests of the plan and its participants and beneficiaries, and is protective of the rights of such participants and beneficiaries. The individual exemptions are only available to the individual requestor on the specific facts and are not generally applicable to other persons.

The applicability of these prohibited transaction rules to futures trading has raised a number of issues. For instance, at first blush it may appear that margin requirements applicable to investments in futures contracts would be considered an extension of credit between the plan and a party-in-interest and, thus, a prohibited transaction. However, there is authority from both the Department of Labor and the Internal revenue Service (IRS) to indicate that such concern is unmerited.

Organizations exempt from tax under Code Section 501(c) are nonetheless subject to tax on income generated from unrelated business activities. This includes income from property acquired through the use of debt ("acquisition indebtedness"). In examining the issue of unrelated business income, the IRS has taken the position in numerous private letter rulings that the use of margin in commodity and financial futures contracts does not constitute acquisition indebtedness because the obligation of the investor is contingent on the delivery of the underlying commodity or financial instrument. In this regard, the futures contract is in the nature of an executory contract to acquire property at a future date. Therefore, the futures contract is not debt-financed property, and the income received from such investment is not taxable as unrelated business income.

It is important to note that these rulings were issued by the IRS regarding unrelated business income as opposed to prohibited transaction issues. The Department of Labor has exclusive authority to rule on prohibited transactions. However, this position of the IRS and its reasoning should be persuasive authority, if the Department of Labor were to analyze whether futures margin was an extension of credit.

In a related vein, the Department of Labor issued an Advisory Opinion to the Futures Industry Association stating that margin funds for futures contracts are not considered plan assets because margin is in the nature of a performance bond. The plan asset is the right "embodied in the futures contract itself as evidenced by a written confirmation and outlined in its agreement with its FCM (futures commission merchant), including such rights as the plan may have to make withdrawals from the account." This opinion clarifies that the futures commission merchant's use of margin will not be considered a prohibited transaction because margin funds are not characterized as plan assets; thus, there is no extension of credit to or from the plan. This ruling also allows futures margin to be held by the plan's broker without giving that broker fiduciary status merely because of its holding such margin, and confirms the inapplicability of the trust requirement, discussed below.

Remedies

ERISA provides that a plan fiduciary who breaches the duties required under ERISA will be personally liable to the plan for any losses resulting from the breach, must restore to the plan any profits made by the fiduciary through the use of plan assets, and will be subject to other equitable or remedial relief as a court may deem appropriate, including removal of the fiduciary. Losses from a breach can occur even when the plan has made money, if it is found that the plan would have made more money were it not for the breach. One form of equitable relief sometimes awarded is the banning of fiduciaries from serving as such to any employee benefit plans for a period of years or, depending on the severity of the breach involved, even permanently. In addition, a fiduciary that engages in a prohibited transaction with respect to the plan assets can be liable for an excise tax under Code Section 4975. This penalty is initially 5 percent of the amount involved in the transaction, for the year during which the transaction occurred. If the transaction exists uncorrected, it can, in certain circumstances, increase to 100 percent of the amount involved.

In response to criticisms about the Department of Labor's enforcement abilities, Congress recently added ERISA Section 502(l). This new subsection calls for a mandatory 20 percent civil penalty to be imposed on judgments or settlements in suits initiated by the Department of Labor involving a breach of fiduciary duties by a fiduciary or a knowing participation in the breach by nonfiduciaries.

PORTFOLIO THEORY

Prior to ERISA, fiduciary standards against which investments were judged were based on principles of common trust law that favored preservation of capital and attainment of adequate return, and these standards were applied to each separate investment in a portfolio. Because of the special nature of employee benefit plans, ERISA espouses the portfolio theory of investment under which individual investments will not be considered per se prudent or imprudent, but instead will be evaluated in light of the whole portfolio of investments that the plan holds. Therefore, it is permissible for an ERISA plan to take some investment risks. "ERISA does not require that a pension fund take no risk with its investments. Virtually every investment entails some degree of risk, and even the most carefully evaluated investments can fail while unpromising investments may succeed." This standard became clear through regulations that the

Department of Labor published in 1979. The regulations took an expansive view of the investment standards a fiduciary must maintain. The preamble to the regulations states that "(1) generally, the relative riskiness of a specific investment or investment course of action does not render [it] either per se prudent or per se imprudent and (2) the prudence of an investment decision should not be judged without regard to the role [it] plays within the overall portfolio."

In this preamble, the Department of Labor gave examples of nontraditional investments that may be prudent under ERISA—small businesses, index funds, guaranteed insurance contracts, art and precious metals—but avoided creating a legal list of permissible investments because no such list could be complete. Instead, the regulations provide a "safe harbor" that stresses procedure and due diligence when determining whether an investment is proper for a plan to make. Despite the characterization of the regulations as a "safe harbor," a fiduciary must still review each investment decision by granting "appropriate consideration" to the relevant facts and circumstances. Appropriate consideration includes a determination that the investment is reasonably designed, as part of the portfolio, to further the purposes of the plan, considering the risk of loss and opportunity for gain, and consideration of the following factors: (1) the diversification of the portfolio; (2) the liquidity and current return of the portfolio relative to the anticipated cash flow requirements of the plan; and (3) the projected return of the portfolio relative to the funding objectives of the plan. Based on this standard of review, an investment could make money and still be imprudent or, conversely, lose money and still be prudent. "The ultimate outcome of the investment is not the yardstick by which the Court must measure the prudence of the fiduciary." "A fiduciary's independent investigation of the merits of a particular investment is at the heart of the prudent man standard." By following this objective standard of review, courts avoid second-guessing the "prudence" of a fiduciary's investment decision.

This approach provides fiduciaries with the flexibility necessary to pursue investments with a variety of characteristics such as the greatest return to meet funding objectives, safety of principal, liquidity for cash flow requirements, and protection against market turns. Having investments with each of these characteristics diversifies a fiduciary's portfolio and thus serves the best interests of the plan's participants and beneficiaries. Therefore, the justification for any investment is the role it plays in the overall plan portfolio.

SPECIAL CONSIDERATIONS

Compensation Arrangements

The form of compensation in which an investment manager will be paid is a matter affected by ERISA. Generally, a flat fee representing a percentage of the assets under management presents no problem. However, if any form of an incentive or performance fee is proposed, significant issues arise under ERISA.

ERISA Section 406 generally prohibits the payment of plan assets to a plan fiduciary and specifically prohibits a plan fiduciary from dealing with the assets of a plan in its own interest or for its own account. Until August 1986, the Department of Labor had indicated, in light of ERISA Section 406, that arrangements providing for payment of incentive fees by a plan to plan fiduciaries were impermissible. In August 1986, the Department of Labor reversed its position, and in two opinion letters indicated that incentive fee arrangements are permissible if certain requirements are met. It is important to note that these letters only apply to securities transactions. There are a few requests for opinion letters on file with the Department of Labor, asking that similar treatment be extended to futures transactions. However, the Department of Labor has yet to rule on any of those requests. Because the relevant aspects of securities and futures trading are virtually identical, it is useful to review the Department of Labor's pronouncements and to structure any futures trading arrangements accordingly.

The first of the two opinion letters concerned the propriety under ERISA Section 406(b) of an incentive fee arrangement proposed by BDN Advisers, Inc., a registered investment adviser under the Investment Advisers Act of 1940. BDN proposed to manage plan investments in securities on a discretionary basis for individual accounts or as the general partner of limited partnerships having employee benefit plan investors. Under the arrangement, each plan would be charged a base fee and an incentive fee for BDN's services. The base fee consisted of a percentage of the net asset value of the client's account at the beginning and end of each quarter during which BDN served as investment manager, and was to be charged without regard to whether BDN had earned an incentive fee. The incentive fee consisted of a percentage of the increase in the value of the assets in the client's account from the beginning of each year of investment management through the valuation date set forth in the contract pursuant to which BDN was retained. All realized and unrealized gains and losses experienced during the year, as well as income received during the year, were taken into account in calculating the incentive fee.

The incentive fee arrangement proposed by BDN contained several other features. First, plans using BDN's investment management services under which the incentive fees were paid had the right to terminate the services on reasonably short notice, as required by Department of Labor regulations. Second, BDN represented that the arrangement would comply with Securities and Exchange Commission (SEC) Rule 205-3 under the Investment Advisers Act, which permits incentive fee arrangements if the investment adviser complies with rules that (1) require that the client make a stated minimum investment or have a stated minimum net worth, (2) establish a permissible incentive compensation formula, (3) require certain disclosures to the client, and (4) require the adviser reasonably to believe that the contract represents an arm's-length arrangement and that the client understands the method of compensation and its risks. Third, BDN represented that the compensation it would receive from plans using its services would be reasonable for the services performed. Finally, BDN said that the decision to retain BDN and to pay an incentive fee to it would be made by a plan fiduciary that was independent of BDN.

Based on BDN's representations, the Department of Labor concluded that neither BDN's act of entering into agreements with plans to provide investment management services nor the payment of incentive fees under those agreements as described would constitute, in themselves, a violation of ERISA Section 406(b). The Department of Labor indicated that the conclusive factor in reaching its decision was that the amount of compensation to be paid to BDN "depends solely on the changes in the value of the securities in the individual account or limited partnership, as determined by readily available market quotations or independent appraisals." The Department of Labor emphasized that any appraisal of securities for which market quotations were not readily available had to be conducted by a person independent of BDN and that the independent appraiser had to make an independent valuation of the securities.

The Department of Labor's opinion also stated that the plan fiduciary authorizing the arrangement with BDN had an obligation to fulfill its fiduciary duties under ERISA Section 404. First, the Department of Labor said that the plan fiduciary must act prudently in making a decision to enter into an incentive compensation arrangement with an investment manager, as well as in the negotiation of the specific formula under which compensation will be paid. Second, a plan fiduciary must fully understand the compensation formula and the risks associated with incentive compensation. Third, the plan fiduciary must monitor periodically the investment manager's actions in the performance of its investment duties. Thus, the Department of Labor said that, in deciding whether to enter into such an arrangement, the fiduciary should take into account its ability to provide adequate oversight of the investment manager. Finally, the Department of Labor advised plan fiduciaries to be aware of the cofiduciary liability provisions of ERISA Section 405, which impose liability on a fiduciary for another fiduciary's breach of fiduciary duty if (1) the fiduciary knowingly participates in or conceals the breach; or (2) by failure to fulfill the fiduciary duties under ERISA Section 404(a)(1), the other fiduciary is enabled to commit a breach; or (3) the fiduciary has knowledge of the breach of the other fiduciary and fails to make a reasonable effort to remedy the breach.

In light of the foregoing, if a plan fiduciary endeavors to structure an incentive fee arrangement with the following points in mind, the arrangement should comply with the requirements identified by the Department of Labor in its letter to BDN:

- The amount of incentive compensation should depend solely on the change in the value of the account, as determined by readily available market quotations. The plan fiduciary should not invest the account in investments that cannot be readily and objectively valued by reference to established markets.
- Either party should be able to terminate the agreement upon 30 days' notice. This satisfies the requirement, under Department of Labor

regulations, that a plan must be able to terminate a service arrangement (including one providing for payment of incentive fees) on reasonably short notice.

- The details of the incentive fee arrangement should be fully disclosed to the independent plan fiduciary who will approve the arrangement. Furthermore, any future changes in the arrangement should be fully disclosed and agreed on. This will satisfy the requirements that full disclosure of incentive fee arrangements must be made to a plan's independent authorizing fiduciary and that independent approval of the arrangement must be given.
- The amount to be paid to the plan fiduciary as an incentive fee must be reasonable in light of the services to be rendered and when compared to fees charged to comparable accounts.
- Finally, the investment manager must comply in all respects with the requirements of SEC Rule 205-3, which provides an exemption from the prohibition against incentive fee arrangements between investment advisers and their clients (Section 205(a)(1) of the Investment Advisers Act). SEC Rule 205-3 lists four basic conditions which, if satisfied, would allow an investment adviser to enter into an incentive fee arrangement. These are:
    - The client must be a person or entity (as defined under the Act) with at least $500,000 under management with the investment adviser, or the investment adviser must reasonably believe the client is a person or entity (as defined under the Act) which has a net worth of over $1 million.
    - The compensation formula must include:
        - in the case of securities for which market quotations are readily available, the realized capital losses and unrealized capital depreciation; and
        - in the case of securities for which market quotations are not readily available, the realized capital losses and, if the unrealized capital appreciation is included, the unrealized capital depreciation;

      and must provide that any compensation is based on gains less losses in the account for a period of not less than 1 year.
    - In addition to the disclosure requirements of Form ADV, the adviser must disclose all material information, including:
        - that the arrangement may create an incentive for the adviser to make riskier or more speculative investments than if no such arrangement existed;
        - that the adviser may receive compensation based on unrealized appreciation as well as realized gains;

  - the period used to measure performance and its significance;
  - the nature and significance of any index used and why the adviser feels it is appropriate; and
  - if unrealized appreciation is included, how the securities will be valued and the extent to which such valuation will be independent.
- The contract must be negotiated at arm's length and the client must understand the proposed method of compensation and its risks.

As noted above, the Department of Labor put much weight on the objective and independent nature of the formula that would ultimately determine the compensation of an investment manager under an incentive fee arrangement. Therefore, it was unclear to those investment managers who wished to use self-developed indexes whether, and to what extent, such indexes would be acceptable as the measurement for an incentive fee.

This concern was addressed in another Advisory Opinion focusing on the particular type of incentive fee formula that may be used. Alliance Capital Management Corporation ("Alliance") requested an opinion from the Department of Labor that its proposed, alternative performance-based fee arrangements for employee benefit plan clients did not violate ERISA Section 406. Alliance set forth three fee formulas: (1) a percentage-of-appreciation fee, (2) a base-plus fee, and (3) a fulcrum fee. The first type of fee simply represented a specified percentage of the asset appreciation in the account. The base-plus fee provided Alliance with a minimum fee and incremental increases for performance above a specified index, up to an agreed-on maximum. The fulcrum fee increased and decreased with the account's performance relative to a specified index, and represented the sole fee for the account.

Alliance indicated that various indexes may be used in the second and third types of fee structures and that the index picked in any particular case would be mutually agreed-on with the client. Alliance asked the Department of Labor to specifically opine on the suitability of an "asset list normal portfolio" for use as an index in the incentive fee formulas. Alliance created this index by selecting screening criteria consistent both with its stated investment philosophy and with empirical analyses of Alliance's historical portfolio characteristics. An independent consulting firm then applied these criteria to a universe of securities. Those securities selected were then assigned portfolio weights, again based on Alliance's investment philosophy and observations. Any criteria Alliance used in this process would be set forth in the investment management agreement and would not be changed without the approval of the plan client.

The criteria and weighing procedures were developed by pure mathematical computations based on objective raw data. Rebalancing of the index was seen as necessary at certain intervals because some securities would no longer meet the criteria and other securities might become eligible. Any rebalancing would be accomplished by an objective mechanism taking place on dates set out in the investment management agreement.

Based on these facts, circumstances, and representations, the Department of Labor issued an Advisory Opinion that the use of the Alliance indexes in the incentive fee formulas would not, in and of themselves, constitute a violation of ERISA Section 406. The Department of Labor focused on the objectivity of the indexes used, as well as the disclosures to and approval by independent plan fiduciaries. Hence, the more objective the arrangement and the more disclosure provided prior to an agreement with an independent plan fiduciary, the more likely are the chances that the Department of Labor will view the arrangement favorably.

Brokerage Arrangements

Until May 1975, securities commission rates were fixed by national securities exchanges. During the period from the early-1960s until May 1, 1975, a substantial number of money managers chose brokerage firms on the basis of execution and research services. Therefore, many brokerage firms developed special research services as a means of competing for institutional business. Investment managers assumed that they could acquire "free" research without raising fiduciary concerns.

However, when fixed commission rates were abolished on May 1, 1975, broker-dealers began to recoup the cost of research services provided to customers through increased commission rates. The difference between the portion of the commission rate charged for the execution of the securities trades and that charged to cover the cost of the research services commonly is referred to as "soft dollars." Because of this difference in cost, many investment managers and broker-dealers became concerned whether an investment manager's fiduciary duty to the managed accounts would still be satisfied if the manager had not paid the lowest commission rates available.

Those concerns over the continued viability of soft dollar arrangements led the SEC to propose legislation (eventually adopted by Congress) allowing investment managers to use their reasonable business judgment when selecting and compensating a broker-dealer. Specifically, the Securities Acts Amendments of 1975 added Section 28(e) to the Securities Exchange Act of 1934 to provide a "safe harbor" for investment managers so that, under the new regime of competitive commission rates, the managers could continue to use "reasonable business judgment" in selecting brokers and causing accounts under their management to pay higher commissions than otherwise might be the case in consideration of appropriate soft dollar services rendered for the benefit of those accounts.

Section 28(e) provides in pertinent part:

> (1) No person using the mails, or any means or instrumentality of interstate commerce, in the exercise of investment discretion with respect to an account shall be deemed to have acted unlawfully or to have breached a fiduciary duty under State or Federal law . . . solely by reason of his having caused the account to pay a member of an exchange, broker, or dealer an amount of commission for effecting a securities transaction in excess of the amount of commission another member of an exchange, broker, or dealer would have charged for effecting that transaction, if such person determined in good faith that such amount of commission was reasonable in relation to the value of the brokerage and research services provided by such member, broker, or dealer, viewed in terms of either that particular transaction or his overall responsibilities with respect to the accounts as to which he exercises investment discretion. This subsection is exclusive and plenary insofar as conduct is covered by the foregoing, unless otherwise expressly provided by contract: Provided, however, that nothing in this subsection shall be construed to impair or limit the power of the Commission under any other provision of this title or otherwise.
>
> • • •

(3) For purposes of this subsection a person provides brokerage and research services insofar as he—
   (A) furnishes advice, either directly or through publications or writings, as to the value of securities, the advisability of investing in purchasing or selling securities, and the availability of securities or purchasers or sellers of securities;
   (B) furnishes analyses and reports concerning issuers, industries, securities, economic factors and trends, portfolio strategy, and the performance of accounts; or
   (C) effects securities transactions and performs functions incidental thereto (such as clearance, settlement, and custody) or required in connection therewith by rules of the Commission or a self-regulatory organization of which such person is a member or person associated with a member or in which such person is a participant.

Investment managers often provide to employee benefit plans services that allow them to direct trades through the broker of the manager's own choosing, and Section 28(e) provides protection to many investment managers in such circumstances. However, the Section 28(e) safe harbor extends only to those persons exercising investment discretion. Therefore, when investment managers are directed by the plan sponsors to use a particular broker, the protections of Section 28(e) are not available. The SEC has also made clear, in a letter to the Director of Enforcement of the Pension and Welfare Benefits Administration of the Department of Labor, that Section 28(e) cannot be used by an investment manager to cover payments for errors made by such managers in placing trades for an account.

Furthermore, the plain language of Section 28(e) indicates that this safe harbor provision applies only to investment managers in connection with the payment of commissions for securities transactions. At the time of the passage of the 1975 Securities Act Amendments, the financial futures contracts presently traded by pension plan accounts were not traded on any futures exchange. Hence, there was no effort by the securities industry or the SEC to have the proposed safe harbor embodied in Section 28(e) cover such futures transactions. The SEC has recently ended any debate over whether futures are covered by Section 28(e) by informing the Department of Labor that the safe harbor does not extend to futures or principal transactions.

Although Section 28(e) does not apply to futures transactions or directed brokerage arrangements, this limitation does not mean that futures commissions cannot be used lawfully in a soft dollar arrangement. Section 28(e) is an exemption, not a prohibition, and cannot by its terms be violated. A person does not violate Section 28(e); rather, by falling outside its safe harbor, a fiduciary must satisfy the otherwise applicable legal requirements, primarily those imposed by ERISA. As the SEC noted, Section 28(e) "provides a *non-exclusive* safe harbor from liability under state or federal fiduciary law to investment managers making reasonable use of client commission dollars to obtain brokerage and research services" (emphasis added). Thus, the fact that futures transactions fall outside the protection of the Section 28(e) safe harbor does not mean that the use of futures commissions to pay for research services is illegal; instead, the affirmative obligations imposed by ERISA and other applicable laws will apply and will have to be satisfied.

Although Section 28(e) is not available as a safe harbor for soft dollar arrangements involving futures, interpretations by the SEC of the Section 28(e) safe harbor nonetheless should be followed as a matter of prudence, when structuring soft dollar arrangements involving futures commissions. For instance, in any such arrangement, the "soft commission" dollars should be used only to purchase "research services" as that term has been interpreted by the SEC.

The term research services as used in Section 28(e) is meant to be broad. "[T]he controlling principle to be used to determine whether something is research is whether it provides lawful and appropriate assistance to the money manager in the performance of his investment decision-making responsibilities." The general availability of a product does not remove it from the ambit of research services, but is relevant to the determination of its value.

Any research services paid for by a plan must be for the benefit of the plan and not for the benefit of the investment manager or other plans for which the investment manager provides services. In some instances, the provision of research services often provides benefits to both the plan and the investment manager.

> Where a product obtained with soft dollars has a mixed use, a money manager faces a conflict of interest in obtaining that product by causing his

> clients to pay more than competitive brokerage commission rates. Therefore, the Commission believes that where a product has a mixed use, a money manager should make a reasonable allocation of the cost of the product according to its use. The percentage of the service or a specific component that provides assistance to a money manager in the investment decision-making process may be paid for in commission dollars, while those services that provided administrative or non-research assistance to the money manager are outside the Section 28(e) safe harbor and must be paid for by the money manager using his own funds. The money manager must keep adequate books and records concerning the allocations so as to make the required good faith showing.

ERISA also requires that services paid for by a plan are not to inure to the benefit of the fiduciary; if this were to occur, it might constitute a prohibited transaction under ERISA Section 406. Where products or services provide benefits to both the fiduciary and the plan, the showing of reasonable allocation of costs will also protect a fiduciary under ERISA.

The SEC views on best execution also should be given great weight in any evaluation of a futures-related soft dollar arrangement. The SEC Release states that an investment manager, as a fiduciary of the managed account, has an obligation to secure best execution of its clients' transactions. The investment manager must "execute securities transactions for clients in such a manner that the client's total cost or proceeds in each transaction is the most favorable under the circumstances." An investment manager should consider the full range and quality of a broker's services when making its determination of best execution. "This includes the value of research provided, execution capability, commission rate, financial responsibility, and responsiveness to the money manager." The SEC also stated that investment managers "should periodically and systematically evaluate the execution performance of broker-dealers executing their transactions." If, after one such periodic evaluation, the investment manager feels the broker is no longer providing best execution for its clients, then it should replace the broker with one that will provide best execution.

If an investment manager advising employee benefit plans covered by ERISA cannot rely on the safe harbor afforded by Section 28(e), for whatever reason (such as the trading of futures rather than securities), the affirmative obligations imposed by ERISA apply. The Department of Labor has set forth its position on soft dollar arrangements in Technical Release 86-1 ("TR 86-1" or "Release"). In its Release, the Department of Labor attempted to provide guidance for arrangements that fall outside the safe harbor—in particular, directed brokerage arrangements. This guidance can be used in the area of futures trading as well. The Department of Labor laid out five sections of ERISA that were felt to be particularly affected by soft dollar arrangements:

- Section 403(c)(1), which provides that the assets of a plan shall be held for the exclusive purposes of providing benefits to the plan's participants and their beneficiaries and defraying reasonable expenses of the plan;
- Section 404(a)(1), which similarly provides that a plan fiduciary must discharge his or her duties for the exclusive purposes of providing benefits to the plan's participants and their beneficiaries and defraying reasonable expenses of the plan, and must act prudently and solely in the interests of the participants and beneficiaries;
- Section 406(a)(1)(D), which prohibits a fiduciary from causing the plan to engage in a transaction if he or she knows or should know that it would constitute a direct or indirect transfer to, or use by or for the benefit of, a party-in-interest, of any assets of the plan;
- Section 406(b)(1), which prohibits a fiduciary with respect to a plan from dealing with the assets of the plan in his or her own interest or for his or her own account;
- Section 406(b)(3), which prohibits a fiduciary from receiving any consideration for his or her own personal account from any party dealing with the plan in connection with a transaction involving the assets of the plan.

ERISA Sections 403 and 404 require an investment manager to discharge his or her duties for the "exclusive purpose of providing benefits" to the managed ERISA accounts. Although there is no hard and fast rule concerning actions that will satisfy this "exclusive benefit" duty, the Pension Welfare and Benefits Administration (PWBA) of the Department of Labor has stated in the foregoing Release that (1) in the case of delegation of investment discretion to an investment manager, "[t]he manager . . . is required to act prudently both with respect to a decision to buy or sell securities as well as with respect to the decision concerning who will execute the transaction" and (2) in the case of a directed arrangement, the plan sponsor has the initial responsibility—and, by implication, the investment manager in other contexts—to determine that the broker-dealer is capable of providing best execution for the plan's brokerage transactions.

> In addition, the sponsor has an ongoing responsibility to monitor the services provided by the broker-dealer so as to assure that the manager has secured best execution of the plan's brokerage transactions and that the commissions paid are reasonable in relation to the value of the brokerage and other services received by the plan. [TR 86-1 at 1008]

The PWBA seems to rely on the notion of best execution to determine whether the fiduciary standards under ERISA are met. Although this phrase is not defined, the PWBA did state that it included the quality and reliability of the execution as well as the cost.

The PWBA then turned its attention to ERISA Section 406 and provided examples of violations of that Section. An employer and named fiduciary for a plan, who does not exercise investment discretion, would normally be prohibited from directing the plan's brokerage transactions through a designated broker-dealer who agrees to utilize a portion of the brokerage commissions received from the plan to procure goods or services for the benefit of that employer. In addition, if a fiduciary does not have the protection of Section 28(e), he or she cannot receive goods or services for his or her own personal account from the broker-dealer dealing with the plan in connection with a transaction involving the plan assets.

In distinguishing these situations from one in which the plan benefits from the provision of goods and services, the PWBA comes close to reiterating the standard of Section 28(e); however, the PWBA explicitly states that the use of this standard does not depend on the availability of Section 28(e).

> [W]here an investment manager directs brokerage transactions through a designated broker-dealer to procure goods and services on behalf of the

> plan, and for which the plan would be otherwise obligated to pay, such use of brokerage commissions ordinarily would not violate the fiduciary provisions of ERISA, provided that the amount paid for the brokerage and other goods and services is reasonable, and the investment manager has fulfilled its fiduciary duty to obtain best execution for the plan's securities transactions. [TR 86-1 at 1008]

Further examples in the Release indicate that, even without the protection of Section 28(e), soft dollars may be used to purchase services that were obligations of the plan to purchase, but may not be used to purchase services that would benefit the fiduciary's own personal account. Finally, without the protection of Section 28(e), a money manager can only look to the benefit of the plan whose commissions are generating the research services to meet his or her fiduciary duties. This particular example goes on to provide that, even if the money manager is protected by Section 28(e), the named fiduciaries of the plan are under a continuing obligation, imposed by ERISA Section 404(a)(1), to periodically review the execution services of the broker-dealer and ensure that the commissions paid are reasonable.

When working with an ERISA account that is the subject of a directed brokerage arrangement, an investment manager should take extra steps to protect itself. Initially, an investment manager must determine whether the direction itself is validly given. To do this, copies of all the relevant plan provisions should be examined to ascertain that the procedures for the authorization of actions by plan fiduciaries have been followed. Any direction the investment manager receives in writing should be memorialized. If the direction complies with all of the procedures for a valid trustee or sponsor action, then the investment manager may assume it is valid. However, if the action does not conform to the procedures in the relevant document, then the investment manager must request a valid direction from the appropriate parties.

After determining that the direction is valid, the investment manager must still be satisfied that the specified broker-dealer will provide best execution for the plan. The things to be considered in determining whether this broker-dealer will provide best execution are similar to the considerations underlying Section 28(e), discussed above. These include the value of research provided, execution capability, commission rate, financial responsibility, and responsiveness to the investment manager. In particular cases, there may be other factors to be considered, but, in the normal situation, these may be taken as inclusive of all the factors to be weighed. The investment manager may secure this information by independent inquiries of the specified broker-dealer and of the plan fiduciary promulgating the direction.

If the investment manager, in light of its knowledge as an expert, finds the commission rate charged is reasonable in light of the execution, research services, and experience provided by this broker-dealer, then its obligation under ERISA is satisfied. However, if the price is not reasonable, this should trigger an inquiry by the investment manager to determine what additional services are being provided by this particular broker-dealer that justify the increased commission rate being charged to the plan. If nothing is uncovered to justify the high rate being charged, the investment manager should inform the directing fiduciary of this problem. In the normal course, the fiduciary will change its direction so as to comply with its fiduciary duties. If, in the rare case, a fiduciary will not change the direction, the investment manager must make "reasonable efforts" to remedy the fiduciary's breach or it will be liable for the breach as a cofiduciary.

Investment managers also have a continuing monitoring function to perform regarding the plan. The investment manager must continually assure itself that the broker being used is providing best execution for the plan. If, at any time, information comes to the attention of the investment manager that the broker may not be affecting best execution, then it must inquire into how this information affects its choice of broker. Examples of such information may be a communication from a cofiduciary questioning the decision; an awareness of an investigation of the particular broker, which may impact on the broker's ability to serve the plan; an increase in the commission rates which appears unjustified; or an awareness of a change in circumstances regarding the financial situation of the broker.

If circumstances have changed, the investment manager should switch to a broker that provides best execution for its discretionary accounts. In the case of a directed account, the investment manager should approach its cofiduciaries with the information and any suggested changes in brokerage. If the continued use of a broker would result in detriment to the plan, the investment manager would have to take additional action if its cofiduciaries refuse to change the direction, because their refusal would be a breach of duty. Such action may involve getting a court order to change the direction or notifying the Secretary of Labor of the breach.

Commingling of Plans' Assets

If an investment manager is granted credits from particular broker-dealers it engages to place trades for the plans it manages, the credits received should be directed to the plans whose transactions gave rise to those credits. If other plans benefit from these credits or if the investment manager itself benefits, the result could be a prohibited transaction under ERISA Section 406. Section 406(b)(3) provides that a fiduciary, with respect to a plan, shall not receive any consideration for his or her own personal account from any party dealing with such plan in connection with a transaction involving the assets of the plan. The commingling of plan funds may also violate a fiduciary's duty of dealing prudently with plan assets, unless there is a tracking mechanism to trace the interest and separately control it.

The SEC also has stated in its Release that it:

> believes that it is illegal, from a securities law fraud perspective, for the money manager or a broker-dealer to use one client's commissions to fund an undisclosed rebate to another client. This problem is particularly acute where a money manager aggregates orders from managed accounts. In this connection, the Commission believes that serious concerns are raised under the anti-fraud provisions of the securities laws where a money manager or broker-dealer aggregates directed and non-directed orders unless the money manager or broker-dealer can demonstrate that it does not disadvantage one client's account in order to fund a rebate to another client. This means that the money manager and the broker-dealer must have a system of controls and a system of records to assure that this commingling does not occur. [Exchange Act Rel. No. 34-23170, 35 SEC Docket 703, 713]

Affiliated Service Providers

ERISA proscribes various acts that a fiduciary may not do. ERISA Section 406(b)(1) prohibits a fiduciary from dealing with the assets of a plan in its own interest or for its own account. Causing the plan to pay brokerage commissions or other service-related fees to an affiliate may be seen as self-dealing by the fiduciary and, thus, a violation of Section 406(b)(1).

Although there are no statutory exemptions from the proscriptions of Section 406(b) and no interpretive regulations under that Section, regulations issued under ERISA Section 408 provide that a fiduciary does not violate Section 406(b)(1) if it does not make use of any of the authority, control, or responsibility invested in it as a fiduciary to cause the plan to pay additional fees for a service furnished by it or to pay a fee to a person in which the fiduciary has an interest. Furthermore, ERISA Section 408(c)(2) provides, in relevant part, that nothing in ERISA Section 406 should be construed to prohibit any fiduciary from receiving compensation for services rendered, or for the reimbursement of expenses properly and actually incurred, in the performance of its duties for a plan.

Individuals seeking other relief from Section 406 may fit within a class exemption or file for individual exemptive relief. In the securities field, the Department of Labor has issued a prohibited transaction class exemption (PTE 86-128), which provides relief, in certain circumstances, from ERISA Section 406(b) for plan fiduciaries who effect or execute securities transactions on behalf of the plan. Similar relief was requested by the Futures Industry Association (FIA) for trading in the futures area. Unfortunately, such relief was denied because the Department of Labor claimed to have too little information upon which to base an exemption. (However, the possibility that an individual exemption would be granted was left open.)

To effect or execute securities transactions in accordance with PTE 86-128, a plan fiduciary must comply with the following requirements:

- Advance written authorization must be received from an independent plan fiduciary who has received all relevant and available information requested at least three months before making the authorization.

- Annual notification that the authorization is terminable at will and without penalty must be given, including a statement that failure to terminate will result in continuation of the arrangement and including a form upon which to effect the termination.
- Confirmation slips or quarterly reports must be provided, upon which all charges are totaled.
- Annual reports must be provided giving a summary of the confirmation slips as well as information on portfolio turnover and the use of commissions to pay for research services.

Some special rules apply if a pooled investment fund is involved.

PTE 86-128 excludes from its coverage fiduciaries who are plan trustees (other than those trustees who act as mere custodians), plan sponsors, and plan administrators. The Department of Labor's reasoning for this exclusion is set forth in the preamble to the regulations. The Department has stated that a position such as that of trustee "may carry with it so great an influence over the general operation of the plan that an independent fiduciary may not be effective in examining critically and objectively multiple service arrangements."

This concern is also implicit in a number of advisory opinions issued by the Department of Labor. Nevertheless, the Department of Labor, in some circumstances, has permitted affiliates of plan trustees to provide services to a plan. In the cited letters, plan fiduciaries requested that the Department of Labor opine that it is not a per se violation of ERISA Section 406(b) for the fiduciary to use affiliated service providers. The fact situations involved offers to employee benefit plans of "bundled" services by a potential plan fiduciary. The services were to include those directly performed by the fiduciary as well as those performed by its affiliates. If a plan hired the fiduciary for the services offered, it was, in effect, hiring the affiliates as well. The Department of Labor granted the requests based on the independent plan fiduciary approval of the relationship at the onset and the application of the regulations under Section 408(b) cited above.

CONCLUSION

ERISA and its regulatory framework impose many obligations and restrictions on ERISA fund managers. Among other matters, ERISA will govern the manager's obligations as a fiduciary, the structure of the compensation arrangement the manager negotiates with a plan, the permitted payment and receipt of brokerage and research services, and the use of affiliated service providers, as well as the prudent use of managed futures for a plan. This is a rapidly developing and complex area of the law.

8 U.S. ACCOUNTING AND TAXATION FOR MANAGED FUTURES AND OPTIONS

Gerald Mangieri
Julia Oliver

The rapid growth of the futures and options markets in the past two decades has given rise to a variety of contracts being used for trading or hedging purposes. The manager of a fund, a pool, or a portion of an institutional portfolio can select from a wide variety of exchange-traded and non-exchange-traded contracts that cover a diversity of products. For exchange-traded products, the diversification in the futures, options, and options on futures marketplace has been dramatic.

Portfolio managers have several means of trading in futures and options for their funds. They can decide to directly trade or hedge in futures and options. Alternatively, they can invest a portion of a fund's assets in an existing managed pool, for trading purposes. Another possibility for the managers is to utilize the services of one or more trading advisers, each of whom would direct the trading strategy of a portion of the fund's portfolio; in this case, trading would be the goal rather than hedging. Finally, a professional futures trader could be utilized to hedge the other assets in the fund's portfolio.

Economic necessity is the mother of invention, in the case of financial product expansion. A long-term reader of the financial press can probably recall the 1973 oil embargo and the subsequent OPEC cartel years; interest rate volatility and its impact on profitability; the rise in agricultural (grains) prices throughout the 1970s and their fall in the 1980s; and, finally, the new and widely discussed trends of synthetic instruments and globalization. Because of economic trends like these, the need for a wide variety of hedges and/or substitutes for holding inventory (and the resulting fluctuating-interest carrying costs) developed. In addition, the opportunity for professional traders and speculators to participate in an expanded number of markets has fed the growth in product expansion.

The marketplace has evolved from a primarily agricultural base to include a diversified arena of financial futures and options (for example, equity indexes, Treasury bills and bonds) and both agricultural and nonagricultural products (for example, the energy complex, metals, meats, and grains). When contracts, the ability to trade in foreign equities and American Depository Receipts (ADRs), and spot or forward foreign currencies are added, the possibilities available to today's fund or pool manager are enormous.

An important factor in trading managed futures is determining how to account for futures, options, and options on futures and how to deal with their tax considerations. This chapter summarizes the accounting and tax perspectives of an institutional investor or a purchaser of units of a managed fund. The chapter represents a general discussion of accounting and income tax issues regarding futures, forwards, and options. As the rules in these areas evolve, investors should discuss specific questions with their accounting and tax professionals.

ACCOUNTING CONSIDERATIONS

Several rules and standards define the accounting for futures, foreign currency contracts, and options. Current accounting rules and practice are stated in the key publications listed in Table 8.1.

TABLE 8.1. **Key publications governing current accounting practice.**

Issuer	Rule or Practice
Financial Accounting Standards Board (FASB)	Statement of Financial Accounting Standards (SFAS) No. 52, "Foreign Currency Translation"
FASB	SFAS No. 80, "Accounting for Futures Contracts"
FASB	SFAS No. 105, "Disclosure of Information about Financial Instruments with Off-Balance Sheet Risk and Financial Instruments with Concentrations of Credit Risk"
American Institute of Certified Public Accountants (AICPA) Emerging Issues Task Force (EITF)	"Accounting for Options" (Issues Paper)

The FASB Statements must be followed by entities that report their financial statement performance utilizing U.S. generally accepted accounting standards (GAAP). The AICPA Issues Paper is not required to be followed, but it does provide guidance for users of U.S. GAAP.

The FASB Statements and the AICPA Issues Paper listed in Table 8.1 address a number of potential circumstances. In addition, the AICPA Emerging Issues Task Force (EITF) has dealt with several issues that touch on hedge accounting. However, for a managed fund or pool engaged in trading activity, the accounting for exchange-traded futures and options would most likely utilize the accounting concept entitled "mark-to-market."

"Mark-to-market" requires that gains or losses are recognized immediately as income. The FASB Statements and the AICPA Issues Paper have been written with many types of businesses in mind. For many businesses—unlike a fund, pool, or institutional trading portfolio—mark-to-market is not the typical accounting methodology. For certain types of businesses, such as producers or servicers, defining whether a transaction is entered into for hedge or speculative reasons is very important in determining the proper accounting treatment. For example, hedge gains and losses may sometimes result in income or loss deferral. Fortunately, for funds and pools trading liquid portfolios and readily tradable contracts, these designations are not important from an accounting perspective.

Before we continue with the discussion of accounting issues and concepts, it is important to explore what it means to mark-to-market in the context of futures and options, as well as forward exchange contracts. Forward contracts are customized, non-exchange-traded agreements to exchange different currencies at a specified future date and rate; a futures contract can either provide for physical delivery of a particular commodity or instrument or call for cash settlement. For an option on a futures contract, the underlying instrument, and therefore the settlement, is still a futures contract. Other options, such as stock index options, may settle in cash only. For foreign currency and other forwards, the principle of future settlement remains the same.

Futures, forwards, and options are executory contracts (i.e., completion of the contract has not occurred). The gross amount of the underlying commodity or equity is not recorded on the financial elements upon the trade date of the contract. Before the settlement date occurs, a number of factors, including volatility, length of time remaining until expiration of the contract, underlying cash or spot commodity prices, interest rates, and other factors will result in changes to the value of these open futures, options, or forward contracts. Because of these conditions, it is very likely that a gain or loss on the open contract will occur. This results in the need to mark-to-market the portfolio and immediately record these gains or losses. A realized gain or loss on closing or settling a previously open contract is also included immediately in the fund's or pool's income.

At this point, it is appropriate to explore some of the accounting rules that address the mark-to-market concept.

Accounting for Foreign Currency Transactions

If a fund's or pool's currency, or the currency of the primary economic environment in which the fund or pool operates, is the U.S. dollar, all transactions entered into, other than U.S. dollar transactions, are foreign currency transactions that may result in foreign exchange gains or losses. This assumes the functional currency is the U.S. dollar. Some typical foreign currency transactions that a U.S. fund could encounter are the sale, purchase, or holding of foreign currencies or related contracts, spot or forward market; sale, purchase, or holding of foreign securities; receipt or payment of interest, tax, or dividend receivables and payables; and payment of certain expenses in a foreign currency.

Under SFAS No. 52, a different accounting treatment is prescribed, depending on: whether a forward exchange contract is entered into for hedge or speculative reasons, what a company's functional currency is, and whether a company's foreign currency gain or loss is a transaction gain or loss or a translation gain or loss. (A transaction gain or loss comes from translating assets, liabilities, income, or expense of a branch or subsidiary from a local foreign currency to a parent's functional currency.)

The problem with SFAS No. 52 from the perspective of a managed fund or pool is that the Statement was written with traditional businesses, like manufacturers, in mind. Managed funds or pools have an entirely different objective and business focus; thus, as discussed earlier, they follow mark-to-market or fair value accounting: all changes in the value of their portfolios must be included in income currently. Therefore, it follows that a change in a portfolio's value resulting from changes in foreign exchange rates is recognized immediately as income or loss; there is no deferral of gains or losses and there is no need to delineate whether a portfolio trading transaction was entered into for hedge or speculative reasons.

Accounting for Futures Transactions

SFAS No. 80 establishes the standards for accounting for futures contracts and sets forth a general principle that changes in market value are recognized when they occur. The Statement also provides that the timing of income recognition is tied to the accounting for associated assets, liabilities, firm commitments, or transactions. If the futures contract qualifies as a hedge of an exposure to price or interest rate risk, the contract reduces the exposure and the contract is designated as a hedge. Arthur Andersen & Co. has published a booklet, *Accounting for Interest Rate Futures, An Explanation of FASB Statement No. 80,* which explains the accounting treatment and hedging examples for this particular futures contract.

Futures contracts may relate to anticipated transactions—transactions the company expects but is not obligated to carry out in the normal course of its business.

For a portfolio manager of managed funds or pools who follows mark-to-market or fair value accounting, SFAS No. 80 provides that, if an entity includes in current income the unrealized gains and losses of a hedged item—that is, the hedged item is already marked-to-market (say, a security included in the portfolio)—then changes in the market value of a related hedge futures contract are also included in income when the change occurs. SFAS No. 80 also provides that if a futures contract does not meet its criteria for hedge treatment, then gains or losses are recorded immediately. In other words, for a managed fund or pool, mark-to-market accounting will always be used whether the contract is entered for hedge or for speculative reasons.

SFAS No. 80 does not address nonexchange forward contracts and thus it does not prescribe any particular method of accounting for such contracts. In the absence of such guidance, if a forward contract has characteristics that are similar to a future, in that there is sufficient contract liquidity, price information or ability to price, and quantifiable credit or nonperformance risk, generally accepted accounting practice considers that contract similar to a future.

Accounting for Options Transactions

Exchange-traded transactions in options involve the payment of a premium for purchased options or the receipt of a premium for written options. For purchased options, the premium is recorded as an asset; for written options, the premium received is recorded as a liability. Entities (like managed funds or pools) that account for other trading positions under the mark-to-market method will record the premium as an asset or liability and should also use the mark-to-market method relative to the income recognition for options.

The AICPA's Accounting Standards Executive Committee released "Accounting for Options" in 1986. The FASB has not specifically addressed option accounting; however, options are part of a long-term

FASB project dealing with financial instruments. The accounting for options outside the speculative arena can be extremely complex. As with futures and forwards, the underlying accounting by an entity for the item being hedged drives the accounting for options. Once again, hedge accounting treatment may apply if an option is a hedge of an existing asset, liability, or firm commitment. Criteria must be met for anticipatory hedges.

There are key differences between the hedge accounting criteria promulgated by the Issues Paper and those in SFAS No. 80. For example, the Issues Paper recommends a "transaction" approach to risk assessment rather than the "enterprise" approach outlined in SFAS No. 80. In other words, for options, it is generally not necessary to determine whether other items or transactions inherent in a company's financial statements already reduce that risk. (Note that, for foreign currency options, the AICPA's EITF Issue No. 90-17 addressed the need for foreign currency options to reduce enterprise risk.) With regard to hedge correlation, the AICPA Issues Paper looks at correlation between changes in the market value of the item or commodity underlying the option and changes in the value of the commodity or item being hedged. SFAS No. 80 looks at the correlation between changes in the value of the option and the hedged commodity or item. Because managed funds and pools are likely to account for options, whether entered into for hedge or speculative purposes using mark-to-market accounting, the mechanical concepts regarding hedge accounting for options for companies not normally following mark-to-market accounting have not been discussed. Arthur Andersen & Co. has published a booklet, *Accounting for Options*, which explores this and other pertinent issues in detail.

OTC Options

Over-the-counter (OTC) options, unlike exchange-traded contracts, do not allow market values to be easily determined by quoted market prices. Determining OTC market value is important from an accounting and business perspective. The determination of market value is often not an easy task, although foreign exchange forwards and exchange-traded futures and options are readily marketable. The holder, therefore, in order to mark-to-market or calculate a fair value, can use an option pricing model, such as Black–Scholes, or obtain a current value quotation from the writer of the option. One should have an understanding of the variables included in the pricing models.

Synthetic Futures

A fund manager can conceivably create a synthetic future by buying a put and writing a call at the same strike price and expiration date (equivalent to a short futures contract), or by buying a call and writing a put at the same strike price and expiration date (equivalent to a long futures contract). If a synthetic demonstrates the same economics as a futures contract, then it would be accounted for in accordance with SFAS No. 80, which results in mark-to-market for managed funds and pools.

Options on Specific Marketable Equity Securities

Managed futures and pools often trade a portion of the portfolio in marketable securities subject to regulators' constraints. For managed funds and pools, because marketable securities are carried at market, options on specific marketable equity securities are also carried at market. Although the Issues Paper does not address these types of options, SFAS No. 12, "Accounting for Certain Marketable Securities," does deal with this issue.

Examples of Accounting Recordation

We have previously discussed the basic concept that a managed fund or pool will record futures, forwards, and options using mark-to-market accounting. Because these are executory contracts, the gross amount of the underlying commodity or item is not recorded on the balance sheet. Only the premium amount for options and unrealized gains and losses are recorded. A few examples should help illustrate these procedures.

Transaction 1

Let us assume that a fund or pool manager has decided to invest in various exchange-traded futures and options contracts with a total initial margin requirement of $50,000. Related commissions have been ignored for this example. The fund has an account with a regulated futures commission merchant (FCM) or an account with a regulated broker dealer. The following entry would need to be recorded:

Debit	Receivable from broker (or FCM) (margin deposit)	$50,000	
Credit	Cash (or securities)		$50,000

On a daily basis, the open contracts are mark-to-market and maintenance, or variation, margin requirements need to be met. At month-end, let's assume, a net favorable price variance of $3,000 has occurred.

Debit	Receivable from broker (open trade equity)	$ 3,000	
Credit	Unrealized profit and loss on open futures/options contracts		$ 3,000

Note that if the amount on deposit had exceeded margin requirements for open contracts, the fund manager could have invested the excess in a broker-sponsored account, withdrawn the excess, or let it remain in the account.

The following month, the fund or pool manager decides to close out the contracts, which have resulted in an additional $2,000 gain.

Debit	Receivable from broker (open trade equity)	$ 2,000	
	Unrealized profit or loss	3,000	
Credit	Realized profit and loss		$ 5,000

The receivable from broker would be closed out as follows:

Debit	Cash	$ 2,000	
Credit	Receivable from broker		$ 2,000

Transaction 2

Let us now assume that the fund or pool manager has decided to enter into a non-exchange-traded forward agreement to buy home heating oil no. 2 in 42 months, with an individual counterparty to be settled in cash. The transaction is entered into at market value on the trade date. In the accounting books and records, only a margin deposit (if any) would be recorded on the trade date. As with futures and options, a daily mark-to-market value should occur. Let us assume the contract is held to maturity. At interim reporting dates, unrealized gains and/or losses should be recorded as follows:

Interim (Assume Loss) Reporting Dates—Years 1, 2, and 3

Debit	Unrealized loss (P&L statement)	$100,000 (or $300,000 in total)	
Credit	Accrued unrealized loss (balance sheet)		$100,000 (or $300,000 in total)

Assume that, in the fourth year, an additional total unrealized loss of $50,000, which ultimately becomes a realized loss, occurs:

Interim Reporting Date—Year 4

Debit	Unrealized loss (P&L statement)	$ 50,000	
Credit	Accrued unrealized loss (balance sheet)		$ 50,000

Settlement Date—Year 4

Debit	Accrued unrealized loss (balance sheet)	$350,000	
	Realized loss (P&L statement)	50,000	
Credit	Unrealized loss (P&L statement)		$ 50,000
	Cash or payable to counterparty (balance sheet)		$350,000

This example assumes no interim margin payments were made to the forward counterparty.

Accounting by Institutional Investors

An institutional investor will acquire either futures and options directly in a managed account relationship or units representing an investment in a pool's or fund's underlying net assets, which would include futures and options. Because financial institutions normally would carry marketable trading account securities at market value, it follows that unit investment in futures and options would be reflected at market, and traded futures and options would be reflected at market. For example, pension funds, brokers, dealers, and bankers would carry marketable trading securities at market value; thus, their positions in futures and options or their units in a fund or pool would follow similar accounting.

A not-for-profit organization may carry marketable securities at market or the lower of cost or market; thus, if the organization also enters into related futures and options activity, the accounting will need to be reviewed for symmetry with the underlying related securities.

If a not-for-profit or any other concern, such as a commercial or industrial company, uses the lower of cost or market accounting, and hedge accounting qualifications are met, then changes in the market value of futures and options that meet the hedge criteria are not reported immediately as income.

For futures, changes in a futures contract market value are deferred and recognized as an adjustment to the carrying value of the hedged item, subject to normal asset realizability tests. For options that qualify as hedges, unrealized gains and losses are also either deferred or recognized in income, depending on the underlying accounting used for the item being hedged. For both futures and options that do not qualify as hedged, mark-to-market accounting is appropriate. Generally, we believe an acceptable alternative for purchased options is the lower of cost or market accounting; an alternative for written options is that they may be stated at the higher of proceeds received or market. The liability recorded for a written option is increased whenever that option is in-the-money. Note that, as an exception, the SEC is requiring commercial companies to utilize mark-to-market accounting for foreign exchange options, if hedge accounting requirements are not met.

For those investors following the lower of cost or market accounting for investment portfolios, their fund or pool units would follow similar accounting.

Disclosure of Off-Balance Sheet Risk and Concentrations of Credit Risk

The FASB has on its agenda a long-term project dealing with recognition and measurement of financial instruments. The project will entail reconsideration of the accounting for all the instruments discussed in this chapter. SFAS No. 105, "Disclosure of Information about Financial Instruments with Off-Balance Sheet Risk and Financial Instruments with Concentrations of Credit Risk" is the first completed paper of the FASB project.

Off-balance sheet (OBS) risk implies that the maximum potential loss that can be realized is not recorded on the fund's or pool's balance sheet as either an asset or a liability. For example, an option writer is exposed to a potential liability that is higher than the premium received from its buyer. SFAS No. 105 describes both market and credit OBS risk.

Market risk is the possibility that future changes in market prices may make a financial instrument more or less valuable because of factors such as interest rate or foreign exchange rate fluctuations. Examples of financial instruments with OBS risk are securities sold short, interest rate swaps, written options, and futures and forward contracts.

Credit risk is the possibility that a loss may occur from the failure of a counterparty to perform in accordance with the terms of a contract. Financial instruments with OBS credit risk include commitments, guarantees, and letters of credit.

Additionally, SFAS No. 105 describes concentrations of credit risk. The term concentrations of credit risk includes both OBS and on-balance sheet risk.

Disclosure requirements for OBS and concentrations of credit risk include:

- For financial instruments with off-balance sheet risk of accounting loss: the face, contract, or notional principal amount and the instrument's nature and terms, including a discussion of credit and market risk, cash requirements of the instruments, and accounting policies.

- For financial instruments with off-balance sheet credit risk: the amount of accounting loss the entity would incur if any party to the financial instrument failed to completely perform according to the terms of the contract and the collateral, if any, proved to be of no value to the entity; a description of the fund's policy of requiring collateral to support financial instruments subject to credit risk; and information about access to the collateral and a brief description of the collateral.
- For concentrations of credit risk: information about the (shared) activity, region, or economic characteristic that identifies the concentration; the amount of accounting loss due to credit risk the fund would incur if parties to the financial instruments that make up the concentration failed completely to perform according to the terms of the contracts and the collateral, if any, proved to be of no value; the entity's policy of requiring collateral or other security to support financial instruments subject to credit risk; and information about the entity's access to the collateral or other security, and the nature of the collateral or other security.

Typically, the fund's trading policies, objectives and a disclosure of trading positions will address many of these requirements.

TAX CONSIDERATIONS

As previously mentioned, today's portfolio managers engage in commodity and commodity-related transactions both for speculative purposes and to hedge or guard against risk of economic loss for existing positions. However, commodity futures were traditionally used, for tax purposes, to create tax benefits that would shelter other types of income by deferring the recognition of capital gains, converting ordinary income into capital gain income, and converting short-term capital gain into long-term capital gain.

In numerous federal tax acts over the past decade, Congress has curtailed the tax benefits of these transactions and provided more definite rules for the taxation of commodities. Table 8.2 lists the pertinent legislation and the resulting Internal Revenue Code (the "Code") Sections.

Beginning with the Economic Recovery Tax Act of 1981 (ERTA), statutory language was added to specifically address the taxation of regulated futures contracts (Code Section 1256, regulated futures contracts) and straddle transactions (Code Section 1092, straddles). ERTA also introduced rules that provided for the carryback of losses from regulated futures contracts (Code Section 1212(c)) and clarified the treatment of gains or losses from certain commodity futures and option terminations (Code Section 1234A). Subsequently, the Technical Corrections Act of 1982 expanded the definition of regulated futures contracts to include cash settlement contracts and foreign currency contracts.

The Tax Reform Act of 1984 (TRA 84) broadened the definition of regulated futures contracts to include nonequity options and dealer equity options. To simplify matters, regulated futures contracts, foreign currency contracts, nonequity options, and dealer equity options were included under Code Section 1256 and, thus, the entire area of the Code was renamed "Section 1256 contracts marked-to-market."

TABLE 8.2. Federal tax acts, 1981–1990, and relevant code sections.

Revenue Reconciliation Act of 1990 (Pub. L. No. 101-508, 101st Congress) (RRA 90)
Tax Reform Act of 1986 (Pub. L. No. 99-514, 99th Congress) TRA 86)
Tax Reform Act of 1984 (Pub. L. No. 98-369, 98th Congress) (TRA 84)
Technical Corrections Act of 1982 (Pub. L. No. 97-448, 97th Congress)
Economic Recovery Tax Act of 1981 (Pub. L. No. 97-34, 97th Congress) (ERTA)
Internal Revenue Code of 1986 as Amended (the Code)
Section 1256: Section 1256 Contracts Marked-to-Market
Section 1091: Losses from wash sales of stock or securities
Section 1092: Straddles
Section 1234: Options to buy or sell
Section 1212: Capital loss carrybacks and carryovers
Section 988: Treatment of certain foreign currency transactions

In addition to these broad-based structural changes, subsequent tax act changes have affected the tax treatment of commodities. The Tax Reform Act of 1986 (TRA 86) eliminated the preferential tax rate for net capital gains for both individual and corporate taxpayers. Code Section 988 (treatment of certain foreign currency transactions) was enacted to clarify the treatment of foreign exchange gains and losses. More recently, the Revenue Reconciliation Act of 1990 (REA 90) marked the return of a spread between the tax rate for individual taxpayers' net capital gains and other types of income.

The first tax issues to be addressed below are those concerning Section 1256 contracts.

Code Section 1256: Contracts Marked-to-Market

The rules require that certain commodity contracts, futures, forwards, and options, known as Section 1256 contracts, held by a taxpayer at year-end must be treated as if sold at their fair market value on the last business day of the taxable year. Any unrealized gains or losses resulting from such contracts are included in the income of the taxpayer.

Gains or losses from Section 1256 contracts are treated as if 60 percent are long-term capital gains or losses and 40 percent are short-term capital gains or losses, regardless of the actual holding period of the contract. This is commonly referred to as the 60/40 rule.

Described more fully below are the types of contracts that have been defined as Section 1256 contracts:

- *Regulated futures contracts* (RFCs) are contracts with respect to the amount required to be deposited with the broker or exchange and the amount that may be withdrawn, depending on a system of marking-to-market. These contracts must be traded on or subject to the rules of a qualified board or exchange, in order to qualify as RFCs. A qualified board or exchange is defined as a national securities exchange that is registered with the Securities and Exchange Commission (SEC), a domestic board of trade designated as a contract market by the Commodity Futures Trading Commission (CFTC), or any other exchange, board of trade, or other market which the Secretary determines has rules adequate to carry out the purpose of Sec. 1256.

- *Foreign currency contracts* are contracts that require delivery of, or the settlement of which depends on the value of, a foreign currency in which positions are traded through regulated futures contracts. These contracts must be traded in the interbank market and entered into at arm's length at a price determined by reference to the price in the interbank market. This definition is broad enough to include interbank forward contracts covering certain regularly traded currencies—Australian dollars, British pounds, Canadian dollars, French francs, German marks, Japanese yen, Swiss francs, and European currency units (ECUs).
- A *dealer equity option* is any listed option that is an option to buy or sell stock purchased or granted by such options dealer in the normal course of dealing in options.
- A *non-equity option* is any listed option that is not an equity option. Generally, this includes options on broad-based stock indexes (i.e., the Standard & Poor's 500), stock index futures, and currency options.

Code Section 1092: Straddles

As part of ERTA, in 1981, Code Section 1092 was added to prevent the use of straddle transactions for deferring income and/or converting ordinary income and short-term capital gains into long-term capital gains.

In general, a straddle is a set of offsetting positions in personal property that substantially diminishes the taxpayer's risk of loss on either position in the straddle. For example, equal long and short positions in the same commodity are probably offsetting and may constitute a straddle.

For purposes of this rule, a *position* means an interest in personal property. An *interest* includes a futures or forward contract, an option (including a stock option, but generally not the stock itself), or an obligor's interest in a foreign currency debt obligation. *Personal property* means any personal property of a type that is actively traded.

Capital Gains and Losses: Tax Reform Act of 1986 (TRA 86)

Prior to TRA 86, individual taxpayers received favorable tax treatment on net long-term capital gains. Specifically, taxpayers could deduct 60 percent of the amount of any net long-term capital gains (the excess of net long-term capital gains over net short-term capital losses). TRA 86 eliminated this benefit; consequently, both ordinary income and net long-term capital gains were taxed at the same effective tax rates. This legislation also eliminated the favorable 28 percent corporate income tax rate that had applied to net long-term capital gains.

TRA 86 also added rules for the treatment of exchange gain or loss for certain transactions denominated in a foreign currency. Under these rules, an election may be made to treat the gains or losses from regulated futures contracts and nonequity options involving a foreign currency as ordinary. Gains or losses on interbank forward contracts involving a foreign currency automatically receive ordinary treatment.

Tax Rates: Revenue Reconciliation Act of 1990 (RRA 90)

In RRA 90, Congress recreated the spread between the tax rates for ordinary income and net capital gains, for individual taxpayers. Under RRA 90, the top marginal income tax rate for individuals increased from 28 percent to 31 percent while the tax rate on net capital gains remained at 28 percent. Again, net capital gain is the excess of the net long-term capital gains over the net short-term capital losses. Long-term capital gain means gain from the sale or exchange of capital assets held for more than one year. (Net short-term capital gains do not receive preferential treatment.) RRA 90 did not alter the taxation for corporations relative to ordinary income versus capital gains or losses.

Tax Treatment Summary

Code Section 1256 governs the tax treatment for transactions in futures and options that meet the definition of a Section 1256 contract. All

Section 1256 contracts either disposed of during the year or marked-to-market at year-end will be subject to the 60/40 rule. Accordingly, gain or loss will be treated as 60 percent long-term capital gain or loss and 40 percent short-term capital gain or loss. The mark-to-market gain or loss on the open positions will be used to adjust their tax basis for purposes of determining gain or loss when the positions are disposed of.

For example, in year 1, Mr. X paid $1,000 to purchase a silver futures contract. The $1,000 amount represents his tax basis. At the end of year 1, the price per ounce has increased and the contract has increased in value to $1,500. Under the mark-to-market rules of Code Section 1256, Mr. X will recognize a $500 gain; 60 percent ($300) will be long-term capital gain and 40 percent ($200) will be short-term capital gain.

The $500 gain will increase Mr. X's tax basis in the open contract to $1,500. Assuming he sells the contract in year 2 for $2,000, an additional $500 gain will result; 60 percent ($300) will be long-term capital gain and the remaining 40 percent ($200) will be short-term capital gain.

In certain cases, a portfolio manager may want to protect a portfolio's positions by entering into offsetting positions in futures and/or options. Prior to ERTA, the portfolio manager was able to take advantage of a lack of tax law guidance and could accelerate losses and defer income. ERTA addressed this practice in Code Section 1092, referred to as the straddle rules.

In general, the straddle rules allow taxpayers to currently deduct recognized losses only to the extent that such losses exceed unrealized gains (if any) from the offsetting position(s). This is referred to as the straddle loss deferral rule. Any loss that is deferred is treated as sustained in the following tax year.

Positions in personal property may be treated as offsetting, regardless of whether the property is of the same kind. A straddle can consist of two positions that do not constitute the same type of interest in property. A straddle may involve a long position in silver (i.e., holding the actual physical commodity) and a futures contract to sell the same amount of silver.

For example, a taxpayer at year-end holds a Section 1256 futures contract to sell silver while also holding physical silver. At year-end, there is a mark-to-market loss in the futures contract of $10,000 and an unrecognized gain in the physical silver of $5,000. Of the mark-to-market loss, $5,000 is currently deductible and the remaining $5,000 is deferred, but may be deducted in the following year. When the futures contract and the physical silver are disposed of, the entire amount of gain and loss is included as taxable income.

The straddle loss deferral rule is not applicable where all the offsetting positions consist of Section 1256 contracts. The logic behind this exception stems from the fact that, because these positions are all mark-to-market, there is no opportunity for deferral of income.

One twist to the straddle loss deferral rule was created by TRA 84. It involves a mixed straddle—a straddle consisting of at least one Section 1256 contract and one or more positions that are not Section 1256 contracts. An election can be made so that the mark-to-market gains and losses from the Section 1256 contracts are not included in taxable income at year-end. Rather, all unrealized gains and losses are deferred until the straddle is closed out. Accordingly, if all positions are open at year-end, then all gains and losses will be deferred.

Generally, if this election is made, the taxpayer determines the net gain or loss for each identified mixed straddle. Net gain upon disposition is treated as 60 percent long-term and 40 percent short-term, if the net gain is attributable to the Section 1256 contract position. On the other hand, if the net gain is from the non-Section 1256 position, then the gain will be short-term or long-term by reference to the holding period of the non-Section 1256 position. The Code and supporting regulations provide the specific rules necessary to make the mixed straddle election.

The following examples illustrate the tax consequences of the mixed straddle election and the straddle loss deferral rule.

Example 1

A trader records the following transactions on the dates noted:

12/1/91	Initiates a long physical silver position and shorts an offsetting position in silver futures.
12/15/91	Sells physical silver at $11 loss.
12/31/91	Has unrealized gains of $10 in futures position.

Tax Results: As a result of the mixed straddle election, the futures are not marked-to-market at December 31, 1991. Accordingly, there is $10 of unrecognized gain in the offsetting position in futures at year-end. Under the loss deferral rule, $10 of the $11 loss realized on the silver sold will not be deductible in 1991 and will be deferred. The remaining $1 loss on the silver will be deductible in 1991: this is the amount of recognized loss that exceeds the unrealized gain.

Example 2

A second trader's transactions had a different time frame:

5/1/91	Has long physical silver and short offsetting position in silver futures.
12/31/91	Closes short position in futures at $8 loss and sells physical silver at net gain of $10. Net gain on straddle is $2.

Tax Results: The loss on the futures will not be subject to the 60/40 rule because of the operation of the mixed straddle election. The net capital gains resulting from the non-Section 1256 position (the physical silver position) will be short-term if this position was not held open for more than one year (current long-term capital gain holding period is longer than one year) prior to the date the account was established.

A taxpayer may also elect to designate a mixed straddle account. In this case, a separate netting rule is applied on a daily basis to an entire account (consisting of a class of related activities) rather than on a straddle-by-straddle basis. Not more than 50 percent of a net gain in the mixed straddle account can be treated as long-term capital gain, even if the net gain results from futures or options contracts subject to the mark-to-market and 60/40 rule. Conversely, no more than 40 percent of a loss may be treated as short-term, even if the net loss results from non-Section 1256 contracts. If the net gain is a result of gains on physical stock, commodities, currencies, or instruments—that is, non-Section 1256 contracts—then the net gain is short-term. Again, very specific rules must be followed to ensure a proper election.

Other special tax issues regarding tax straddles, mixed straddles, and related tax strategies may need to be considered.

Straddles and TRA 84 are involved in the rules regarding qualified covered calls. TRA 84 exempted from the Code Section 1092 rules tax strategies involving *qualified covered call options* and the stock underlying such options. A qualified covered call option generally means any option granted by the taxpayer to purchase stock owned by the taxpayer, if the option fulfills certain requirements. These requirements focus on the option's not being deemed to be "deep-in-the-money" (a call option likely to be exercised by the holder because the strike price is below certain defined benchmarks).

Code Section 1234: Options

The preceding discussion focused on futures and options that are subject to the mark-to-market and 60/40 rules. However, these rules are not always applicable, especially in the instance where a transaction involves equity options or non-exchange-traded options and futures. Gains and losses from the sale or exchange of options that do not qualify as Section 1256 contracts are governed by Code Section 1234. These usually include options on stock (e.g., equity options). Gain or loss from these types of transactions will be capital in nature and can be long-term or short-term, depending on the length of time the option has been held. If the option is not exercised, it is deemed to have been sold or exchanged on the day it expires. Transactions involving offsetting positions in stock and the related option may also be subject to the straddle loss deferral rules.

Code Section 1091: Wash Sales

Another tax issue that may affect the investor or risk manager is the wash sale rules contained in Code Section 1091. The purpose of the wash sale rules is to preclude a taxpayer from recognizing a loss for tax purposes if the taxpayer has not sustained an economic loss or if the taxpayer's economic position remains unchanged.

In general, any loss from the sale or other disposition of securities will be disallowed if, within a period beginning 30 days before the sale date and ending 30 days after that date (the *61-day prohibited period*), the taxpayer acquires in a taxable event substantially identical securities. The basis of the substantially identical securities acquired within the 61-day period will be increased by the amount of the disallowed loss.

A contract or option to acquire substantially identical securities within the 61-day prohibited period will be treated as an actual acquisition for purposes of the wash sale rules.

Code Section 1212(c): Capital Loss Provisions

Generally, the tax law allows an individual to deduct annually up to $3,000 of capital losses in excess of capital gains. Any excess is carried forward on a year-by-year basis. Carrybacks of net capital losses are not permitted. However, a special provision allows an individual to elect to carry back a net loss from Section 1256 contracts three years and to apply the loss against prior years' Section 1256 contract gains.

For example, in 1988, an investor had a $100,000 long-term capital gain from the sale of stock and a $25,000 gain from a Section 1256 contract. In 1991, the taxpayer has a $25,000 loss from a Section 1256 contract. Assume no other capital transactions in 1991.

The taxpayer can elect to carry back the $25,000 loss, to eliminate the $25,000 gain in 1988.

Institutional Investor Issues

In addition to the preceding discussion regarding the taxation of futures and options, a few other issues that affect the institutional investor and the entity involved with managed futures should be briefly mentioned.

For the corporate institutional investor (and for individuals), the issue of how to treat capital losses may arise. Under the general tax rules, corporations may only use capital losses to offset capital gains. Any excess is available to be carried back three years to offset capital gains (if any), and then any remaining amount can be carried forward for five years. As previously mentioned, both a corporation's capital gains and other types of income are currently subject to the same income tax rates.

One type of institution that has recently become an investor in managed futures is tax-exempt entities. Although tax-exempt entities are generally not subject to federal income tax, there are certain instances where this may not be the case. The tax law provides for a tax on a tax-exempt entity's unrelated business taxable income (UBTI). UBTI includes certain types of income that Congress and the IRS have determined to be unrelated to that of the business and investing income of the tax-exempt entity. The tax law allows these types of entities to make investments and not be subject to tax on the related earnings, but the rules become clouded where the particular investment is leveraged or the investment vehicle itself uses leverage. It is extremely important for the tax-exempt entity to carefully analyze the tax law with its advisers, prior to engaging in these transactions.

An investor should also be aware of what effect the type of entity used to manage the futures and options will have on the character and timing of income and losses. Generally, if the entity is an individual money manager or a partnership, the character of the gains and losses from these transactions will flow through directly to the investor. On the other hand, if the managing entity is a corporation, the character of gains and losses and the timing into taxable income by the investor may be affected.

General tax law does not tax a corporation's shareholders until amounts are actually distributed by the corporation. When earnings are distributed as dividends to the shareholders, they are taxed. Dividend treatment is required even if the corporation's earnings consisted solely of capital gains and losses. However, corporations have available to them two elections that can more or less equalize the tax treatment to an investor in a partnership versus a corporation. The two elections are the regulated investment company (RIC) election and the S corporation election.

The RIC election has the effect of treating distributions to shareholders as dividends to the extent of the corporation's ordinary income—for example, interest and dividends, as well as short-term capital gains. On the other hand, long-term capital gains will maintain their character as capital gain when distributed to shareholders. The key to the RIC election is that no corporate income tax will be paid by the RIC, provided it distributes annually substantially all of its earnings.

The S Corporation election is most likened to a partnership, in that items of income maintain their character as they flow to the shareholders.

Ordinary income, including interest and dividends as well as short-term and long-term gains and losses, can maintain its character as it flows to the shareholders. The key here, as with a partnership, is that amounts are taxed annually to the shareholder and not to the electing S corporation, whether amounts are distributed or not.

CONCLUSION

As a result of the tremendous growth in the use of futures and options, both the accounting and tax communities, along with the respective regulatory and legislative bodies, have responded to provide guidance. Their responses have included the issuance of accounting pronouncements and the passage of tax laws necessary to provide a consistent approach to reporting gains and losses.

From an accounting perspective, GAAP generally follows a mark-to-market approach for exchange-traded futures and options. SFAS No. 52, SFAS No. 80, and the AICPA Issues Paper provide for this approach, which requires that gains and losses be recorded at year-end prior to the time when the specific transaction is terminated or disposed. When a non-U.S.-dollar-based transaction is involved, the accounting rules require that foreign currency exchange gain or loss be recognized. If futures and options are being used as hedging devices, the method of reporting the underlying transaction will guide the accounting treatment for the hedge.

From a tax perspective, the rules regarding futures and options are detailed and specific. The taxpayer must determine whether the future or option is taxable as a Section 1256 contract. If Code Section 1256 applies, all open positions must be marked-to-market at year-end and combined with other Section 1256 contracts positions disposed of during the year, for purposes of applying the 60/40 rule. Depending on whether the transaction is entered into for speculative or hedging purposes, the straddle loss deferral rules may apply, and a determination must be made regarding the mixed straddle elections. Finally, an analysis may be needed regarding whether, and to what extent, the foreign currency gain or loss rules, the wash sale rules, or the carryback election provisions may apply.

The institutional investor is faced with a few accounting and tax considerations that need to be analyzed prior to engaging in managed futures transactions.

The subject matter in this chapter has not represented an all-inclusive discussion of the accounting and taxation of futures and options, but rather has been aimed at providing the financial professional with a general overview of the major accounting and taxation issues covering this evolving area.

9 MANAGED FUTURES: THE CONSULTANT'S VIEW

Henry Marmer

Some U.S. pension sponsors and consultants have begun to propose futures as a possible alternative asset class. They have recommended employing managed futures as a portfolio management strategy in which to introduce futures as a "new asset class" into the mix decision. This chapter presents the consultant's view of introducing futures into the asset mix decision. The focus here is on the issues pension plan sponsors should consider when evaluating futures as a nontraditional asset class and employing a managed futures strategy.

Various problems are involved when contemplating futures as an asset class. Any new asset class usually poses several issues of concern that must be effectively resolved before it can be included in the investment decision-making process. Considered as a new asset class, futures raise particular practical problems that an investor must evaluate before considering futures as an investment.

An investor pondering the addition of a new asset class to the portfolio mix must have a clear understanding of what the proposed asset class is. More specifically, the investor must have a firm grasp of the historical risks and rewards, the correlations, and the underlying factors that drive these numbers. With such a base of knowledge, the portfolio manager can then build capital market expectations for the new asset class and consider the feasibility of including it in the portfolio mix. This chapter summarizes the academic work that has examined the historical performance of futures as an asset class and the use of commodity futures funds as an investment strategy.

The chapter closes with some relevant comments for Canadian pension sponsors.

FUTURES AS AN ASSET CLASS: PRACTICAL ISSUES OF CONCERN

Investors realistically considering the potential of a new asset class often encounter several issues of concern, including:

1. Fuzzy definition of asset class
2. Problems developing benchmarks for performance measurement
3. Inaccurate data
4. Lack of market history
5. Market illiquidities
6. Significant structural changes in the market.

Futures as a new asset class presents investors with a number of similar issues.

ASSET CLASS DEFINITION

Can futures, like other well-established asset classes, be lucidly defined as an asset class? Traditional asset classes, such as stocks, bonds, and bills, are clearly perceived in the investment community as asset classes. These asset classes are represented by broad-based indexes (for example, the S&P 500 Index) composed of numerous securities, with each security representing a financial claim on assets. In recent years, broad-based indexes have been further refined and developed into an assortment of narrow specialty indexes (e.g., S&P 400 Mid Cap Index).

A futures contract also can be clearly defined as a derivative asset—an instrument whose value is derived from some other asset, known as the underlying asset. This underlying asset can be a commodity, a financial asset, or a derivative asset. However, the specific identification of a particular asset class called futures is a "fuzzy" issue that currently has a number of unanswered questions. These questions include:

- What composes a futures assets class—commodity futures, or financial futures, or both?
- How do you weight various futures contracts to compose a futures asset class?
- Are margins ignored or treated as part of a futures investment?

PERFORMANCE MEASUREMENT AND DATA ACCURACY

The issue of appropriately identifying a futures asset class has important implications for performance measurement. The performance of an investment manager cannot be effectively measured without a clear and concise identification of the asset class or the universe of securities from which the manager selects investments. What is the appropriate benchmark or bogey for the futures investment manager?

Some futures advisers have attempted to address this performance measurement problem by suggesting that the Managed Accounts Reports (MAR) Index may be considered as a performance bogey. This index is a composite of the returns of all publicly offered commodity funds sold to retail investors that are listed in MAR.

However, the biggest practical issue in using MAR as a bogey for managed futures accounts is that the index does not represent the universe of securities from which the manager selects investments. Effective performance measurement in terms of security selection and asset timing abilities necessitates benchmarking the manager against a passive index of securities from which the manager selects investments.

Futures adviser Abughazaleh points out that there are three unique MAR indexes:

Public Funds Index—the aggregate performance of the Public Futures Funds.

Equal Weighted Index—the combined performance of 25 selected commodity trading advisers (CTAs).

Dollar Weighted Index—the dollar adjusted version of the Equal Weighted Index.

Because each index is computed differently, results among indexes will vary. For example, over a 9-year period ending December 1988, Abughazaleh reported the following average calendar year returns for the indexes:

MAR Index	*Average Calendar Year Return*
Public Funds	13.04%
Equal Weighted	26.57
Dollar Weighted	24.47

Abughazaleh also warns investors that index returns can be calculated in at least six distinctive ways, with each method yielding different results. For example, yearly returns based on average monthly results multiplied by 12 will be significantly different from yearly returns derived from average monthly results compounded by 12.

Both academics and practitioners have raised several other general issues about MAR indexes:

- The indexes may be incomplete because there are publicly traded commodity funds that are not included in MAR.
- The integrity of the indexes may be questioned because commodity trading advisers (CTAs) voluntarily submit their results to MAR, and they are not verified by an independent third party.
- The indexes display survivorship bias: managers who do poorly simply stop submitting their results.
- MAR averages the returns across accounts, which can bias results upward.

MARKET HISTORY

Historical asset class data are an important source of information for investment professionals seeking to build return and risk expectations for asset classes and for manager performance expectations. Traditional asset classes usually have at least 35 years of historical information. Unfortunately, financial futures, which are the predominant futures contracts traded in today's marketplace, were only developed in the 1980s. The MAR Index also has a limited history of approximately 10 years.

LIQUIDITY

Liquid markets are one of the key cornerstones for efficient markets. The liquidity of futures contracts varies from market to market and can be easily found in any newspaper. What is less well known is that the depth of managed futures developed over the past five years. For example, in 1985, there were 94 funds with $600 million under management. By 1988, there were 130 funds with over $2 billion under management. By 1991, about $20 billion was in managed futures funds. If managed futures continues to illustrate such enormous growth, then the liquidity of futures contracts should continue to soar.

STRUCTURAL CHANGES

The structure of the futures market has significantly changed over the past 15 years, shifting from a predominantly commodities-dependent market to a financials-based market. The possible development of a long, historical, representative asset class series for futures could be hindered to some degree by the ongoing significant change in the types of contracts actively considered and traded by participants in the market.

ACADEMIC STUDIES

Nevertheless, despite these practical issues, a number of good academic research efforts are being directed toward empirically investigating the concept of futures as an asset class and the use of managed futures as a strategy in this market. The work in this area has developed into two different schools.

The first school of thought suggests that futures can be considered an asset class with a role to play in the asset mix decision. From a practical perspective, it is worth noting that the asset class proxy employed by the academics as a benchmark for futures performance changes from study to study. Hence, the academics provide little help for solving the initial pragmatic issue of defining a futures asset class.

The second school of thought concludes that investing in commodity futures funds is not an effective or efficient investment strategy.

FUTURES IN THE ASSET MIX

The inclusion of futures contracts in the portfolio mix progressed with a pioneer paper in 1980 by Bodie and Rosansky. When they examined the performance of 23 individual commodities from 1949 through 1976, they found that a benchmark portfolio of commodity futures had approximately the same mean (13.83 percent vs. 13.05 percent) and standard deviation (22.43 percent vs. 18.95 percent) of returns as equities. However, the distribution of commodity returns was significantly more positively skewed than that of stocks, because commodities had a higher maximum and a higher minimum annual return relative to stocks.

The commodity portfolio was a significantly better hedge against inflation than stocks. The correlation between commodity futures returns and inflation was 0.58; stock returns and inflation had a negative correlation of −0.43. A negative correlation was found between stocks and the commodity portfolio. To the portfolio manager, this suggests that there are potential diversification benefits to including a basket of commodity futures in the portfolio mix.

Bodie (1983) extended his work by utilizing modern portfolio techniques to examine the risk–return tradeoff of adding commodity futures to a portfolio of traditional asset classes (stocks, bonds, and bills). Bodie employed mean–variance analysis (MVA) to examine this issue and concluded that essentially, MVA is based on the belief that rational investors choose investments that maximize expected return for a given degree of risk and minimize risk for a given expected return. Given this rule, an optimization model is implemented to determine the efficient frontier: a curve that contains all the portfolios that maximize expected return at each level of risk. Risk is measured as the variance or standard deviation of returns.

To generate an efficient frontier, one requires forecasts of expected returns, risk, and correlations among the asset classes under consideration. The assumptions used by Bodie are shown in Table 9.1.

Bodie's results are displayed in Figure 9.1. The efficient frontier on the lower right side of Figure 9.1 includes all the optimal portfolios available to an investor who can invest in stocks, bonds, and bills. If the investor can also take a position in commodity futures, then the efficient frontier shifts above the original curve. More specifically, combining commodity futures with investments in traditional asset classes yields a new efficient frontier with a superior risk–return tradeoff relative to the frontier based on stocks, bonds, and bills. Based on Bodie's return, risk, and correlation assumptions, these results reveal diversification benefits for traditional asset mixes by including commodity futures.

Lee, Leuthold, and Cordier continued the work of Bodie and Rosansky by examining the performance of the Commodity Futures Index (CFI) produced by the Commodity Research Bureau (CRB) ("the CRB

TABLE 9.1. Bodie's assumptions on asset class risk–return.

Asset Class	Expected Real Return	Risk
Bills	0%	1.7%
Bonds	3	7.4
Stocks	7	19.5
Commodity Futures	2	17.4

	Correlation Coefficients			
	Bills	Bonds	Stocks	Commodity Futures
Bills	1.00			
Bonds	.43	1.00		
Stocks	.25	.19	1.00	
Commodity Futures	−.51	−.23	−.21	1.00

FIGURE 9.1. Risk–return tradeoff curves.

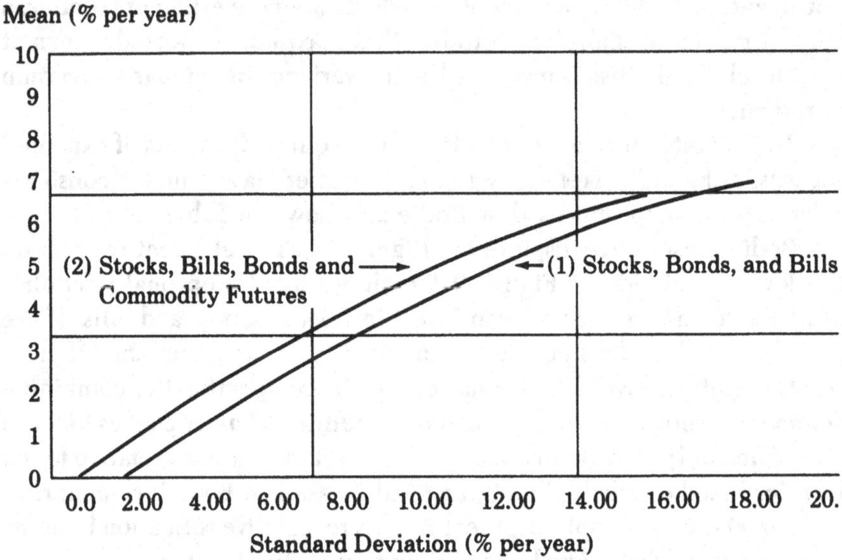

futures index"). At the time this research was conducted, the Index was comprised of the futures contract prices of 27 commodities. The period of analysis was 1978 through 1981. Over this time frame, the stock market, as proxied by the S&P 500, performed marginally better than the CFI. However, once again, commodity futures returns were found to have little relationship to stock market returns. Hence, further support was provided for the concept that commodity futures included in a stock portfolio may help to reduce portfolio risk and provide for a more efficient asset mix.

The New York Futures Exchange (NYFE) hired a futures research house to conduct a study that further advanced this concept of including a basket of commodities in a traditional investment portfolio. The research examined whether the CRB futures index futures would enter the efficient frontier of a U.S. investor.

Because the CRB futures index futures only began trading in June 1986, the historical returns were simulated. It was conservatively assumed that 10 percent of the investors' money was kept in cash to back a long position in the CRB futures index futures and the remaining 90 percent was invested in Treasury bills (T-bills). In essence, the investors' returns were composed of the return on the CRB futures plus 90 percent of the return on the T-bills.

The following traditional asset classes were considered in the risk–return efficient frontier analysis: U.S. stocks, U.S. corporate bonds, U.S. government bonds, and three different indexes of foreign stocks. Three different scenarios were employed where the asset class weight of the simulated CRB futures index futures was restricted to 10 percent, 20 percent, and 30 percent of the portfolio. In all scenarios, combining the simulated CRB futures index futures with the various asset classes shifted the efficient frontier up and to the left of the efficient frontier derived from investing only in the traditional asset classes.

Figure 9.2 displays the shift in the efficient frontier that occurs when the simulated CRB futures index futures are combined with U.S.

FIGURE 9.2. Efficient frontier (with constraints).

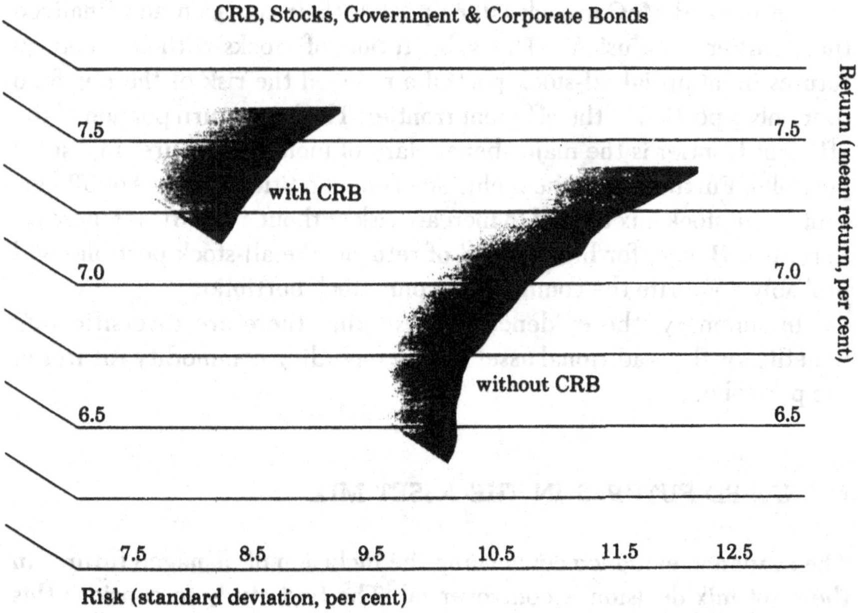

stocks and bonds. The efficient frontiers including the synthetic CRB futures dominate the pure stock–bond efficient frontier. In other words, the risk–return tradeoff of a traditional portfolio improved when the simulated CRB futures index futures were included. Furthermore, the risk–return ratio continued to be enhanced as the percentage allocated to the CRB index was increased.

Herbst and McCormack examined the portfolio risk and return implications of including futures and stocks in the asset mix. The procedure these authors employed was to compare portfolios of randomly selected stocks with portfolios of randomly selected stocks and futures contracts. They found that "the addition of commodity futures reduces risk for each stock portfolio, up to a point where commodities comprise more than 70 percent of the portfolio."

More importantly, stock portfolios combined with futures can at times dominate pure stock portfolios. These writers concluded that "portfolio managers should consider including some proportion of futures in their common stock portfolios." It is important to note that their research did not recommend an appropriate weighting of futures contracts in the stock portfolio.

Herbst and McCormack later updated their research and finalized their earlier conclusions. The substitution of stocks-with-commodity-futures in an initial all-stock portfolio reduced the risk of the portfolio over only a portion of the efficient frontier. The low-return portion of the efficient frontier is the major beneficiary of including futures in a stock portfolio. Furthermore, the inclusion of commodities in excess of 30 percent of the stock mix tended to increase risk without a significant increase in return. Hence, for higher level of returns, the all-stock portfolio will probably dominate the commodities-plus-stock portfolio.

In summary, the evidence suggests that there are diversification benefits for the traditional asset mix by including commodity futures in the portfolio.

MANAGED FUTURES IN THE ASSET MIX

The academic evidence concerning the inclusion of managed futures in the asset mix decision is controversial. The first study to consider this issue was undertaken by the renowned John Lintner. Although his study was never formally published because of his untimely death, the Lintner study became widely quoted in the industry.

Basically, Lintner concluded:

> [T]he combined portfolio of stocks after including judicious investments in appropriately selected sub-portfolios of investments in managed futures or funds shows substantially less risk at every possible level of expected return than portfolios of stocks or stocks and bonds alone.

One criticism of Lintner's study was that his results were based on only eight publicly traded funds examined over a 3½-year period.

Irwin and Brorsen employed advanced statistical measures (for example, stochastic dominance) beyond MVA to evaluate the performance of public commodity funds relative to different degrees of investor risk tolerance levels. Results were consistent with expectations: generally, risk-seeking investors preferred commodity funds relative to T-bills or stocks. As risk aversion increased, investors preferred T-bills and stocks relative to commodity funds.

Three academics who have spent a significant amount of time investigating the performance of publicly offered commodity funds are Elton, Gruber, and Rentzler (EGR). Their first paper presented some interesting results for futures funds over the period July 1979 through June 1985. They generally found that the typical commodity fund had a standard deviation twice as large as the stock market and three times larger than the bond market, and that its average return was significantly lower than either traditional market. The correlation between commodity funds and stocks and bonds was negative.

Criticisms directed toward the EGR paper include:

- Limited sample period of six years, with a limited number of funds;
- Using June-to-June returns could bias returns downward.

In 1990, EGR responded to these criticisms and updated their work using calendar-year data over the period January 1980 through December 1988. Once again, EGR found that commodity funds had a low return (2.4 percent per year) with a high risk level (10.4 percent monthly standard deviation). Furthermore, as revealed in Table 9.2, commodity

TABLE 9.2. Summary of return on assets, by asset class.

Asset Class	Yearly Return	Standard Deviation of Monthly Return
Commodity Funds	2.4%	10.4%
Common Stocks	14.9	4.9
Long-Term Corporate Bonds	11.8	3.8
Long-Term Government Bonds	11.4	4.2
Treasury Bills	8.6	0.3

funds were a poor alternative asset class on a risk–return basis, relative to other traditional asset classes.

On a risk–return basis, commodity funds are not attractive, but as stand-alone investments they may provide diversification benefits for portfolios. Although the correlation between commodity funds and stocks and bonds was approximately 0, EGR concluded that commodity funds did not prove to be useful diversifiers that should be included in the portfolio mix.

EGR also found that commodity funds were negatively correlated with inflation—an indication that they are not good inflation hedges.

Schneeweis and Savanayna developed two creative approaches to examining commodity fund performance. First, an independent outside manager was used to select a set of "preferred commodity funds for investment"; 14 funds were chosen, and their performance results were analyzed over a 5-year period. Three trading strategies were then employed to pick superior managers.

Results indicated that, after estimated transaction costs and manager fees, it was questionable whether the 14-commodity-funds set would be a valuable addition to a traditional (stocks and bonds) portfolio mix. However, the funds selected employing two of the trading strategies would probably be beneficial to the traditional asset mix.

Marmer proposed several issues of concern pertaining to the innovative approach of Schneeweis and Savanayna. Ex post (after the fact) selection of commodity funds results in survivorship and selection bias. Survivorship bias occurs because commodity funds that have failed and gone bankrupt cannot be available for selection. Selection bias transpires when the independent outside manager chooses the commodity funds because their superior performance was known ex post.

Furthermore, inappropriate benchmarks were used as a means of testing performance. More specifically, the best active commodity funds ex post were compared against passive buy and hold indexes for stocks and bonds. It would have been more fitting to compare these superior commodity funds to the best performing actively managed equity and bond funds.

PULLING IT ALL TOGETHER

The empirical work discussed to this point focuses on either futures or managed futures within the asset mix. Irwin and Landa pulled together both futures and managed futures in the asset allocation decision and produced some interesting results. Employing mean–variance analysis, they examined seven investment alternatives: U.S. T-bills, U.S. T-bonds, common stocks (S&P 500), real estate, gold, the CRB futures index, and a composite value-weighted index of public commodities futures funds.

The input parameters for the efficient frontier are displayed in Tables 9.3 and 9.4 and are based on historical real return data obtained over the period 1973 through 1985. The risk approximations for real estate and futures funds were appropriately increased to more closely reflect "real" expectations.

Figure 9.3 displays the efficient frontier results. Frontier A represents optimal portfolios based on traditional asset classes of bills, bonds, and stocks. Frontier B represents the optimal portfolios when the investment opportunities expand to include futures, futures funds, gold, and real estate. Frontier B dominates frontier A over every level of risk.

For the sponsor considering futures, the issue now is: what role did futures play in the efficient frontier? Table 9.5 displays the efficient portfolio proportions for points along frontier B. Buy-and-hold futures had a small role in attaining the minimum variance point, with futures composing 3.6 percent of the asset mix. Further out along the frontier, futures rapidly diminish from the asset mix.

Public futures funds indexes tell quite a different story. Futures funds are held in all portfolio mixes along the efficient frontier, and the

TABLE 9.3. Annual real rates of return for alternative assets, 1975–1985.

Year	Treasury Bills	Treasury Bonds	Common Stocks	Real Estate	Buy-and-Hold Futures	Futures Funds	Gold	Inflation Rate
1975	–1.1	2.0	28.3	6.0	–12.5	3.5	–29.7	7.0
1976	0.3	11.4	18.2	4.7	2.2	–25.6	–8.5	4.8
1977	–1.6	–7.0	–13.1	4.0	–8.3	55.3	14.8	6.8
1978	–1.7	–9.4	–2.3	5.3	4.2	19.3	25.7	9.0
1979	–2.6	–12.9	4.5	4.7	9.1	40.9	104.6	13.3
1980	–1.0	–14.7	17.9	0.8	–2.5	13.4	0.1	12.4
1981	5.3	–6.7	–12.8	–3.7	–24.1	7.8	–37.7	8.9
1982	6.4	35.1	16.8	3.8	–11.6	–4.7	10.0	3.9
1983	4.8	–3.0	18.1	3.2	14.3	–13.9	–19.6	3.8
1984	5.7	11.1	2.2	0.7	–15.4	3.3	–22.3	4.0
1985	3.7	26.1	27.2	5.7*	–9.6	10.1*	3.0	3.9
Arithmetic Mean	1.6	2.9	9.5	3.2	–4.9	9.9	3.7	7.1
Geometric Mean	0.1	1.8	8.5	3.1	–5.6	7.8	–1.6	7.0
Standard Deviation	3.5	16.3	14.7	2.9	11.5	22.9	38.8	3.5

* Preliminary estimate of return.

Sources: Bills, bonds, stocks, and inflation rate: *Stocks, Bonds, Bills, and Inflation.*
Real estate: Ibbotson and Siegel; Ibbotson Associates.
Buy-and-hold futures: Commodity Research Bureau.
Futures funds: Irwin and Brorsen.
Gold: Sherman (1984); *The Wall Street Journal,* various issues.

TABLE 9.4. Correlation coefficients.

	Bonds	Stocks	Real Estate	Buy-and-Hold Futures	Futures Funds	Gold	Inflation Rate
Bills	0.63	0.07	−0.46	−0.42	−0.54	−0.53	−0.66
Bonds		0.46	0.25	−0.33	−0.47	−0.23	−0.77
Stocks			0.51	0.22	−0.56	−0.15	−0.29
Real Estate				0.49	0.07	0.41	−0.18
Futures					−0.03	0.52	0.18
Futures Funds						0.58	0.55
Gold							0.55

FIGURE 9.3. Efficient risk–return frontiers.

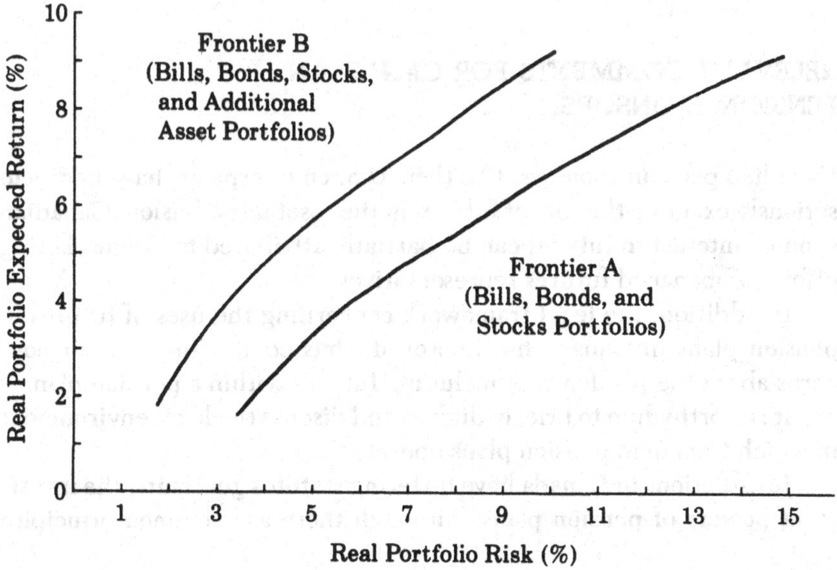

TABLE 9.5. Efficient portfolio proportions (percent).

Expected Return	Risk	Proportions: Real Estate	Buy-and-Hold Futures	Futures Funds	Gold
1.9	1.8	19.7	3.6	3.8	0.0
2.0	1.9	19.6	3.0	4.0	0.0
3.0	2.4	12.5	0.0	6.3	0.0
4.0	3.4	0.0	0.0	9.1	0.0
5.0	4.5	0.0	0.0	11.2	0.0
6.0	5.8	0.0	0.0	13.2	0.0
7.0	7.2	0.0	0.0	15.3	0.0
8.0	8.6	0.0	0.0	17.4	0.0
9.0	10.0	0.0	0.0	19.4	0.0

proportion of total asset mix allocated to futures funds steadily increases to a maximum of 19.4 percent. Irwin and Landa warned that "the impressive performance of futures funds, however, must be viewed cautiously because of the short sample period."

RELEVANT COMMENTS FOR CANADIAN PENSION SPONSORS

Canadian pension sponsors, like their U.S. counterparts, have begun to seriously examine the role of futures in the asset mix decision. Canadian sponsor interest in futures can be partially attributed to the marketing efforts of managed futures representatives.

In addition, the legal framework concerning the uses of futures in pension plans in Canada has improved, thus comforting sponsor concerns about the prudence of including futures within a pension plan.

It is worthwhile to briefly digress and discuss the legal environment in which Canadian pension plans operate.

Jurisdictions in Canada have differing statutes governing the investment powers of pension plans. Although there are common principles underlying the laws of all jurisdictions, each pension plan must abide by the laws of the jurisdiction it is registered under.

For example, pension plans in Ontario that are registered under the Pension Benefits Act "may use futures and options contracts where appropriate, if the statement of investment policies and goals for the plan permits such use." Pension plans in Manitoba that are registered under the Pension Benefits Act "may use futures and options contracts where appropriate, if the trust document governing the pension fund permits such use."

Canadian sponsors contemplating some role for futures in their pension portfolios should also consider that all the research in this area, as discussed above, has been based on the U.S. investor's perspective. Hence, Canadian investors should consider how the foreign exchange rate risk of investing in U.S. markets would alter the results presented. In addition, Canadian sponsors should perform their own optimal asset mix tests employing futures and traditional Canadian asset classes.

CONCLUDING COMMENTS

As pointed out at the beginning of this chapter, the investor considering the introduction of a new asset class into the portfolio decision-making process must have a clear perception of the risks, rewards, and correlations of that asset class. In his classic book, *Investment Policy,* Charles Ellis proposed that "thoughtful, objective study of the past is the best way to develop an understanding of the basic nature of investments and markets." This chapter has attempted to give an overview of both the practical issues and the academic studies concerning the potential of futures as an asset class within the historic framework of this very young market.

To place some perspective on the material presented here, it is useful to point out, as a case study example, two other asset classes that once raised difficulties in analysis similar to those discussed here in relation to futures as an asset class. The two asset classes I refer to are junk bonds and real estate, two markets that have experienced significantly different outcomes with respect to their development as asset classes.

Although the real estate market is currently undergoing some difficulty today, no one would question the validity of real estate as an asset class. The same can certainly not be said about junk bonds. Time will tell in which direction futures as an asset class will develop.

The current evidence suggests that both pension plan sponsors and consultants should investigate more seriously the potential of futures as an alternative asset class.

FOR FURTHER READING

Abughazaleh, A. T. "Indexes Are Not Created Equal." *Intermarket*, April 1989, pp. 53–54.

Bodie, Z., and Rosansky, V. "Risk and Return in Commodity Futures." *Financial Analysts Journal*, May–June 1980, pp. 27–39.

Browne, M. "Commodity Futures as an Asset Class." *New York Futures Exchange*, January 1990.

Ellis, C. *Investment Policy: How to Win the Loser's Game*. Homewood, IL: Dow Jones-Irwin, 1965.

Elton, E. J., Gruber, M. J., and Rentzler, J. "Professionally Managed, Publicly Traded Commodity Funds." *Journal of Business*, 60:2 (1987), pp. 175–199.

———. "New Public Offerings, Information, and Investor Rationality: The Case of Publicly Offered Commodity Funds." *Journal of Business*, 62:1 (1989), pp. 1–15.

———. "The Performance of Publicly Offered Commodity Funds." *Financial Analysts Journal* (July–August 1990), pp. 23–30.

Herbst, A. F., and McCormack, J. P. "An Examination of the Risk/Return Characteristics of Portfolios Combining Commodity Futures Contracts with Common Stocks." *Center for the Study of Futures Markets* (January 1986), Working Paper Series CSFM-125.

———. "An Examination of the Risk/Return Characteristics of Portfolios Combining Commodity Futures Contracts with Common Stocks." *Review of Research in Futures Markets*, 6:1 (1987), pp. 416–431.

———. "A Further Examination of the Risk/Return Characteristics of Portfolios Combining Commodity Futures Contracts with Common Stocks." *Center for the Study of Futures Markets* (February 1988), Working Paper Series CSFM-167.

Irwin, S. H., and Brorsen, B. W. "Examination of Commodity Fund Performance." *Review of Research in Futures Markets*, 4:1 (1985), pp. 84–105.

Irwin, S. H., and Landa, D. "Real Estate, Futures and Gold as Portfolio Assets." *Journal of Portfolio Management* (Fall 1987), pp. 29–34.

Lee, C. F., Leuthold, R. M., and Cordier, J. E. "The Stock Market and the Commodity Futures Market: Diversification and Arbitrage Potential." *Financial Analysts Journal* (July–August 1985), pp. 53–60.

Lintner, J. "The Potential Role of Managed Futures Accounts (and/or Funds) in Portfolios of Stocks and Bonds." Paper presented at Annual Conference of Financial Analysts Federation, Toronto, Canada, May 1983.

Marmer, H. "A World of Difference." *Benefits Canada* (October 1990).

———. "Commentary on Multi-Manager Commodity Funds: A Risk Return Analysis." *Selected Papers of the Fifth Canadian International Futures Conference and Research Seminar*, Canadian Securities Institute, 1990.

———. "When Fact and Opinion Collide." *Risk Magazine* (September 1989).

Moore, P. M. "Legal Uses of Futures and Options Contracts by Pension Plans, Insurance Companies and Trust Companies in Canada." Paper produced for The Montreal Exchange and The Toronto Stock Exchange for use by their member firms, April 30, 1990.

Newcastle Capital Management Inc. "Ambiguity in Managed Futures Studies." *Derivative Portfolio Manager*, 2:5 (October–November 1990).

Schneeweis, T., and Savanayna, U. "Multi-Manager Commodity Funds: A Risk/Return Analysis." *Selected Papers of the Fifth Canadian International Futures Conference and Research Seminar*, Canadian Securities Institute, 1990.

10 THE FINANCIAL CONSIDERATIONS OF FUTURES EXECUTION AND CLEARING

Phil Bennett

A futures contract can be defined as "a standardized contract for the purchase or sale of a commodity for future delivery, traded or executed on a regulated contract market." By highlighting certain key characteristics of futures markets—namely, standardization, future delivery, execution, and regulated markets—it is possible to isolate areas that involve financial considerations for futures market participants.

Although these considerations include both potential disadvantages and advantages, the overwhelming weight of evidence indicates that, in general, the advantages of these markets predominate. This conclusion is supported by the explosive growth in futures trading volume in recent years and by current developments, which point to continued market expansion. However, before addressing these financial issues in detail, it is worthwhile to discuss briefly how the futures markets have grown and the mechanisms under which these markets operate.

GROWTH AND CHANGE IN THE INDUSTRY

The 1980s witnessed unprecedented growth in the volume of futures contracts traded. During that decade, futures trading volume in the United States grew by 290 percent. In 1990, for the 23rd consecutive year, annual volume increased, reaching a total volume of over 276 million contracts traded. The volume of exchange-traded options also grew proportionately, reaching a record volume of over 64 million in 1990, an increase of 16 percent above the previous record established in 1989.

During the past few years, in addition to the growth of volume in the United States, the establishment of futures markets has grown rapidly outside the United States. In the 1980s, futures markets were created in Australia, Japan, Singapore, France, Switzerland, Germany, and Sweden, and existing markets in the United Kingdom and the Netherlands were expanded and diversified. Countries with current plans to establish futures markets now include Spain, Italy, Taiwan, Korea, and Mexico.

Of equal significance in this market evolution has been the dramatic shift in the volume mix from the dominance of traditional commodities, such as agricultural commodities and precious metals, to the new generation of predominantly financial contracts. The increase in financial futures has fueled industry growth in recent years. Comparatively, traditional commodity futures, linked in most cases to underlying physical transactions, have remained static or have exhibited modest growth. Only the energy complex (heating oil and gasoline particularly) has shown rates of growth equivalent to those of interest rate futures. However, much of the growth has been driven by financial institutions that have used energy futures as a hedging mechanism for a variety of derivative, off-exchange financial products, such as options and swaps.

NEW CUSTOMER PARTICIPATION

Commensurate with this change in volume mix has been a change in the nature of customer participation. A decade ago, the futures industry was dominated by physical commodity hedgers and speculators. Market volume was fueled by speculative interests that established the high-water marks for gold, silver, sugar, and copper prices in the late-1970s and early-1980s. In turn, these price movements reflected high levels of inflation and were prompted by a broad-based retail interest fleeing negative real interest rates and bearish equity markets. This period's sharp conclusion in 1980 was precipitated by recession and by the bursting of the speculative bubble, exemplified, among other things, by the dramatic and publicized collapse of the silver futures market.

During the 1970s, the futures industry had prospered and had indulged itself in relatively inefficient, high-cost operations. The sharp contraction of traditional market volumes, associated with the changing economic environment in the early-1980s, has a parallel in the contraction of equity market activity in the late-1980s. Consequently, the futures industry went through a period of contraction. The inefficient high-cost producers with their swollen overheads were, in the main, absorbed by the more efficient firms. By the mid-1980s, therefore, the industry was generally leaner and better structured.

At the same time, the nature of industry participation began to change. A period of deflation, positive interest yields, a strong bond market, and, in the mid-1980s, a vibrant equity market drew a significant portion of the traditional retail base away from the futures markets. The rapid rise in U.S. government deficit financing and the acceleration of financial innovation expanded a group of clients who began to consider the futures market as a readily available and liquid means of managing risk in their underlying cash businesses.

NEW PRODUCTS AND APPLICATIONS

During this era, the now common phrase "derivative products" was first coined. Not only were large banks and securities firms able to hedge significant risk positions in futures, thus facilitating the underwriting and distribution of major debt and equity underwritings, but they were able to use their futures expertise as a means of structuring a widening range of over-the-counter products. These products, in turn, were supplied to corporate clients, who lacked similar expertise. As the 1980s progressed, events stemming from financial deregulation, international expansion, and globalization all created new opportunities for financial innovation and challenges in risk management. The resulting uncertainty again focused attention on the futures markets.

In addition to this form of financial engineering, the developing relationship of large liquid futures markets and significant global cash markets enabled portfolio managers to monitor and evaluate periodic aberrations between these markets. These aberrations were then arbitraged in order to improve yields on their underlying cash portfolios. Finally, as the market became increasingly sophisticated, individual investors, recognizing the natural disadvantage at which they were now placed when attempting to participate in the market, sought to even these odds by pooling resources in a variety of managed futures products. This evolution emulated the growth of mutual funds that evolved in the equity markets in the 1970s.

By the end of the 1980s, therefore, the futures market had become dominated by large commercial and financial institutional users who dealt, in many cases, for their own account as conventional hedgers and in support of a wide range of derivative products. Business was also being generated by the increasingly large participation of portfolio managers and fund traders seeking to establish futures as an asset class capable of providing a legitimate alternative to traditional equity and fixed income investment vehicles. This expanded volume of business was being transacted by the large, and in most cases, efficient, producers who benefited from the industry consolidation that occurred during the mid-1980s.

These developments are significant because many have had an impact on the financial parameters that a futures market participant must evaluate. Among the most important of these are global markets, global networks, capital adequacy, systems capability, integration with cash markets, and efficient, low-cost clearing operations.

HOW FUTURES MARKETS OPERATE

Despite these major structural changes, the fundamental market mechanism has changed little in the past 10 years. Nevertheless, it requires careful consideration by the market user.

Futures and options contracts are traded principally on regulated markets. In the main, particularly in the United States, the two major components of these marketplaces are the exchanges on which the contracts are executed and the clearinghouse that processes and matches the trades, and provides a guaranty of performance of the transactions. Several financial issues are associated with this process. In order to evaluate them, it is beneficial to examine the various stages involved.

The majority of current futures and options orders are still executed on the trading floors of the respective exchanges on which they are traded, although certain new exchanges, particularly SOFEX (Switzerland) and the DTB (Germany), are promoting all-electronic access, and other markets, such as the ICCH (London), provide "after hours" electronic access. The electronic movement promises to change the industry in the future. However, the level of transactions currently entered in this way is small.

Although the implications of electronic access are significant, the majority of trading today is done through the traditional method of order entry and execution. In this method, a futures order may be entered either directly to the exchange floor or through an intermediary located off-the-floor—usually a representative of the firm (called the futures commission merchant (FCM)) who will clear the transaction for the client.

The order is then relayed to a floor broker by the phone clerk who receives the order. The execution of the futures order involves two floor brokers, one representing the buyer and one representing the seller. Both brokers must be exchange members. The brokers engage in open and competitive bidding, shouting bids and offers in what is called the "open outcry" trading system. Whenever a bid and offer correspond, a contract is formed and a trade is consummated. At this point, the transaction consists merely of a contract between two independent individuals; the exchange has not witnessed or recognized the transaction. This later stage can only be done by "clearing" the trade.

The respective brokers can execute the orders, but they cannot clear the trade. Only market members who are also members of the clearinghouse can submit trades for clearance. Consequently, the broker must now give up the trade to a clearing member for this purpose.

The clearing process is unique. When a trade is executed, the buy side and the sell side of the trade are distinct, but once the clearinghouse accepts a trade for clearance, the individualized nature of the trade changes and the clearinghouse becomes the buyer to every seller and the seller to every buyer. Essentially, the trades are commingled at this point. Furthermore, once the trade is accepted by the clearinghouse, the floor brokers who entered into the trade are removed from the process, and the client for whom the brokers executed the trade can only look to the clearinghouse for performance. The floor broker and the client no longer have any obligation to their counterparts in the transaction. The feature of the clearinghouse becoming a party to every trade is one of the essential elements of the clearing process and should be regarded by clients as a key element in considering financial risk.

At the end of the trading day, the clearinghouse computes the number of contracts presented for clearance by each clearing member. These trades are broken down by customer name and by the name of the clearing member firm responsible for carrying the customer's account. The clearinghouse then compares the current day's transactions in each of these accounts with the balance of trades in the account on the previous day (the assessment of this position or change in position gives rise to the critical margining process). However, although the clearinghouse assesses the changing account balance and continues to recognize the existence of the customer, it deals only with the clearing member firm. The clearing member firm then becomes responsible to the clearinghouse for any financial obligations of the customer in respect to those positions.

In summary, the customer places the order and has it executed and given to the clearinghouse where it is matched by the clearinghouse and reported back to the clearing member firm.

It is important to analyze the various financial considerations associated with this initial stage of the clearing process, but, before doing this, an essential feature of the futures clearing process—the margin—deserves comment.

MARGIN

Futures and options are leveraged instruments. In exchange for a modest "deposit," a client can control a substantially greater level of assets.

In the case of Treasury bond futures, for example, a deposit of as little as $2,000 enables the client to control a position with a face value of $100,000 and to ultimately benefit (or suffer) from price movements applicable to the full face value of the position.

To control the risk of leverage, the clearinghouse adopts a practice of charging margins. There are two principal types of margin:

- Initial margin—the amount of money (or securities) that must be deposited upon an opening of or an increase in a futures position.
- Variation margin—the amount of money paid by the client to the clearinghouse, or the amount of money received by the client from the clearinghouse (both payments having been directed by the client's clearing member firm), as a result of the daily price fluctuations, whether positive (a profit) or negative (a loss) of the underlying position held by the client.

In the majority of cases, initial margin takes the form of either cash or U.S. Treasury bills. These are carried at 100 percent of face value. However, variations exist between exchanges concerning the acceptability of collateral. The Chicago Board of Trade, for example, will accept certain Treasury notes as initial margin on financial futures contracts traded there.

Unlike the equity market, where margin represents partial payment for the position, the initial margin of a futures position represents only a good faith margin. Typically, the margin represents approximately 1 to 5 percent of the face value of the underlying contract and is defined as "a demand on the part of the clearinghouse that the clearing member (on behalf of a client) make a security deposit to ensure that the clearinghouse will receive performance on the contracts that it has accepted for clearing." The amount of initial margin required by the clearinghouse is determined by comparing the current day's open trades in each customer account with the balance of trades in the accounts from the previous day. Initial margin calls are made to members on the basis of any net new positions established during that period. Conversely, in the event that the net number of positions was reduced, the initial margin requirement would decline and the corresponding dollar amount would be available for return to the clearing member firm for the client's account.

Variation margin is a "demand by the clearinghouse that the clearing member pay any losses that a member has suffered as a result of an adverse movement." The reverse is true in the event of profits. In this case, the clearing member is entitled to receive the amount of any profits incurred as a result of a positive market movement. One of the principal characteristics of the futures market, and one that differentiates it strongly from the majority of cash markets, is that profits and losses are realized each day in full, which means that variation margin payments, for example, are *payments,* not deposits, and represent actual losses. Realization of losses or profits applies irrespective of the maturity of the contract being traded. As a result, the client does not have to wait until the maturity of the respective contract in order to receive profits (and cannot wait until the contract's maturity in order to pay losses).

As indicated previously, in the case of both initial and variation margin payments, the clearinghouse looks to the clearing member firm to provide the requisite funds. Although the clearing process reconciles individual customer accounts, the clearing firm does not recognize individual customers for the purpose of settling trades or receiving funds. This obligation rests squarely on the shoulders of the clearing firm, which must put up the margins in order to maintain a customer's positions. The clearing member firm in turns looks to the customer for reimbursement.

Although many futures clients are not exposed directly to the execution or the clearing and settlement process (both are accessed through the sales representative), this process represents the first category of financial considerations that the client must address. Other considerations are economic or basic policy decisions concerning a client's willingness to deal in futures, vis à vis alternative financial markets. At this point, it is appropriate to look at each component and focus on some specific considerations.

Order Execution

Order execution is provided by individuals who are members of the relevant exchange (U.S. exchanges limit membership to individuals). Within this group, there is a distinction between independent brokers—brokers who are self-employed and in most cases have no allegiance to any particular clearing firm—and brokers who also may be employees of a clearing firm. (These brokers are not precluded from executing orders and delivering them to clearing firms other than their employer.)

From the client's point of view, the significance of the broker's status relates to the nature of financial risk associated with execution. The client's overriding concern is whether an order placed into the market has been communicated accurately and can be executed expeditiously at a satisfactory price. The ability of the broker to execute consistently at price levels specified by the client can only generally be measured by assessing the reputation of the individual or the company for which that broker works. Most clients have the means of monitoring execution price performance by comparing the execution price of their orders against the general level of prices reported by the market at the time of execution. Any queries a customer may have concerning the efficacy of these executions can be addressed by referring to a Time and Sales Report, which is a precise record maintained by the exchanges of each price level at which the market traded at a specific time during the trading day.

Although certain market conditions (specifically, "fast market" conditions) may interfere with this normal process, measuring execution accuracy is relatively efficient. It is likely that the methodology of measuring futures execution efficiency will be further developed. This will provide support, comfort, and credibility, which are particularly important to clients such as pension funds, whose fiduciary responsibilities require them to ensure that independent verification of execution efficiency can be relied on.

In conjunction with measuring order execution efficiency, the client should be conscious of potential conflicts associated with the choice of the executing and clearing broker. Particular attention should be paid to order execution procedures, to ensure that no conflict exists between the handling of proprietary and customer business. Selecting a broker who does not trade principal positions offers one solution to this potential conflict.

Assuming that the order is executed accurately and efficiently, it must also be reported accurately to the client and written accurately on the completed order ticket prior to the latter's submission for clearing.

The potential risks here are a function of the operational efficiency of the executing broker.

Many large institutional clients maintain a constant telecommunications link with their "upstairs" traders or floor brokers, which facilitates execution and trading. However, care also must be taken to establish a consistent routine for confirming that orders have been executed. Failure to implement this essential operational state will result in a failure to detect discrepancies that sometimes occur in the order execution process. Common discrepancies (e.g., "buys" instead of "sells," transactions executed in the wrong amount, or a price disagreement between client and broker) result in the cleared trade's being incorrect and could expose the client to considerable loss when correcting the error.

Similarly, if the executing broker's administrative procedures are poorly organized, it may prove impossible for the broker to submit the day's trading activity to the clearing firm in a timely manner. This could prevent that day's trading activity from being processed on the same day and would result in reporting an incorrect position on the following morning. This situation would severely compromise the client's management and financial reporting and could easily compound a problem, given the nature of the current marketplace, which is becoming increasingly global and is trading on a 24-hour basis.

Clearing

After the order has been executed, confirmed back to the customer, agreed on, and submitted to the clearing firm for further processing at the clearinghouse, the obligation of the executing broker and the client is eliminated, as is the obligation of that executing broker to the opposite executing broker and, in turn, that broker's client.

The clearinghouse now becomes a party to every trade. Furthermore, although the clearinghouse recognizes the existence of the customer, it deals only with the clearing member firm in matters pertaining to the maintenance and margining of the client's positions. The client's financial risk, therefore, now shifts clearly to the member firm and the clearinghouse.

Member firms of clearing organizations in the futures markets are referred to as futures commission merchants. FCMs are defined as:

> an individual, association, partnership, corporation or trust that engages in the solicitation or acceptance of orders for the purchase or sale of any commodity for future delivery or is subject to the rules of any contract market, and that in or in connection with such solicitation or acceptance of orders accepts any money, security, or property (or extends credit in lieu thereof) to margin, guarantee or secure any trades or contracts that result or may result therefrom.

Although all clearing members of the exchange are FCMs, not all FCMs clear exchanges, nor does an FCM have to be a member of every exchange. Indeed, relatively few FCMs are members of all exchanges. Furthermore, a nonclearing FCM may be a client of a clearing FCM.

The FCM plays the role of financial intermediary between the customer and the clearinghouse. This function requires that the client make certain financial decisions when selecting an FCM. It also places risk on the FCM, which in turn must determine the financial integrity of its clients.

The clearinghouse looks to the FCM to provide the margin to support its client's position. The FCM, in turn, must look to the customer for reimbursement of monies which it has transferred to the clearinghouse in respect of those positions. To the extent that the clearinghouse aggregates and commingles client positions and funds, the FCM must also assume the responsibility for maintaining accurate books and records for individual customer accounts for which it separately pays and receives funds. It must reconcile these to the aggregate position it maintains at the clearinghouse on behalf of its clients. As a result of these varying responsibilities, several financial considerations must be addressed by prospective clients. A majority of these involve an assessment of financial risk.

The futures industry in the United States (and to a large extent elsewhere), in conjunction with the appropriate regulatory bodies, has established a number of checks and balances aimed at protecting clients from the financial risks associated with the clearing process. Among the most important are the following:

1. Capital (financial) requirements for clearing member firms
2. Legal separation ("segregation") of customer balances from the clearing firm's own funds

3. Conservative financial reporting
4. Specific internal control requirements monitored by regular audit procedures
5. Guarantees of client balances available through the guarantee pool maintained by the clearinghouse
6. Availability of additional member funding, in the event of financial difficulty at the clearinghouse.

As a result of these various levels of protection, FCM insolvencies have been infrequent in recent years, and insolvencies causing losses have been even more rare. Nevertheless, each client should be aware of the mechanism provided by the following protective devices.

Capital Requirements

Regulation establishes the amount of capital that an FCM must maintain. The more important measure of capital is "net capital," broadly defined as the sum of immediately available liquid funds which the firm could realize to resolve any immediate financial need. This requirement measures the continuing ability of the FCM (in its capacity as the intermediary responsible for the maintenance of margin levels at the clearinghouse) (a) to meet margin levels required by customer positions before being reimbursed (in the normal course of business) by the client whose position created the margin call; or (b) following the occurrence of a potential loss resulting from the failure on the part of an individual client to remit the funds necessary to support its positions (as a result of which, positions are liquidated at a loss), thereby ensuring that the overall integrity of client funds is not compromised.

As already indicated, from an operational standpoint, the clearinghouse will look for payment by the FCM of the daily margin calls prior to the FCM's receiving confirmation that customer funds have been received. In addition, in periods of extreme market volatility, the clearinghouse may accelerate the margin process, resulting in interim (intraday) margin calls that must be met by the FCM.

The need for adequate capital has been emphasized by the emergence of global markets in recent years and by the expansion of the customer base to include multinational concerns. An interim margin call, for example, often cannot be met promptly, if a client is operating in a time zone different from that of the trading market. Although the client's trading desk which is responsible for executing the orders may be functioning, the client's domestic banking channels could be closed. Many such clients have diversified their banking operations to cater to funding requirements in different time zones, but the FCM must be prepared to "bridge" this intraday need if necessary. Accordingly, the liquid resources available to a futures firm are of even greater importance than before.

There is a relationship between the likely calls on liquid capital and the overall level of customer activity. Accordingly, the principal measure of net capital links the level of net capital to customer segregated funds.

The minimum percentage required under this formula is 4 percent (of net capital to customer funds), although a decline in this percentage to below 6 percent is regarded as an early-warning indicator of potential capital shortfalls. The adjusted net capital computation involves the deduction from statutory GAAP (Generally Accepted Accounting Principles) capital of assets defined by the regulatory authorities as illiquid. This would include, for example, fixed assets, exchange memberships, receivables from unregulated markets, and any past-due receivable or debit balance being carried by the FCM.

This measure of "liquid net worth" is important to the client and provides a true measure of liquidity. The importance to the FCM of maintaining an adequate level of liquid net worth is in sharp contrast to many other business enterprises, where cash liquidity is less crucial. Its response to the daily monitoring of volatility and risk is one of the essential benefits and risk management tools of this industry. The net capital computation is monitored by the Self Regulatory Organization (SRO) of the member firm, which can obtain daily reports of the calculation. The exchanges also use the daily payment and collection data for individual firms, as well as position information (indicators of future margin calls), to monitor capital adequacy and anticipate unusual or volatile market events that may represent a threat to capital.

The futures industry has always been conservatively capitalized. For example, the aggregate adjusted net capital of member firms, in a survey conducted by the National Futures Association in 1986, exceeded 80 percent of total segregation requirements (that is, the amount of client funds on deposit). This substantial liquidity percentage clearly indicates that capital levels in the aggregate provided more than satisfactory support for customer activity, thus ensuring the continuing liquidity of the market and the preservation of customer positions at the clearinghouse.

Segregation of Customer Funds

All FCMs are required to segregate all equity belonging to clients. (Equity is defined as the combination of cash and securities carried for the benefit of an individual customer account.) To this end, the FCMs maintain customer funds in special accounts to satisfy their obligation to customers. Furthermore, and as an important distinction between the futures and the securities industries, FCMs, unlike broker/dealers, cannot use funds to help finance their own businesses.

The effect of segregating customer funds has been powerful in ensuring the integrity of customer equity at the clearing firm. However, some important elements associated with segregation should be pointed out. First, although the FCM carries individual accounts for each client (this account records the specific activity, position reporting, and cash balances for the client), these customer funds are commingled as a group and placed with certain preapproved and designated banks for investment purposes. Furthermore, client funds are not segregated by individual client at the clearinghouse; the aggregate cash or securities attributable to an FCM's client positions are commingled.

Although the track record of the industry with respect to maintaining the integrity of customer funds is excellent, there is a circumstance in which the bankruptcy of the FCM could create a deficiency in the combined customer equity account. If, for example, a customer default was so large that it exceeded the net capital of the FCM, resulting in the failure of the FCM to make the margin calls necessary to support the positions of its remaining clients, and subsequently the FCM was liquidated in order to generate the cash necessary to make those margin calls (and the amount of liquidated capital of the FCM was insufficient), then any shortfall in the margin payment would be met from the remaining customer segregated pool.

This pool retains a preference in liquidation, vis à vis any and all other creditors of the FCM, but a degree of loss could be experienced by clients. It would then become necessary for the clearinghouse and/or exchange to intervene with guarantees or financial support that it has available, to ensure that clients were fully compensated.

Clients should be aware of this issue, even though, in recent history, circumstances have never arisen in which a deficiency has existed and not been cured. This is testimony not only to the effectiveness of regulation, but also to the tendency on the part of exchanges to reimburse clients in the event of such shortfalls.

FCM Internal Controls

The adequacy of an FCM's internal controls is audited by the member firm's SRO at least annually. These audits are supplemented by the fiscal audit conducted by the company's outside accountants. Spot audits, conducted periodically, address specific aspects of control. The client also may monitor the effectiveness of the controls by evaluating bad debt or error loss performance over a period of years. A pattern of consistent profitability is also indicative of sound operating systems and controls.

In recognition of the importance of systems in dealing with the rapid increase of futures volume in recent years, the exchanges have worked with member firms to streamline order processing and clearing systems with a view to reducing manual input and the rate of errors. The manual writing-up of trades and the manual monitoring of daily discrepancies have been replaced by electronic matching systems, thus eliminating the labor-intensive practices that would have prevented the industry's expansion to its current levels.

Margining

Creditworthiness and the credit risk assumed by the FCM are also functions of the FCM's control procedures, policies and due diligence concerning credit assessment, and, in particular, margining. Margining is one of the cornerstones of the futures industry and is the principal vehicle through which the industry controls leverage.

As with customer equity, there are significant differences between margining procedures in the securities industry and the futures industry. Unlike securities trading, futures margins do not represent down payments, as they do in equity margins. Instead, futures margins are good-faith deposits made to secure ownership of a contract, and the margin level requirement is based largely on volatility.

All exchanges establish a minimum margin structure for client activity. This is generally defined by type of customer (hedger or speculator). The FCM has the right to impose whatever margin levels it deems appropriate above the exchange's minimum requirement. The FCM also can establish its own operating procedures with clients, to ensure both that margins are met and that the FCM could take requisite action in the event margins are not met. FCMs can, for example, give customers as little as one hour to meet a margin call before liquidating a customer's position.

THE CHANGING CLIENT MIX

As noted earlier, the futures industry has changed significantly in recent years. Nowhere is this more evident than in the mix of client business. The more typical retail (largely speculative) account, which was an important element in the futures industry in the late 1970s and early 1980s has been replaced by an overwhelming percentage of large, sophisticated institutional accounts and fund managers. This influx has improved the risk profile and the margining structure of the industry. The exchanges have worked with the FCM community in adapting margin techniques to reflect a wider and more sophisticated range of futures and, particularly, options contracts. Such margining systems have sought to modify margin requirements based on volatility and other measures. The combination of sophisticated software and improved client credit quality has, therefore, vastly improved the credit profile of the customer base and the bad-debt performance of the industry.

The prospective client should be aware of these margining procedures, in order to gain the maximum benefit from the use of these markets. The client should also recognize that significant cash management issues arise from the need to make margin calls on a periodic basis. Both the initial margin, which may be provided in the form of cash or eligible securities, and the variation margin, which must be deposited in the form of cash, require constant monitoring and sufficient liquidity. The need to increase the efficiency of the cash management associated with margin calls has also led large sophisticated clients to review and rationalize the clearing process wherever possible.

Clients should seek to avoid, for example, having offsetting positions at different futures firms. This situation would increase the margin requirements by requiring both sides of the transaction to be margined independently, rather than on a net basis. By consolidating these positions at one firm, the margin requirements could be significantly reduced. This alternative has given rise to a strong interest on the part of clients to centralize clearing activities with one global clearing firm.

Most FCMs employ a comprehensive system of checks and balances designed to detect credit exposure and the credit suitability of clients. The account documentation itself provides background information and, when supplemented by a growing network of credit references and an analysis of financial statements, the financial worth of clients can be better determined in order to maintain a suitable customer profile. In certain cases, credit limits are established for customer accounts, based on the client's credit standing and the potential volatility of the markets on which the client trades.

Clearing Association Default

The clearinghouse is responsible for the day-to-day settlement of accounts and transactions. More importantly, a major goal of the clearing process is to reduce the risk attached to passing trades through the clearinghouse as an intermediary. Effectively, the clearinghouse guarantees the integrity and performance of contracts and provides customers with protection against defaults by other market participants. As a result, the customer is dependent on the clearinghouse to ensure that both the member firm carrying its positions and the clearinghouse maintain their financial integrity and avoid losses on a level that could interrupt the performance of the contracts owned by the customer.

The chief aims of the clearinghouse are efficiency and safety. The faster and more accurately a trade can be processed, the sooner the same capital can be reinvested at a lower cost, with less risk to investors. Because capital will flow toward markets that are most attractive on a risk–return basis and have efficient and reliable clearing and settlement systems, there is a constant incentive for the clearing organizations to pursue these aims. To ensure safety, clearing organizations have devised a hierarchy of protections for both the clearinghouse and, indirectly, the clearinghouse members.

The clearinghouse controls the risk of the clearing and settlement process through its interface and relationship with the clearing members. If the financial integrity of individual members is maintained, then the aggregate financial integrity of the clearing organization will be preserved. To police the financial integrity of the member firms, the clearinghouse has devised a number of financial measures and tests. They include the following:

- Minimum capital requirements.
- Position limits (usually determined as a function of capital).
- The requirement that clearing member firms place deposits with the clearinghouse to form a guarantee fund. The amount determined for these deposits is based on the volume of transactions and the capital of the clearing firm in question. The guarantee fund sits to cover default by a specific member that individually is unable to meet its obligations to the clearinghouse.
- Daily and periodic reporting requirements and the right to conduct a spontaneous audit. Both create an incentive for member firms to manage their capital and funds efficiently.
- In the event of a member firm's failure, and should the failure be of a size sufficient to fully draw down the proceeds of the guarantee fund, the clearinghouse may also have the ability to assess its membership for additional funds to adequately fund the default.
- The financial structure of clearing is aimed at minimizing the amount of capital at risk. The clearing organization settles all members' accounts daily to a net gain or loss position. Balances on its books, therefore, are settled daily to zero, and all gains and losses are paid and collected on a daily basis. The nature of this settlement and collection is aimed at protecting the clearing organization against the subsequent risk of default on a contract. The clearing organization monitors the daily fund flows, position information, and large trader reports, in order to help assess and project risk. It monitors

the previously established position limits and concentration risks associated with customer activity, and reviews these based on the firm's capital. The clearinghouse estimates pro forma margin calls based on price movement, to access the potential call on member firms' liquidity. During periods of extreme price movement, the clearinghouse may make intraday rather than next-day margin calls.

A client contemplating the level of exposure that might be experienced can, therefore, rely on the fact that, in addition to the capital of the clearing firm carrying a specific customer's position, a comprehensive series of safety nets exists to preserve the financial integrity of the client's position and protect those cash assets (in the form of initial margin), any variation profits due, and ultimately the performance of the underlying contract.

In summary, the order of protection afforded specifically by the exchange includes, first, the guarantee fund subscribed to by the membership and monitored by the clearing organization. Next is the overcall provision, which, under certain circumstances, permits the clearing organization to make additional calls for capital from its membership, the proceeds of which would be used to remedy deficiencies. Finally, there is the financial strength of the clearing organization itself, which could, in the worst case, cover a member's deficiency.

It is not surprising to learn there has never been a default of a domestic futures clearing association in the United States. Furthermore, to the extent that the model of the U.S. clearing organization has been widely adopted by foreign markets, the same basic protections also exist there. When contemplating use of the U.S. market, a client can rely heavily on these levels of protection to defend any financial exposure that may exist.

OTHER KEY FEATURES OF THE FUTURES MARKETS

The combined financial structure of FCM and clearinghouse is a crucial element in the consideration of the use of futures markets. It represents the principal difference between the futures market and the variety of cash and OTC markets, many of which offer similar products.

In the OTC markets, the client is required to make an independent evaluation of each counterparty's credit standing and ability to perform. This evaluation must consider any major or minor differences in the specifications and tenor of a contract, and the terms of its ultimate settlement or delivery.

In the futures contract, the client is spared this burden. The clearinghouse becomes a party to every contract, assuring the client of the payments due and the ultimate performance under the terms of the contract. Theoretically, this feature should provide a basis for substantial continued growth of this industry as the primary alternative to a great many markets that heretofore have been available only in an OTC format. This aspect of the futures and options market is probably underestimated and undervalued. However, it should provide great comfort to potential users of the market who are seeking the most independent guarantees of financial integrity and performance.

It is a characteristic of futures and options that they span a wide range of financial and operational considerations. At the macro level, the development of this market as an essential financial tool has facilitated the extraordinary pace of financial innovation in recent years. Many of the sophisticated derivative products now trading, including swaps, OTC options, CAPS, floors, and portfolio insurance programs, owe their existence to the ability of the seller of such products to hedge risk in the futures marketplace. To this extent, futures and options have become an integral part of the globalization of financial markets. At the other end of the spectrum, a comprehensive knowledge of the detailed workings of the market is essential in order that the efficiency of these strategies is assured and the financial controls necessary to monitor risk can be supervised competently.

The financial implications of the use of futures involve an equally wide spectrum. At the macro level, the client must consider the policies associated with the use of these markets, including the financial security and the creditworthiness of the clearing broker selected to provide access to the marketplace. The client's comfort level should, at the very least, be equal to that currently experienced when dealing with traditional (e.g., equity and fixed income) markets. Indeed, certain characteristics of futures markets suggest a greater security of financial performance. Included among these are: the role of the clearinghouse as a party to each transaction and as a guarantor of financial performance, the checks and balances that have been established to protect customer assets, and the role of regulation in monitoring the financial structure of member firms.

These characteristics eliminate the need to make individual credit assessments when accessing the market. Indeed, as has already been suggested, this is one vital aspect of the futures industry that has generally been undervalued by the market-at-large. In the long run, the guarantee of performance by independent financial entities may prove a more productive means of facilitating transactions than multilateral counterparty relationships.

The futures industry provides the advantage of allowing the client to compartmentalize the financial implications of accessing the market. While evaluating these implications, the client can take comfort from the historical performance of an industry that has demonstrated an effective balance of risk and cost while providing a sound environment for the responsible use of futures by a wide range of financial institutions.

11 INFLATION HEDGING WITH UNLEVERAGED FUTURES

Steven H. Hanke
Christopher L. Culp

Opportunities to trade unleveraged futures dramatically expand the portfolio choices open to today's institutional and individual investors. One of the most interesting applications of unleveraged futures is their role in hedging against the devastating effects of unanticipated changes in the price level. By investing in a diversified basket of internationally traded, unleveraged commodity futures whose price appreciation equals or exceeds cost-of-living increases, investors can protect themselves, at least in part, against the scourge of inflation.

The basic principle underlying the use of commodity futures as an inflation hedge is a simple one: movements in spot commodity prices are closely associated with present and future movements in the generalized

The authors wish to thank Chuck Epstein, Todd Petzel, Mark Powers, and Frank Warnock for their comments and assistance in the preparation of this chapter. The usual disclaimer applies.

price level. However, investment in commodities is cumbersome and costly. Fortunately, futures contracts on commodities provide low-cost substitutes for holding the commodities themselves. This chapter examines the justification behind using unleveraged futures as a hedge against inflation. Some of the relevant theory and evidence on this subject is surveyed, and one practical application of the theory—the Inflation Hedge Account operated by Friedberg Commodity Management, Inc. (FCMI)—is discussed.

With the development of that account, a new investment vehicle was available to investors for exploiting the relationship between commodity prices and inflation. Not only can such a well-managed portfolio of commodity futures offset losses from inflation, but proper fund management can lead to an appreciation of the commodity futures portfolio, which actually exceeds the rate of increase in general prices. A comparison of the performance of the Inflation Hedge Account with similar portfolios of cash, stocks, and bonds reveals that such speculative returns from this new investment opportunity are quite respectable.

This chapter is not an attempt to survey the literature on commodity futures and inflation hedging. That literature is far too broad to be included in this text, and it lacks definitive conclusions. Rather, we hope to show that inflation hedging with unleveraged commodity futures is theoretically desirable, and that it is possible in practice.

INFLATION HEDGING AND COMMODITY FUTURES

It was formerly thought that holding common stocks was a good way to protect future consumption opportunities from uncertain changes in the price level. To a large extent, this theory was based on the notion that, because ownership of capital goods was ownership in some physical production process, the returns from such investments would be invariant to the general price level. However, that relationship has not withstood empirical scrutiny. On the contrary, much research now suggests that changes in the inflation rate are often *negatively* correlated with returns on stock portfolios. Not only do stocks fail to provide an adequate hedge against inflation, but they also tend to deteriorate in value in response to unexpected price changes. We should mention that, unlike stocks, bonds have never been touted as inflation hedges. Indeed, it is well known that unanticipated inflation results in capital losses on bonds. It is therefore prudent to examine other alternatives for protecting future consumption opportunities and existing asset portfolios from inflation.

Examining the Relationship

With the financial deregulation of the 1980s, the relationship between the growth of monetary aggregates and the growth of nominal GNP became less reliable. In consequence, several important members of the Federal Reserve Board of Governors began to advocate the use of price information from commodity markets as targets or guides for the conduct of monetary policy. This stimulated a great deal of research within both the Federal Reserve System and multinational financial institutions about the relationship between commodity prices and more general measures of inflation. These studies have confirmed that there is a significant and direct linkage between changes in commodity prices and future generalized inflation. Thus, there is reason to believe that holding an inventory of commodities might be one appropriate means of protecting one's wealth against unexpected price level changes.

However, as noted earlier, the cost of storing and holding commodities is often high. Hence, the strategy of holding an inventory of spot commodities as a hedge against future price inflation is often intractable and almost always inadvisable. Fortunately, the existence of organized markets for the future delivery of such commodities provides investors with a relatively low-cost substitute for holding commodities themselves.

To clarify why holding futures is a suitable substitute for holding physical commodity inventories, it is necessary to briefly examine the economic theory underlying the existence of futures markets. Futures markets operate as loan markets for commodities. As such, they operate in a manner that is similar to money markets. When handlers of commodities purchase a commodity and simultaneously sell a futures contract, they are temporarily borrowing a commodity. This procedure is much like borrowing money from a bank with the promise to pay back the loan in the future. The sale of a futures contract, in conjunction with the purchase of a commodity in the spot market, allows handlers to borrow a commodity now and repay it later. These simultaneous buy–sell transactions are, therefore, implicit commodity loans.

The array of futures contracts, from immediate delivery to the most deferred, allows for an active loan market for any given commodity. The spreads between contract prices represent the cost of borrowing a commodity. Like the term structure of interest rates for money that is borrowed in different periods, the differences in the spreads between different pairs of futures contracts represent a term structure of "commodity interest rates" for a given commodity. These commodity interest rates reflect the relative cost of having a commodity in the present versus keeping it in inventory for the future.

Because of the existence of an implicit loan market for commodities, the relationship between futures and spot prices for commodities is very well defined. In particular, the price of a commodity for future delivery is as follows:

$$F_{0,t} = S_0 + w_t + r_t - c_t$$

where $F_{0,t}$ = price at time 0 for delivery in time t
S_0 = price for immediate delivery at time 0
w_t = warehouse and storage fees from time 0 to t
r_t = capital cost of holding inventory from time 0 to t
c_t = convenience yield of holding inventory from time 0 to t

A market is said to be "in full carry" when the futures price exceeds the spot price by exactly the physical and capital costs of storage. In such situations, the cost of borrowing a commodity is negative because the borrower is buying nearby at a relatively low price and selling a more distant contract for a higher price.

However, commodity markets are not often in full carry because of the final term in the above equation (c_t), the "convenience yield." Businesses hold stocks of commodities for much the same reason they hold cash: they want to keep their processing plants running smoothly in the face of uncertain timing of both arrivals for their input supplies and orders for their outputs, and they want to avoid the high costs of temporary shutdowns. Hence, businesses are willing to incur a cost for holding (borrowing) inventories because inventories generate a convenience yield. Just as the loan market for money guides funds into the hands of those who have the greatest need, the futures markets allocate (lend) commodity inventories to the dealers and handlers who have the most immediate need.

When the convenience yield for commodities is sufficiently strong that it outweighs the "cost of carry" for the commodity (w_t and r_t), futures prices can fall below spot prices. When that happens, the market is said to be in backwardation, and the cost of borrowing a commodity is positive because the borrower is buying nearby at a relatively high price and selling a more distant contract at a lower price.

Futures as an Inflation Hedge

Given the relationship between futures prices and commodity prices, we should examine how a portfolio of futures contracts might prove useful as an inflation hedge. An asset is an inflation hedge if its real rate of return (without inflation) is independent of the rate of price inflation. This implies a positive correlation between the nominal rate of return on the inflation hedge and the rate of inflation, with stronger correlations indicating a better hedging device.

Futures themselves are not assets, but the spot commodities on which the futures contracts are based are assets. Thus, when we look for an asset whose returns are correlated with the rate of price inflation, we must look to the returns from holding an inventory of physical commodities. That return can be measured crudely by the percentage change in the price of the spot commodity over some prespecified time horizon, minus the costs of its storage.

We then recognize from the economic theory of futures markets that holding a long futures contract is equivalent to being synthetic long the spot commodity. Thus, the asset acting as an inflation hedge when an unleveraged futures contract is held in a portfolio of other assets is actually the underlying commodity. Moreover, the price inflation of the futures contract should reflect the price appreciation in the underlying commodity, because the two are separated only by the cost of carry. As was shown earlier, the futures price is clearly a function of nominal storage costs and the convenience yield. Assuming the convenience yield does not change because of inflation, the *real* relationship between the spot and futures prices will be unaffected by price level increases. Any inflation-induced spot price appreciation in the commodity will be reflected in the futures price. This implies that both commodity prices and futures prices should be correlated with the rate of inflation.

Commodity Prices and Inflation

We can gain insight into the relationship between commodity prices and inflation by looking at the price index maintained by the Commodity Research Bureau (CRB Index). This index was created in the 1950s to facilitate the fundamental analysis of broad commodity price trends. Since 1986, the CRB Index has been traded as a futures contract in New York. The CRB Index represents a weighted average of 21 commodity prices. Table 11.1 shows the simple correlation statistics between the CRB Index and two broad measures of inflation: the producer price index (PPI) and the consumer price index for all urban wage earners (CPI-W). The correlations shown are based on lagged values of the CRB Index—4 months for the PPI and 6 months for the CPI-W. The results indicate that the CRB Index is positively associated with broad changes in the price level. Moreover, changes in the CRB Index precede changes in the price level, suggesting that commodity prices are a forward-looking inflation hedge.

In addition to using commodity futures as a consumption hedge, it may be possible to combine commodity futures positions with a portfolio

TABLE 11.1. Correlation statistics—CRB index vs. PPI and CPI-W.

Index	15 Years	10 Years	5 Years	1 Year
CRB	76.01:90.12	81.01:90.12	86.01:90.12	90.01:90.12
PPI*	68.5%	47.5%	62.4%	73.0%
CPI-W**	55.8%	14.2%	39.0%	70.0%

All data are percentage changes from the same period, one year earlier. The CRB Index values represent monthly averages of daily cash values. CPI-W refers to the CPI Index for all urban wage earners.

* PPI correlated against cash values of the CRB Index, lagged 4 months.

** CPI-W correlated against cash values of the CRB Index, lagged 6 months. *Source:* Haver Analytics, New York, NY.

TABLE 11.2. Correlation statistics—CRB Index vs. 10-year Treasury yields and NYSE composite index.

Index	10 Years	5 Years	1 Year
CRB	81.01:90.12	86.01:90.12	90.01:90.12
10-Year Yields*	80.5%	72.5%	32.0%
NYSE Composite**	−61.3%	30.7%	−35.0%

All data are monthly averages of daily cash values. 10-year yields are yields on actively traded issues adjusted to a constant 10-year maturity, as reported in the Federal Reserve's Statistical Release G.13.

All correlations based on actual levels.

* Current 10-year yields correlated against cash values of the CRB Index, lagged 4 months.

** Current cash values of the NYSE Composite correlated against cash values of the CRB Index, lagged 9 months.

Source: Haver Analytics, New York, NY.

of assets, such as stocks and bonds. As mentioned, stock and bond returns are negatively correlated with the rate of inflation. Therefore, it is possible to combine synthetic long positions in spot commodities, via long futures contracts, with a well-diversified portfolio of stocks and bonds to at least partially offset the cost of inflation. Table 11.2 reveals to some degree the strength this portfolio hedge can have. Evidently, the CRB Index is negatively correlated with stock prices, measured by the NYSE Composite Index, and positively correlated with yields on 10-year bonds (hence, the CRB Index is negatively correlated with the value of a bond portfolio). To the extent that the CRB Index reveals the relationship between commodity prices and inflation, the returns on an investor's portfolio may be enhanced (or the losses made smaller) by holding synthetic long positions in commodities as a hedge against inflation.

THE FCMI INFLATION HEDGE ACCOUNT

Friedberg Commodity Management's Inflation Hedge Account is designed to exploit the relationship between commodity prices and inflation, outlined above. The goal of the Inflation Hedge Account is to *outperform* inflation through the judicious analysis of technical and fundamental factors. In this manner, investors are allowed to hedge the uncertainty associated with future changes in the generalized price level *and* to engage in speculation with managed futures.

The mechanics of the inflation hedge account are relatively straightforward. The account manager selects a diversified portfolio of internationally traded commodity futures contracts whose total face value does not exceed the amount invested plus accumulated profits (or minus accumulated losses). Consistent with the desire to be synthetically long the spot commodities, no short speculation is done. Trades are only from the long side and, at any given time, the account is always invested in at least three different commodities traded on established and recognized exchanges. Thus, by only trading long unleveraged futures contracts, the product has some rather unique attributes.

Because the performance of the account is directly related to inflation, it is sometimes prudent for the Inflation Hedge Account manager to hedge against the risk of generalized price declines in the required long futures positions. As a general rule, the manager will hedge with CRB Index futures when downward pressure on commodity prices is thought to come from poor business conditions, as in a recession. However, when downward pressure on commodity prices is thought to come from a rising U.S. dollar, the adviser will hedge via the sale of major foreign currency futures. In both cases, the face value of the hedge does not exceed the face value of the portfolio of commodities held in the account.

At present, the standard account size for the Inflation Hedge Account at FCMI is $130,000. The funds required to maintain margin on an account fully invested in unleveraged commodity futures with that face value ($130,000) is no more than $15,000. The balance of the money in the account, or excess funds, will either earn a rate of return approximately equal to the 3-month T-bill rate or it can be placed in various other interest-bearing instruments. Such instruments may include a wide variety of foreign-currency-denominated bonds. Hence, the desirable features of portfolio diversification also are captured in the account.

FCMI's Hedge Account

Because FCMI's Inflation Hedge Account has been in operation for only the past 5 years, a detailed time-series analysis of the account's performance would be meaningless. Table 11.3 details the performance of a pilot account managed by FCMI. This account was opened on February 19, 1986, with a face value of $150,000. Fifty-seven months later, on December 31, 1990, the account had a closing equity of $295,200. At the time of the account's opening, the CRB Index stood at 210.27. On December 31, 1990, it had increased to 222.64. The managed account earned a respectable 96.8 percent in a period when commodity prices, as reported by the CRB Index, increased 5.88 percent. The overall performance of the pilot account is shown in Figure 11.1.

From its inception in February 1986 to January 1991, the FCMI Inflation Hedge Account outperformed similar accounts comprised of cash, bonds, and stocks, respectively, when measured by total returns. The results are presented in Table 11.3.

An account such as the FCMI Inflation Hedge Account can be useful in several ways. First, it provides a comfortable means of hedging the risk of future uncertainty in consumption prices by exploiting a well-defined and well-established economic theory, the economic theory of futures markets. By holding a portfolio of commodity futures, investors are effectively holding a synthetic long position in spot

TABLE 11.3. Performance of FCMI inflation hedge account vs. alternative investments.

	Cash*		Bonds**		Stocks†		Inflation Hedge	
Year/Month	**$**	**%**	**$**	**%**	**$**	**%**	**$**	**%**
1986.01	150,000		150,000		150,000		150,000	
1986.12	159,450	+ 6.3	187,125	+24.8	174,000	+16.0	167,550	+ 11.7
1987.12	169,050	+12.7	182,091	+21.4	179,400	+19.6	271,200	+ 80.8
1988.12	180,300	+20.2	199,699	+33.1	204,000	+36.0	285,150	+ 90.1
1989.12	195,750	+30.5	235,865	+57.2	262,800	+75.2	303,150	+102.1
1990.12	211,200	+40.8	251,102	+67.4	248,550	+65.7	295,200	+ 96.8

* 3-month T-bills.
** Long-term government bonds.
† S&P 500 stocks.
Percent columns represent cumulative increases in total returns.
Starting date is February 19, 1986, when a unit of the FCMI Inflation Hedge Account was equal to $150,000.

FIGURE 11.1. Friedberg Commodity Management's Inflation Hedge Account.

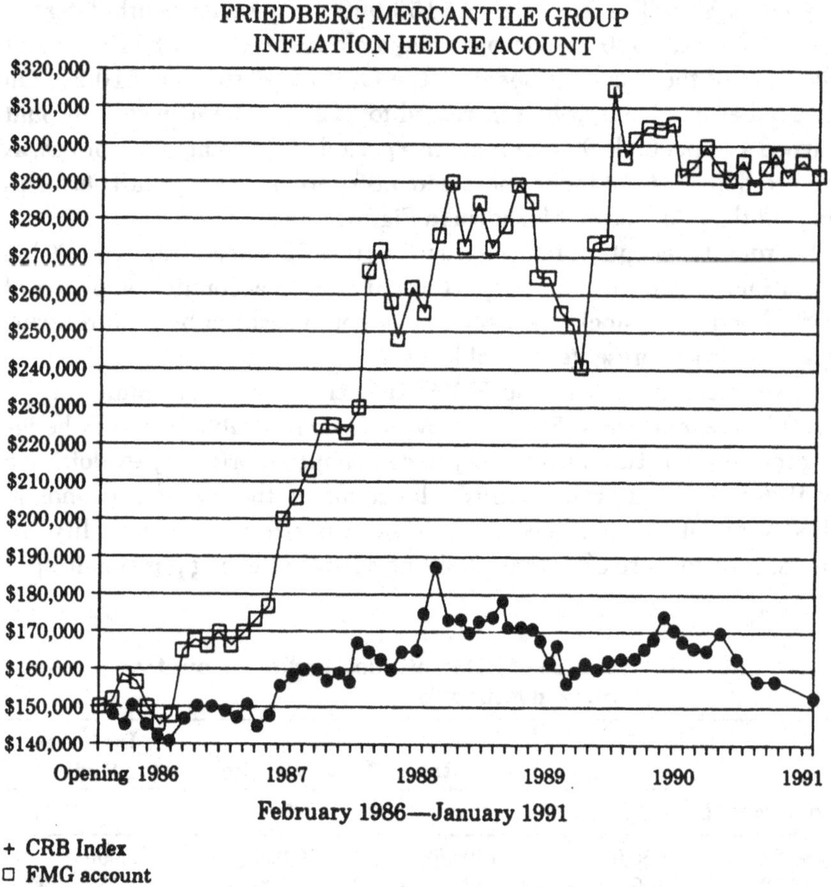

commodities and protecting their wealth against unexpected increases in the general price level.

Second, the Inflation Hedge Account offers as an attractive alternative to investors a way to increase their speculative returns above and beyond simply hedging against inflation. By further capitalizing on the relationship between commodity prices and inflation, a well-managed portfolio of commodity futures can be designed so that its price appreciation exceeds increases in the cost of living, creating an additional source of income for institutional or individual investors. Table 11.3 confirms that these additional income flows are quite respectable compared to alternative investment opportunities.

Third, it may be possible for the returns generated from an Inflation Hedge Account to be used in a portfolio context to lower the total variance on a portfolio of assets such as stocks and bonds. Because the returns from stocks and bonds are negatively correlated with the rate of inflation, an account that generates a positive return from price level increases can improve the attractiveness of an otherwise well-diversified portfolio of assets.

CONCLUDING OBSERVATIONS

The explicit economic relationship between spot commodity prices and futures prices makes holding long futures contracts synthetically equivalent to holding long positions in the commodities themselves. We exploit that price relationship and create an opportunity for investors to hedge their assets against future price level increases. The method that we advocate is to hold synthetically long positions in spot commodities via lower-cost futures contracts.

The Federal Reserve Board's renewed interest in the relationship between commodity prices and the future level of price inflation suggests that using commodity futures in this manner may become even more effective in the future. As the Fed becomes increasingly attentive to monetary policy indicators emerging from commodity prices, the Fed's focus on commodity prices will, if anything, strengthen the relationship outlined earlier.

The FCMI Inflation Hedge Account illustrates how effective strategies based on the relationship between commodity prices and inflation can be. The performance of the account suggests that a well-managed portfolio of futures contracts can both insulate investors from some costs of inflation and enhance the returns from an investment in the futures markets.

12 FUTURES VERSUS STOCKS: A RISK COMPARISON

Peter Matthews
Pascal I. Magnollay

The immediate reaction of most people when someone says that he or she trades in the futures markets is something like "Oh, that must be very scary. How do you sleep at night? I couldn't do it." This view is not particularly surprising, given that the media tend to portray the futures markets as wild and crazy gambling dens.

There seem to be two reasons for this bias. First, there is a natural tendency for the media to look to the sensational side of any issue. Not too many readers want to see a study of the relative volatility of futures versus stocks. They are interested in reading how some small investors lost their shirts trading pork belly futures. Second, it is a matter of fact that the vast majority of investment managers, brokers, and individual investors participate in the stock and bond markets and not in futures. The media thus may be in the position of legitimizing the view of their readers rather than pointing out the merits of an alternative investment field.

Regulators have generally considered futures investments as speculative products not suitable for "widows and orphans." Prospectuses for public futures funds are extremely costly to produce: they require extensive disclosure, numerous risk statements, detailed performance tables, and, in most cases, fulfillment of individual state constraints in addition to the conditions of the Securities Exchange Commission (SEC) and the Commodity Futures Trading Commission (CFTC). In effect, regulators have imposed high hurdles for potential funds, on the assumption that they are protecting the investor from a high-risk speculation.

Institutional investors, such as pension funds, often have internal investment policies that explicitly prohibit the use of futures in the investment mix. Some of these investors have relaxed their policies in order to use stock index futures or bond futures in a legitimate hedging function, but they are still opposed to exploring futures as an investment alternative.

THE PROBLEM: MISPERCEPTION OF LEVERAGE VERSUS RISK

Much of the resistance to futures can be attributed to confusion between the leverage available in futures markets and the volatility of the underlying instrument. Because one can buy or sell futures contracts on margin of 5 percent (the actual margin percentage varies by futures market), a 5 percent move in the underlying futures price can result in a 100 percent loss of the initial margin deposit. This is clearly "risky," by anyone's definition.

However, the leverage employed in futures is a matter of choice: an investor could purchase the same futures contract at the full price, for example, by putting up the whole amount in cash, or, equivalently, by putting up 5 percent in cash and holding the remaining 95 percent in Treasury bills as a reserve against price fluctuations. In this case, a 5 percent movement in the futures price results in a 5 percent movement in the total amount set aside for this investment.

Although the issue of volatility is sensational, it is a totally separate feature from leverage. For example, it is possible to compare the volatility of futures bought at "full price" (100 percent of the face value of the contract) with the volatility of stocks purchased without margin. It is then possible to compare the price volatility of cattle futures selling for $65 per hundred pounds with a stock selling for $65 per share, without using the fact that the futures contract could be bought on 5 percent margin and the stock on 50 percent margin. More generally, it is possible to compare futures as a group with stocks.

PREVIOUS RESEARCH

Other researchers have examined the issue of futures volatility, although most have looked at it in the context of a futures portfolio as part of the overall mix. That is, the researchers have been interested in determining whether a futures component in an overall portfolio improves the reward : risk characteristics. However, the studies do provide some insight into the relative volatility of futures and stock portfolios.

For example, Bodie and Rosansky constructed a "buy-and-hold" futures portfolio in which an equal dollar amount of each commodity's face value was purchased using a combination of margin and Treasury-bill deposits so that no leverage was involved. They compared this portfolio with a stock portfolio over the years 1949 through 1976, with the results shown in Table 12.1.

Standard deviation is a statistical measure of risk. Basically, it measures the variation of the actual performance around an average. The actual formula involves adding up the squared differences between each period's actual return and the average for the period, and then taking the square root of that sum. In effect, the formula penalizes (through the squaring function) large deviations from the average relative to small deviations.

The standard deviation turns out to be a useful measure because, under reasonable conditions, the information can be used to make probability statements about the range of returns. For example, there is a 68 percent chance that in any given year the annual return will be within one standard deviation of the average. In Table 12.1, there is a 68 percent

TABLE 12.1. Stocks vs. futures: 1949–1976.

1949–1976	Stocks	Futures
Annual Return	13.05%	13.83%
Standard Deviation	18.95	22.43

chance that the return on stocks would be between −5.9 percent and +32.0 percent. Alternatively, one can work out the chances of having a losing year in stocks. In this case, the probability would be 25 percent, quite close to the actual percentage of years in which stocks have had net losses in the past.

Thus, the stock portfolio provided less return with less risk. Nonetheless, the futures portfolio's risk was only 18 percent more than that of the stocks. Bodie and Rosansky go on to show that, if the risk is measured according to measures of loss experience rather than standard deviation, the futures portfolio comes out better than the stock portfolio. That is, they found that the risk in futures, as measured by the standard deviation, comes about because a number of years were far above average (hence penalized a lot), whereas the losing years were less frequent. The futures returns then showed what is called in statistics "positive skewness."

Many investors, given the choice, might well prefer to take the chance on the unusually high returns, as long as the likelihood of large negative returns is lower. This chapter focuses on the standard deviation, the most commonly used measure of risk given in investment literature, but it is worth noting that futures markets have this characteristic of positive skewness.

Further, most of the investment managers in the futures world tend to have trading strategies that are designed to accentuate the skewness (strategies that cut losses and let profits run), so the distribution of returns will tend to have a very different shape from the distribution of returns from a stock portfolio.

Bodie extended the results to cover the period from 1953 through 1981, and changed the methodology so that results were in terms of excess returns versus Treasury bills. In this comparison, the volatility of futures came out lower than that of stocks, as indicated in Table 12.2.

It may seem strange that the results were switched around—that futures show a lower risk profile over this time period—but the results can be explained by the fact that a buy-and-hold futures portfolio's returns tend to be related to inflation (or, more precisely, to anticipated inflation increases). The large positive returns for futures tended to occur in years of sharp rises in the inflation rate; lower returns occurred in years of flat or deflationary trends.

TABLE 12.2 Stocks vs. futures: 1953–1981.

1953–1981	Stocks	Futures
Annual Excess Return	6.68%	5.69%
Standard Deviation	19.48	17.36

Because the Treasury-bill rate moves up or down with the actual inflation rate, the excess returns for futures are less variable than the gross returns. Conversely, stock returns tend to be highest in periods of low or stable inflation and lowest in periods of rapid inflation. This means that the bad years for stocks come out worse: a −10 percent return with a 10 percent inflation rate, for example, becomes a 20 percent return.

Based on these patterns of returns, Bodie concluded that the futures portfolio is both an effective inflation hedge and a stock market hedge; it tends to perform well when stocks perform poorly.

Irwin and Landa used the Commodity Research Bureau (CRB) futures price index, a geometric average of commodity futures prices (excluding financial futures such as bonds, stock indexes, and currencies), as a proxy for an unleveraged futures portfolio. For the decade 1975 to 1985, they found that the annual standard deviation of the CRB futures index was 11.5 percent versus 14.7 percent for stocks.

Barbanel, Lipsky, and Zumbrum also constructed an unleveraged buy-and-hold portfolio of futures. Their research covered the period from 1960 through 1982, with the results shown in Table 12.3. According to Barbanel et al., futures had higher returns and lower risk than a portfolio of stocks.

Although the studies varied in their methodology and in the time period covered, the results all showed that the unleveraged futures

TABLE 12.3. Stocks vs. futures: 1962–82.

1962–1982	Stocks	Futures
Annual Return	8.71%	11.71%
Standard Deviation	17.65	17.17

portfolios' standard deviation is on an order of magnitude similar to that of a portfolio of stocks.

This research makes it possible to take a more direct look at the volatility of futures versus stocks, without constructing portfolios. It also provides the framework for investors to ask a basic question: "Are futures less risky than stocks?" If the answer is "Yes," many more investors should be interested in the possible role of futures in their investment basket.

METHODOLOGY

The approach adopted to address the question of stocks versus futures volatility is quite straightforward: a measure of price risk or volatility is defined and then the average on that measure for futures markets is compared to the average for stocks.

Specifically, price volatility for a stock or futures contract is defined as the standard deviation of daily prices over the past 60 days, divided by the average price over the past 60 days, divided by the average price over the same 60-day period. The ratio of the standard deviation to the average is known as the coefficient of variation and is useful when comparing items with different units or, in this case, price levels.

This measure was calculated for all futures in this study's data base at the end of each quarter from June 1970. The number of futures markets ranged from a low of 8 in the second quarter of 1970 to 50 in the most recent quarter.

Similarly, the coefficient of variation for each stock in the data base was calculated. To eliminate stocks whose volatility may be at least partially a function of illiquidity, the portfolio was restricted to the top 50 percent of market capitalization. The number of stocks in the calculation varied from 1,051 to 3,469. As suspected, stock volatility decreases as market capitalization increases, so the restriction to the top 50 percent of market capitalization stocks results in lower volatility figures than would be obtained from the full data base. Thus, if anything, the results will be more favorable to stocks than they would have been if the full universe had been used.

The stock data base was developed by combining the COMPUSTAT and CRSP (Center for Research in Security Prices) tape from the

Graduate School of Business of the University of Chicago files. COMPUSTAT contains fundamental data on stocks. For every calendar quarter, the market capitalization of each stock was calculated in order to determine its percentile market capitalization among the stocks available during that quarter. The CRSP data base was used for daily prices and daily price changes, taking into account stock splits, dividends, and other adjustments. In particular, every time a split occurred, prices were retrospectively adjusted for the prior 60 days in order to have a consistent measure of price volatility.

BASIC RESULTS

Figure 12.1 illustrates the quarterly coefficient of variation for stocks and futures respectively. Each quarterly observation in the graph represents the average coefficient of variation for the prior quarter, for stocks and futures.

To avoid any bias associated with extreme values, which can sometimes be a problem with small samples, the median coefficient of variation was determined quarterly for futures and stocks. The median is defined as the value at which 50 percent of the sample is below that number and 50 percent is above. The median numbers are illustrated in Figure 12.2.

Overall, the results in Figures 12.1 and 12.2 show that futures volatility (coefficient of variation) is, on average, consistently lower than that of stocks. Specifically, futures volatility averaged 4.9 percent over the past 20 years, versus 7.2 percent for stocks; that is, futures volatility has been about 32 percent lower than stocks on average. The same result is found if we look at the median volatility: the median volatility (averaged over all time periods) is 6.5 percent for stocks versus 4.2 percent for futures, so futures volatility is about 35 percent lower.

VOLATILITY BY TIME PERIOD

As noted, the findings are quite stable over time. Figure 12.1 shows that the average volatility for futures is higher than that for stocks in only five quarters, four of which are in the 1973–1974 period, when prices rose

FIGURE 12.1. Volatility, futures vs. stocks, 1970–1989.

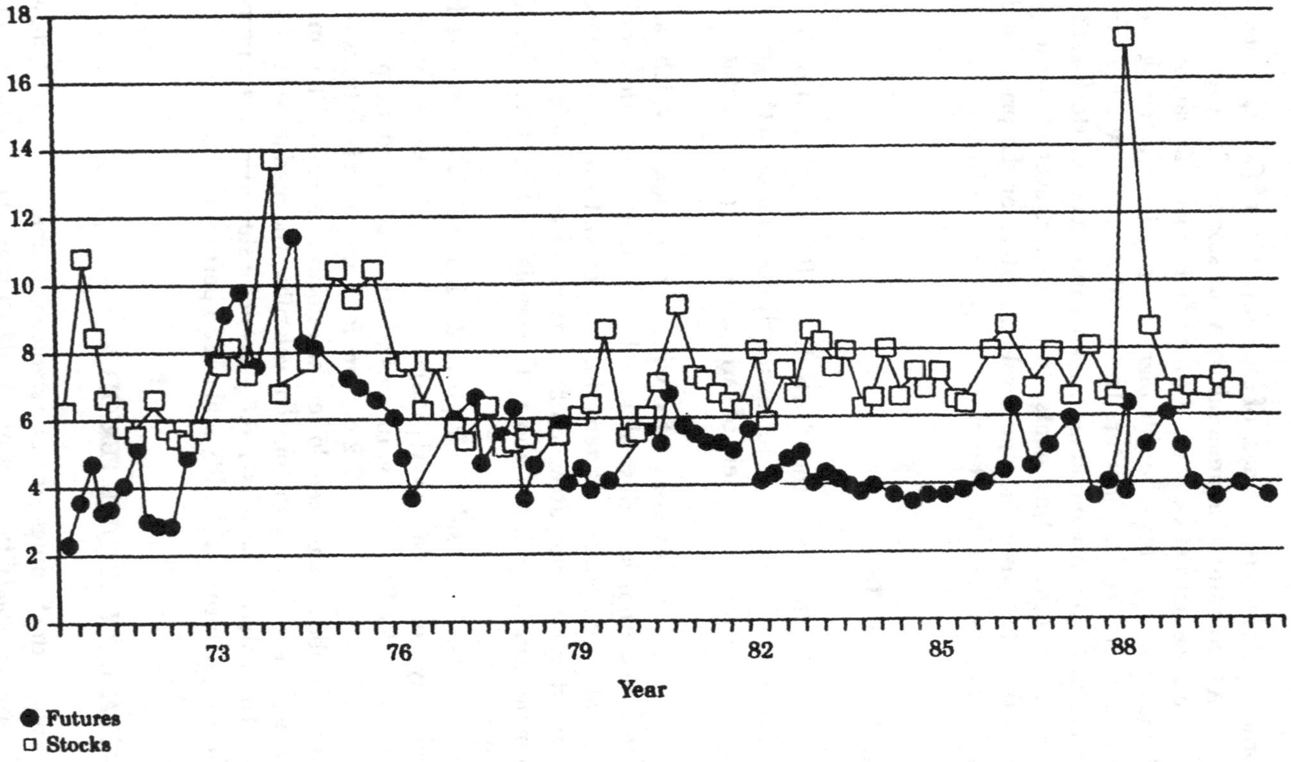

FIGURE 12.2. Median volatility, stocks vs. futures, specific months, 1970–1989.

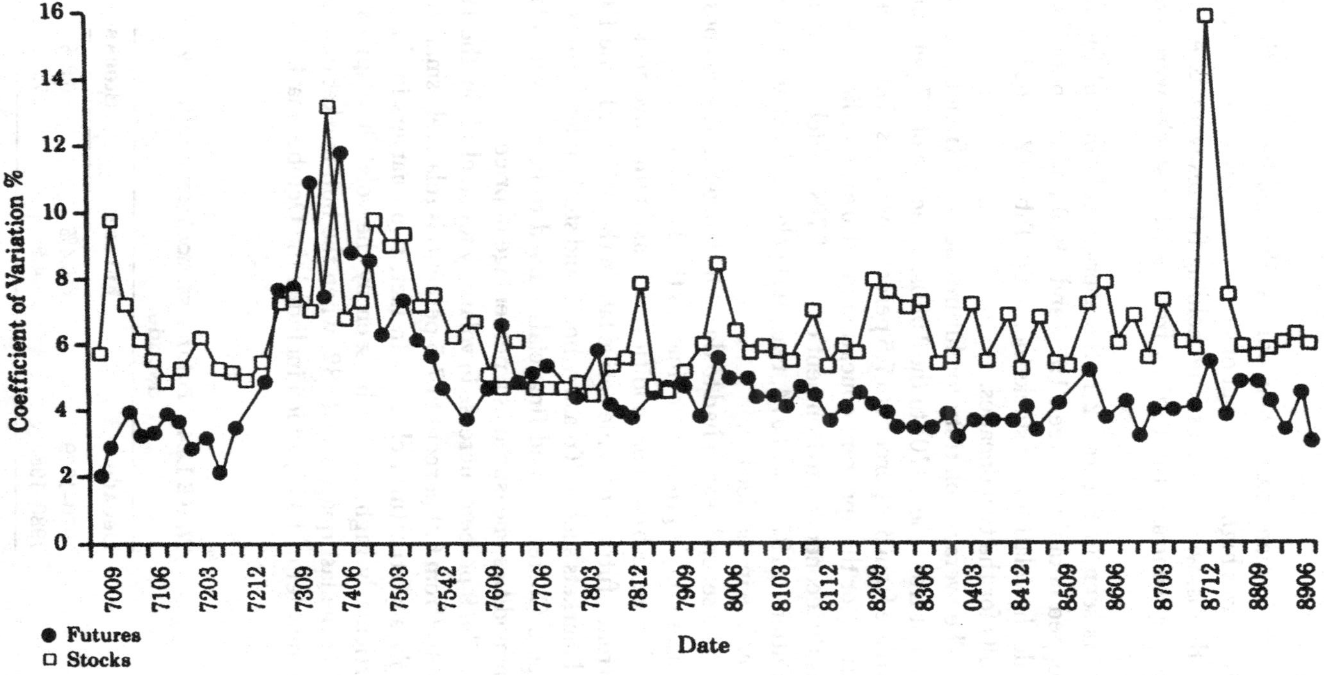

sharply in many basic commodities. Put another way, the volatility of futures was higher than that of stocks exactly when one would want it to be, that is, when returns from holding futures were exceptionally high (and, by contrast, the returns from holding stocks were exceptionally poor).

As seen in Figure 12.1, the average volatility of futures markets dropped notably between 1970 and 1979 and the period since 1980, while the volatility for stocks increased. Table 12.4 shows the computed results for the two decades.

The average volatility for futures declined from 5.4 percent to 4.5 percent from the 1970s to the 1980s, a decline of 17 percent versus an increase from 6.9 percent to 7.5 percent for stocks. There were two main reasons for the apparent education in futures volatility. The first reason was the economic environment of the 1970s, which saw unusually high inflation in 1973 and 1974, two oil shocks, and a sharp rise in gold and silver late in the decade.

The second reason had to do with changes in the composition of the futures sample group over time. In the 1970s, most futures markets in the list were basic commodities such as grains, livestock, and metals; currency futures became active late in the decade. In the 1980s, financial markets such as Treasury bonds and stock index futures were introduced. Currencies and financials tended to have lower volatility than commodities, measured as a percentage of price.

The 9 percent increase in volatility for stocks from the 1970s to the 1980s (from 6.9 percent to 7.5 percent) is relatively small and does not imply any structural change. In fact, two quarters in the 1990s were particularly high, as can be seen by the volatility "spikes" in Figure 12.1: the last quarter of 1982, when the bull market took off, and the last quarter of 1987, which included the October market crash.

TABLE 12.4. Futures vs. stocks: volatility by decade.

Decade	Futures	Stocks
1970–1979	5.4%	6.9%
1980–1989	4.5	7.5

Nonetheless, the gap between average stock and average futures volatility widened in the 1980s, with futures turning out to be 40 percent less volatile than stocks. Given that the trend in futures markets worldwide is for more and more financial futures to be introduced (they have been a tremendous success in terms of volume and liquidity), it is unlikely that the gap will narrow back again because of this industry evolution. The traditional agriculturals and "hard" commodities will tend to represent a declining slice of the futures pie.

STOCK VOLATILITY BY MARKET CAPITALIZATION

It is generally believed that there is a relationship between market capitalization and volatility, that the higher the market capitalization, all other things being equal, the lower volatility is likely to be.

This issue was examined directly by dividing the stocks each quarter into the following categories: top 50 to 66 percent of market capitalization; top 66 to 84 percent of market capitalization; and top 84 to 100 percent of market capitalization. The average and median coefficients of variation were then computed in each group.

The average volatilities for the three groups were 8.7 percent, 6.8 percent, and 5.6 percent respectively. However, the differences in median volatilities are somewhat less pronounced: 7.2 percent, 5.9 percent, and 5.0 percent were the median figures in the three groups.

The important point is that even within the top 16 percent of market capitalization stocks, the average (5.6 percent) and median (5.0 percent) volatilities for these stocks are still higher than the corresponding average (4.5 percent) and median (4.2 percent) for futures.

Stock volatility is also a function of price levels; that is, we would expect low-priced stocks to have higher variability around their price level than high-priced stocks. This is reflected in the fact that margin requirements for low-priced stocks (less than 45, typically) tend to be higher.

To examine this expectation, stock prices for each quarter were divided into the following price ranges: $0 to 5; $5 to 15; $15 to 30; $30 to 60; $60 to 120; $120+. The overall average and median results by price category are summarized in Table 12.5.

TABLE 12.5. Stock volatility by price level.

Price Range	Average	Median
$ 0– 5	11.1%	9.8%
$ 5– 15	8.5	7.3
$15– 30	6.5	5.6
$30– 60	5.7	5.0
$60–120	5.3	4.7
$ 120	4.9	4.5

From Table 12.5, the following conclusions can be drawn:

1. Stock volatility decreases consistently as the average price level of the stocks on which it is measured increases.
2. Average/median futures volatility is below the volatility of the lowest volatility stock group (those stocks with an average price above $120).

It is also worth noting that if one restricted stock purchases to those trading at a high absolute price level in order to reduce volatility, there would be a penalty in terms of expected annual return. Again, this study is restricting its analysis to the basic question of relative volatility.

STOCK VOLATILITY BY MARKET CAPITALIZATION AND PRICE

Because average stock volatility decreases as both market capitalization and price increase, it makes sense to combine the two categories. The methodology is the same: in each quarter, the average volatility for the 18 subgroups is calculated (three market capitalization groups versus six price groups; for example, stocks between $15 and $25 with market capitalization in the top 16 percent).

Table 12.6 provides the summary results (averaging across quarters) in terms of the median volatility by subgroup (mean numbers are not presented because of the small number of stocks in some subgroups).

Table 12.6 again shows a fairly consistent decline in average volatility as the price range increases or the market capitalization percentile

TABLE 12.6. **Median stock volatility by market capitalization and price.**

	Market Capitalization Percentile		
Price Range	**50–66%**	**66–84%**	**84–100%**
$ 0– 5	10.2%	10.2%	NA
5– 15	7.5	7.0	5.7%
15– 30	5.9	5.7	5.1
30– 60	5.1	5.2	4.9
60–120	NA	5.5	4.7
120	NA	NA	4.7

increases. As expected, the highest volatility numbers occur in the top left corner of the table, and the lowest volatility numbers occur in the bottom right corner (the highest capitalization stocks trading above $120 per share). Even this subgroup, which represents a highly restricted universe of 14 stocks as of September 1989, for example, does not have lower average or median volatility than the corresponding figures for futures.

IMPLICATIONS OF THE FINDINGS

The results of this analysis show that the average (median) futures market volatility, measured by the coefficient of variation, is consistently lower than the average (median) for stocks, even when we consider the least volatile subsets of equities in terms of price level and market capitalization.

Thus, the common perception of futures markets as being risky and dangerous is not founded in fact. The actual risk one faces in futures is related to the leverage applied, the diversification across markets employed, and the approach used to construct the portfolio. But the same is true of equities: investors can buy equities on 50 percent margin; elect to diversify the portfolio or not diversify; or increase the risk substantially by electing to buy low-price, low-market-capitalization stocks instead of high-price, high-market-capitalization stocks.

This means that no one should ignore futures simply because of fears about risk. Instead, the data clearly indicate that the underlying risk of futures can be minimized. The real issue facing investors is how to use futures to improve the overall reward : risk ratio of their investment portfolio.

FUTURES IN THE INVESTMENT MIX: BUY-AND-HOLD VERSUS RISK MANAGEMENT

There are two distinct ways for including futures in the investment mix. One is the buy-and-hold approach: buying an equal dollar value of each separate futures market on an unleveraged basis. The second approach involves making buy/sell/stand-aside and position-size decisions on each futures market according to some objective or subjective criterion. Leverage might or might not be involved in this approach.

BUY AND HOLD FUTURES PORTFOLIOS

The first approach is the simplest and is consistent with the academic studies discussed earlier in the chapter. The researchers demonstrated that (excess) returns for futures compared favorably to stocks with similar volatility. Furthermore, the returns for stocks and futures were not correlated so that a combined portfolio of stocks and futures would provide a better return : risk tradeoff than either portfolio alone.

This is perhaps the obvious approach, but it may not be the optimum approach among buy-and-hold strategies. For example, it may be appropriate to use historical return series for each futures market, to determine the correct weighting of each market in the portfolio going forward. As noted earlier, the number of futures markets available to trade is expanding, and the weighting of commodity (nonfinancial) markets is declining relative to financial futures.

If the aim is to construct an optimum portfolio of equities, bonds, and futures, it is unlikely that overweighting in financial futures will be particularly helpful. Similarly, it may not make sense to give equal weight to soybeans, soybean meal, and soybean oil (whose returns are highly correlated) versus gold because this gives the soybean complex a weight of 3 : 1 relative to gold.

The benefit of a buy-and-hold futures portfolio within the overall investment mix comes primarily from its role as an inflation hedge: it helps to mitigate losses that could occur in stocks and bonds during periods of high inflation. Thus, the futures portfolio should have most of its weight oriented toward markets that would provide the best protection.

It should be pointed out that two of the three studies of the futures buy-and-hold approach covered a period through 1981. For most of the early and mid-1980s, there was a general deflationary trend in most commodity futures as the overall inflation rate declined. The few years immediately after 1981 would have been poor ones for a buy-and-hold approach, although, in the context of an overall stock/bond/futures portfolio, the above-average stock returns would have offset any futures losses in this period.

RISK MANAGEMENT-BASED FUTURES PORTFOLIOS

A buy-and-hold futures strategy may not be the optimum approach to portfolio construction. As seen earlier, futures tend to perform well at different times than stocks. In particular, some characteristics of futures markets suggest that a different approach might be more appropriate.

First, futures display better trending behavior than stocks. The main reason related to supply-and-demand disruptions that cause unusually large moves from time to time. Consistent with the findings in this chapter, futures markets are less volatile than stocks on average, but the futures volatility is made up of two components: long periods with very low volatility because supply and demand are in balance, and occasional sharp increases in volatility because the market gets out of balance.

One example is the live cattle market. In the late-1970s, the market had a sustained rise from the 35 cents per pound (mid-level) to 80 cents per pound (because of a sharp drop in the supply of cattle). The price never exceeded 80 cents in the next 11 years and has generally oscillated between 55 and 75 cents over the entire period. Similarly, grain markets had been quiet for several years, but in the summer of 1988 there was a major bull market because of the drought in the United States.

If this trending behavior is indeed characteristic of futures markets, then it is possible to develop trading strategies that seek to detect these trends, hence reducing participation during nontrending periods, which ties up capital for no benefit.

A corollary of this observation is that, in the presence of trends, it makes sense to consider short as well as long positions. If the trend detection method is consistent, it will limit losses on short positions: if the market moves up instead of down, sooner or later an uptrend will be signaled. In this sense, the risk of long and short positions is equivalent. Furthermore, supply-and-demand changes are just as likely to cause price reductions as price increases—for example good growing weather will increase the production of a crop.

The second important characteristic of futures markets is their lack of correlation from one market to another; that is, the population of futures markets is heterogeneous compared to stocks. Soybeans can be in a raging bull futures market while sugar prices are plummeting. Stocks tend to move as a group. In a general bull market, nearly all of the stocks will go up; in a bear market, nearly all will go down. The difference is more one of degree. Furthermore, as has been increasingly clear in recent years, most of the world's major stock markets move together. Limited diversification is available from investing in global equity markets.

Futures, by contrast, offer significant diversification potential. Not only can one construct a portfolio of reasonably uncorrelated futures markets, but one can take long positions in some and short positions in others, to extend the diversification.

It is fair to say that futures portfolio managers believe they have a significant advantage over buy-and-hold stock and bond investors. To the futures manager, stocks (or more precisely, stock index futures) and bond futures are simply two possibilities within a spectrum of futures markets. Looking just at the major groups of futures, one can trade energy markets, precious metals, base metals, grains, oilseeds, foodstuffs (cocoa, coffee, sugar), currencies, long- and short-term interest rate contracts in the United States and overseas, various global stock market indexes, and livestock markets. Within at least some of these groups, one will probably find at least one good bull market and one good bear market prevailing at any time.

The third characteristic of futures markets is the finding that risk can be managed effectively. This finding is related to the trending behavior of futures, but it has its theoretical underpinnings in the role of futures markets.

Futures markets came about because producers and users needed a mechanism to protect themselves against adverse price movements. The futures markets provide this hedging facility. Successful futures managers are the ones who take on and manage the price risk that hedgers are trying to avoid. For example, the futures manager can spread risk by participating in a wide variety of markets, can tailor the risk taken on to the particular situation, and can get out of markets if the actual loss exceeds predetermined limits.

Thus, a futures portfolio may best be constructed around a risk management model rather than a simplistic buy-and-hold model.

SUMMARY

A growing body of literature demonstrates that a well-constructed futures portfolio within an overall investment mix of stocks, bonds, and futures lowers the portfolio risk while enhancing return. The results seem to be quite robust, holding true across a range of futures portfolio constructions, from simple buy-and-hold (unleveraged) to a leveraged portfolio with futures bought or sold short according to the prevailing market trend.

To date, institutional investors do not seem to have taken these results seriously, possibly because their fear of the riskiness of futures has overwhelmed their need or desire to achieve better risk-adjusted performance. Today, it's possible to see futures risk in a direct way, demonstrating that futures price movements are less risky than those of equities. This viewpoint should help in the effort to bring futures into the mainstream of investment alternatives.

FOR FURTHER READING

Barbanel, Jack, Phil Lipsky, and John Zumbrum. "Why Futures Belong in Institutional Portfolios." *Futures*, December 1983.

Bodie, Zvi. "Commodity Futures as a Hedge Against Inflation." *The Journal of Portfolio Management*, Spring 1983.

Bodie, Zvi, and Victor Rosansky. "Risk and Return in Commodity Futures." *Financial Analysts Journal*, May–June 1980.

Irwin, Scott, and Diego Landa. "Real Estate, Futures, and Gold as Portfolio Assets." *The Journal of Portfolio Management*, Fall 1987.

CHAPTER NOTES

Page **Chapter 1**

2 "Preoccupation with these concerns . . ."

P. L. Taylor, Jr., A. Cooper, and D. Morris, "The Use of Futures In Connection with Hedging and Other Asset Management Transactions for Institutional Investors," a paper presented before 1990 Annual Symposium on the Institutional Uses of Managed Futures, New York, June 1990.

8 "Traditionally, the differences in the cost structures . . ."

M. Baratz, *The Investor's Guide to Futures Money Management*, Futures Trading Group, Columbia, Md., 1984.

9 "In a survey conducted by . . ."

F. Pusateri and J. Stapleton. "A Case Study in Translating Statistics," presented at the seminar, "Managed Futures Investing," presented by the Institute for International Research, July 1990, New York.

11 History of Managed Futures:

R. T. Northcote, "Highlights in the Managed Futures Industry," Managed Futures Trade Association Journal, January–

February 1990. The author would like to thank Mr. Northcote for contributing large portions of this history.

11 "The managed futures industry . . ."

M. Baratz, Presentation at Managed Account Reports 12th Annual Conference on Futures Money Management, Orlando, Fla., February 1991.

18 "Transaction costs are comprised of . . ."

For a complete description of transaction costs on the New York Stock Exchange see "The Total Cost of Transactions on the NYSE," Stephen Berkowitz, Dennis Logue, and Eugene Noser, *Journal of Finance,* March 1988.

18 "Since the first index fund began trading in 1973 . . ."

C. Epstein, "Big Board Blues," *Global Custodian Magazine,* December 1990.

19 "According to a 1991 study . . ."

Presentation by William Toy, vice president, equity derivative products, Goldman Sachs & Co., "Portfolio Trading Strategies Using Futures on Indexes," at a conference, "Swaps, Synthetics, Derivatives on International Stock Indexes," February 1991, New York.

19 "These same cost efficiencies exist . . ."

G. Gastineau and J. Hornblower, "Stocks versus Futures for the International Investor: Trading Costs and Withholding Taxes." Salomon Brothers Equity Options and Futures Research Report, August 31, 1988.

19 "In a Salomon Brothers Equity and Options Research Report . . ."

"Stocks vs. Futures for the International Investor: Trading Costs and Withholding Taxes," August 31, 1988.

20 "Another Salomon Brothers research report states . . ."

R. S. Salomon et al., "Investment Policy Weekly: The Rising Cost of Changing Your Mind," Salomon Brothers, September 4, 1990.

23 "A partial reason for this slow start is . . ."

In early-1990, Chemical Futures, Inc. a subsidiary of Chemical Bank, began plans to launch a $100 million off-shore commodity pool, one of the largest bank offerings ever attempted. Due to changing market conditions, the war in Kuwait and a reliance on Middle East funding sources, the pool was unable to break escrow. The pool attempt was disbanded in late-1990.

28 "In July 1989, Commodities Corporation . . ."

The Wall Street Journal, March 1, 1991.

28 "In March 1991, Paul Tudor Jones . . ."

The Wall Street Journal, March 1, 1991.

29 "Jones has posted a 75% rate . . ."

Private conversation.

30 "Among the major national wirehouses, managed . . ."

Ken Tropin, president, John W. Henry & Co., Inc., presentation at the Sixth Canadian International Futures and Options Conference, Montreal, October 1990.

31 "The success of guarantee funds also could . . ."

PaineWebber Group Inc. managed futures fund was cancelled because it failed to provide a guaranteed return on principal feature, according to a PaineWebber executive.

Chapter 2

36 "Modern Portfolio Theory": This section draws heavily from S. Irwin, "Diversification Dampens Volatility To Your 'Satisfaction' Level." *Futures.* April 1987, pp. 45–47.

37 "The basic premise of MPT . . ."

H. M. Markowitz, *Portfolio Selection.* New York: John Wiley and Sons, 1959.

38 "To quote Burton Malkiel . . ."

B. G. Malkiel, *A Random Walk Down Wall Street.* 2nd ed., New York: W. W. Norton, 1981.

46 "Investment Performance of Public Commodity Pools": This section draws upon Chapter Two of T. R. Krukemyer, *The Investment Performance of Public Commodity Pools: 1979–1989.* Unpublished M. S. Thesis, The Ohio State University, 1990.

46 "Harvard Professor John Lintner was the first academic researcher to examine . . ."

J. Lintner, "The Potential Role of Managed Commodity-Financial Futures Accounts (and/or Funds) in Portfolios of Stocks and Bonds." Paper presented at the Annual Conference of the Financial Analysts Federation, Toronto, Canada, May, 1983.

47 "Irwin and Brorsen analyzed returns from 84 commodity pools . . ."

47 "Murphy evaluated the performance of 11 commodity pools . . ."

J. A. Murphy, "Futures Fund Performance: A Test of the Effectiveness of Technical Analysis." *Journal of Futures Markets.* 6(1986):175–185.

47 "Irwin and Landa updated the database . . ."

S. H. Irwin and D. Landa. "Real Estate, Futures, and Gold as Portfolio Assets." *Journal of Portfolio Management.* (1987):29–34.

48 "Elton, Gruber, and Rentzler studied the monthly returns . . ."

E. J. Elton, M. J. Gruber, and J. C. Rentzler. "Professionally Managed, Publicly Traded Commodity Funds." *Journal of Business.* 60(1987):175–199.

48 "Elton, Gruber, and Rentzler produced a second study in 1990 . . ."

E. J. Elton, M. J. Gruber, and J. C. Rentzler. "The Performance of Publicly Offered Commodity Funds." *Financial Analysts Journal.* (1990):23–30.

49 "Irwin, Krukemyer, and Zulauf examined monthly return data . . ."

S. H. Irwin, T. R. Krukemyer, and C. R. Zulauf. "The Investment Performance of Public Commodity Pools: 1979–1989." Working paper, Department of Agricultural Economics and Rural Sociology, The Ohio State University, January 1991.

51 "By comparison, investment costs of stock mutual funds are about . . ."

W. Sharpe, *Investments*. Englewood Cliffs, NJ: Prentice-Hall, 1981.

51 "Basso estimated the operating costs . . . ."

T. F. Basso, "A Review of Public and Private Futures Funds - 1988." Working paper, Trendstat Capital Management, 1989.

51 "Further, Irwin and Brorsen show that the costs imply . . ."

S. H. Irwin and B. W. Brorsen. "Public Futures Funds." *Journal of Futures Markets*. 5(1985):463–485.

51 "Institutions have negotiated much lower . . ."

L. Hecht, "The Commodities Conundrum." *Institutional Investor*. December 1989, pp. 191–195.

Chapter 4

81 Notes about the Chapter:

The three primary forms of investment in professionally managed commodity trading products are publicly traded commodity funds, private commodity pools, and individually managed commodity trading accounts. Publicly traded commodity funds and private commodity pools are organized as vehicles for pooling investments, like mutual funds, and involve the allocation of investment funds to at least one and, often, two to five commodity trading advisors (CTAs). In addition, commodity trading advisors (professional traders who trade in one or a variety of commodity markets following technical, fundamental, or hybrid trading strategies) take individually managed accounts from investors. While initial minimum investments in public funds and commodity pools are often as small as $5000, initial investment minimums for individually managed accounts range from as little as $10,000 to as much as $1,000,000 or more.

Since this chapter tests the return performance of commodity traders these results are not strictly comparable with earlier studies which have tested the performance of publicly traded commodity funds. If portfolios of commodity traders can be formed which offer suitable returns after adjustments for typical costs of forming a fund, then a rational basis for the existence of various commodity vehicles can be assumed.

For an additional discussion on the costs of establishing a multi-manager CTA commodity portfolio, see S. Angrist, "How to Get Help for That Big Plunge Into Commodities," *The Wall Street Journal,* (March 16, 1990). As discussed in the article, for large accounts all fees are negotiable.

81 "In this chapter, we analyze the performance . . ."

Asset allocation across mutual funds in different subsets of securities has been called diversification of style Sharpe (*Investments,* Prentice Hall, 1984). Asset allocation across managers within a single subset of securities (e.g., multi-manager has been called diversification of judgment).

Survival bias may represent one reason for the superior performance of existing funds. However the funds studied represent a sample of those funds which have existed for the period and results indicate superior performance within the set of existing funds. In addition, given the management review, few funds approaching bankruptcy would have been in the set.

In order to offer a check on the management search process a second set of commodity investments funds was selected from a second independent management firm. The funds were selected for the period 1984–1987. Results are similar and are available from authors.

The CTAs were chosen for examination in October, 1987. The authors examined the results of the 14 CTAs selected in the 18 months following the original study. The performance over this subsequent period was not available at the time the original 14 were selected. Return on investment (1.54%) and standard deviation (7.28%) for the full period is similar to the original period studied. Further, the reduction in standard deviation resulting from looking at the portfolio returns rather than the average standard deviation of the individual CTAs was consistent in the two periods (30%). A common criticism of the ability of management consultants (e.g., Frank Russell, Evaluation Associates) to select superior performers is that the firms could use the private information of a superior performer to its own advantage instead of offering the information externally in the form of managed funds. However, the return to the management consultant from selling the information may produce a more profitable alternative.

Since many commodity vehicles (e.g., funds, pools) are not traded on a central exchange, this paper assumes that the past performance of a CTA and a pool or fund formed by that CTA is indicative of future performance. While the relationship between past and future performance by CTAs had been debated in the literature (see F. Edwards and A. Ma, on p. 101) historical analysis of stock and bond funds likewise assumes a relationship between past and future performance.

For a full discussion of problems in return measurement for commodity funds see Ginger Szala in bibliography on p. 102.

83 "These composite rates of return include . . ."

Markowitz's optimization was done for the CTA sample using historical correlation and return/variance inputs for the period studied. As expected, the portfolio outperformed the simple equal weighting scheme used in this analysis. The inputs used, however, assume perfect foresight of the correlation and return forecasts for the period.

Under the assumption of no risk-free rate the marginal benefit of the multi-manager CTA portfolio is generally greater since the impact of adding the risk-free rate restriction is removed. For example, for the whole period while the minimum/maximum return for the average CTA is −20.67/24.15, the CTA with the greatest minimum/maximum return was .98/39.44. Other individual CTAs had even greater minimums or maximums. In terms of CTA correlations with S&P 500, while the average correlation was .07, individual CTA correlations ranged from −.15 to .26.

97 "For the whole period (1983–October 1987), the correlation . . ."

For the full commodity portfolio versus stocks break-even analysis, Elton et al. used a stock return of 1.3% and a standard deviation of 4% for their 6-year sample (7/1979–6/1985). For our analysis (January/1983–October 1987), we use a stock return of 1.39% and a standard deviation of 5.% (see table). While Elton et al. used the average of the correlation coefficients between individual commodities funds and the S&P 500 stock portfolio (the average across funds of the correlation of each fund with the stocks) in their break-even analysis, in our calculations of break-even returns we use the correlation coefficient between the commodity portfolio and the S&P 500 stock portfolio for the years January 1983–October 1987. The correlation coefficients used in Elton et al. and our analyses are .121 and .056, respectively. For the entire period of analysis, the risk-free rates used in Elton et al. and our analysis are .85% and .50% per month, respectively.

The stability of individual CTA correlations and returns with comparison assets is examined in T. Schneeweis and D. McCarthy, "Manager Selection and Commodity Performance" Working Paper, University of Massachusetts, 1990.

Chapter 5

106 "Managed futures has been one of the fastest growing areas . . ."

F. Helmut Weymer, "Extraordinary Growth," *FIA Review*, January/February 1990. p. 10.

106 "Many researchers who use measures of portfolio rewards . . ." Studies include "The Potential Role of Managed Commodity Financial Futures Account in Portfolios of Stocks and Bonds," John Lintner, Annual Conference of Financial Analysts Federation,

Toronto, Canada, May 1983; Scott Irwin and Diego Landa, "Real Estate, Futures, and Gold as Portfolio Assets," *The Journal of Portfolio Management*, Fall 1987; Robert D. Arnott and Dr. Roger G. Clark, "Active Asset Allocation," *Portfolio and Investment Management*, 1989.

106 "A recent study conducted by . . ."

Mitchell Rock and Joseph Rosen, "Does Money 'Barrier' Alter Trading Styles Returns?" *Futures Magazine*, April 1990, p. 48. The authors concluded that the amount of equity under management and risk adjusted rate of return are not correlated. (Unadjusted returns were negatively correlated.)

107 "According to the National Futures Association . . ."

Earl Farkes, an information services representative for the National Futures Association, noted that as of April 30, 1990, there were 2,517 CTAs registered with the CFTC.

110 "By contrast, 1990 provided this same group of advisors . . ."

Ginger Szala, "Managed Money: Capitalizing on the Trends of 1990," *Futures Magazine*, March 1991, pp. 44–48.

121 "Some of the systems also offer data with . . ."

Ginger Szala, "Want a Traders? Should You Let Software Do The Walking," *Futures Magazine*, February 1991, pp. 42–43.

131 "In both of these cases, critics argue, the performance . . ."

Joel Rentzler, "Some Institutions Buy Futures to Cut Risks," *The Wall Street Journal*, December 10, 1990, p. C1.

Chapter 7

147 "This 62% increase . . ."

Sherman, *Pension Planning and Deferred Compensation* (1985).

147 "As of 1990, $2 trillion . . ."

Leo Melamed, "Telecommunications, markets: Shaping the world in the 1990's," *Futures: The Magazine of Commodities and Options* (November 1990).

149 "These provisions, . . ."

Welfare benefit plans are plans that provide for life, health, disability, other insurance-type benefits, severance benefits, vacations, and other employee benefits.

149 "However, the fiduciary standards . . ."

Self-employed individuals are defined in Code Section 401(c)(1). See *Schwartz v. Gordon,* 761 F.2d 864 (1985).

149 "Investment managers, . . ."

See the discussion under "Delegation of Duties," below.

151 "In contrast, a broker . . ."

See *Stanton v. Shearson Lehman/American Express,* 631 F. Supp. 100, 7 Employee Benefits Cas. (BNA) 1579 (N.D. Ga. 1986).

151 "Even though a client . . ."

Stanton, 7 Employee Benefits Cas. at 1581, 1582.

152 "A venture capital operating company . . ."

29 C.F.R. § 2510.3-101.

156 "If look-through investment vehicles . . ."

A look-through investment vehicle includes (1) an investment company described in Section 3(a) or 18(f) of the Investment Company Act of 1940 or any segregated portfolios of such company; (2) a common or collective trust fund or a pooled investment fund maintained by a bank, a bank deposit, or a guaranteed investment contract of a bank; (3) a pooled separate account or a guaranteed investment contract of an insurance company qualified to do business in any state; or (4) any entity whose assets include plan assets by reason of a plan's investment in the entity.

157 "This point was emphasized . . ."

See *Dardaganis v. Grace Capital, Inc.*, 889 F.2d 1237 (2d Cir. 1989).

158 "Mere resignation of the fiduciary . . ."

29 C.F.R. § 2509.75-5 FR-10.

159 "However, the fiduciary cannot be relieved . . ."

See Conf. Comm. Rep., Pub. L. 93-406, Pensions (P-H), ¶ 93,095.

159 "The Department of Labor, reaffirming . . ."

See DOL Adv. Op. 82-39A (August 5, 1982).

160 "Because the liquidity needs . . ."

Investment managers should be aware of *GIW Industries, Inc. v. Trevor, Stewart, Burton & Jacobsen, Inc.*, 895 F.2d 729 (11th Cir. 1990), where a need for large distributions from a plan required the liquidation of many U.S. Treasury bonds held for the plan by the investment manager. This unplanned liquidation caused large losses to the plan. The court found that the investment manager had breached its fiduciary duties to the plan by not independently keeping itself informed of the liquidity needs of the plan and diversifying the assets accordingly.

160 "The matter of obtaining a bond . . ."

The plan itself cannot indemnify a fiduciary for liability resulting from violation of its fiduciary duties. The SEC also has limited the ability of an investment adviser to be indemnified for violation of the federal securities laws.

160 "Fee arrangements . . ."

Both of these important issues are discussed in detail under "Special Considerations."

160 "Although not held responsible . . ."

See DOL Tech. Rel. 86-1 and the discussion beginning on page 176.

161 "These 'prohibited transactions,' . . ."

Similar provisions are found in Code Section 4975.

161 "In general, a party-in-interest . . ."

This grouping of fiduciaries and parties-in-interest is referred to as "disqualified persons" under Code Section 4975.

163 "In examining the issue . . ."

See, e.g., Priv. Ltr. Ruls. 87-17-066 (January 30, 1987) and 83-38-138 (June 24, 1983).

163 "Therefore, the futures contract . . ."

In *Elliot Knitwear Profit Sharing Plan v. Commissioner*, 614 F.2d 347, 2 Employee Benefits Cas. (BNA) 2330 (3rd Cir. 1980), the court ruled that securities purchased on margin by a profit-sharing plan were "debt-financed property" within the meaning of Code Section 514 and, thus, income realized on the purchased and sale of the securities was unrelated business income and subject to tax. The court based its decision on the assumed fact that the securities were purchased through the use of "acquisitions indebtedness." The decision did not, however, affect the tax-qualified status of the plan.

163 "The plan asset . . ."

DOL Adv. Op. 82-42A (September 21, 1982).

164 "Losses from a breach . . ."

See *Donovan v. Bierwith*, 754 F.2d 1049 (2d Cir. 1985).

164 "One form of equitable relief . . ."

In *Donovan v. Williams*, Civil Action No. 82-912-Civ-J-B (N.D. Fla. August 19, 1983), The Department of Labor filed suit against trustees of a benefit plan for, among other things, failure to establish a reasonable method of accounting for travel expenses, fees, and other administrative costs, in violation of ERISA's exclusive benefit and prudence standards. A consent order was entered into, barring Williams (one of the trustees) from serving as a fiduciary of an ERISA benefit plan. The other trustees were required to implement procedures to account for the plan expenses.

164 "Virtually every investment . . ."

See, *Marshall v. Glass/Metal Association and Glaziers & Glassworkers Pension Plan*, 507 F. Supp. 378, 384, 2 Employee Benefits Cas. (BNA) 1006 (D. Haw. 1980).

164 "This standard became clear . . ."

29 C.F.R. § 2550.404a-1.

165 "Appropriate consideration includes . . ."

See *Donovan v. Mazzola,* 716 F.2d 1226, Employee Benefits Cas. (BNA) 1895 (9th Cir. 1983).

165 "The ultimate outcome . . . ."

See *GIW Industries, Inc. v. Trevor, Stewart, Burton & Jacobsen, Inc.*, 10 Employee Benefits Cas. (BNA) 2290 (D. Ga. 1989).

165 "A fiduciary's independent investigation . . ."

See *Fink v. National Savings & Trust Co.*, 772 F.2d 951, 957, 6 Employee Benefits Cas. (BNA) 2269 (D.C. Cir. 1985).

166 "The first of the two opinion letters . . ."

See DOL Adv. Op. 86-20A (August 29, 1986). The second DOL letter, to Batterymarch Financial Management (DOL Adv. Op. 96-21A (August 29, 1986)) involved essentially the same type of performance-based compensation arrangement and will not be separately discussed.

168 "The Department of Labor emphasized . . ."

The DOL declined to indicate whether the arrangement would violate the prohibited transaction provisions of ERISA Section 406(a), which provide, among other things, that a plan fiduciary may not cause a plan to engage in a transaction that constitutes a "transfer to or use by or for the benefit of a party-in-interest, of any assets of the plan." The DOL noted that ERISA Section 408(b)(2) provides an exemption from Section 406(a)'s restriction for any contract or reasonable arrangement with a party-in-interest for office space or legal, accounting, or other services if no more than reasonable compensation is paid. The DOL also said that whether the requirements of ERISA Section 408(b)(2) are met is a factual question and that is ordinarily does not issue opinions on such questions. Despite the narrow wording of ERISA Section 408(b)(2), the DOL has indicated that this provision does not exempt customary securities and futures transactions from ERISA Section 406(a), if the reasonable compensation test is met. See Part C of release accompanying adoption of Prohibited Transaction Exemption 86-128 (November 18, 1986), and Part B of Letter of DOL to the Futures Industry Association (August 16, 1985).

169 "Finally, the investment manager . . ."

Investment managers should note that most states have adopted their own versions of Rule 205-3 and these must be reviewed before transacting business in any given state.

170 "This concern was addressed . . ."

See DOL Adv. Op. 89-28A (September 25, 1989).

172 "Specifically, the Securities Acts Amendments . . ."

See Senate Comm. on Banking, Housing and Urban Affairs, S. Rep. No. 75, 94th Cong., 1st Sess. 69-71 (1975); and SEC Rel. No. 34-12251 (March 24, 1976).

173 "The SEC has also made clear, . . ."

See *Charles Lerner* (October 25, 1988).

173 "The SEC has recently ended . . ."

See *Charles Lerner* (July 25, 1990).

174 "As the SEC noted, . . ."

See *Charles Lerner* (October 25, 1988).

174 "[T]he controlling principle . . ."

Exchange Act Rel. No. 34-23170, 35 SEC Docket (CCH) 703 (April 23, 1986).

175 "The money manager must keep . . ."

Id., SEC Docket at 706.

175 "ERISA also requires . . ."

See *Capital Institutional Services, Inc.* (October 16, 1989) [1986 Transfer Binder] Fed. Sec. L. Rep. (CCH) ¶ 78.107.

175 "Where products or services . . ."

If an investment manager could take advantage of Section 28(e), it would allow him or her to consider the benefit provided to all the managed accounts when making a good faith determination as to the reasonableness of the commissions paid to the broker. Id. at 713. Therefore, because Section 28(e) preempts ERISA, falling under the safe harbor provisions of this Section provides an investment manager with the additional benefit of considering as a small group all of its managed accounts when making the determination of best execution.

175 "The SEC Release states . . ."

An investment manager's fiduciary duty to secure the best execution for the plan's transactions is not relieved by the direction of the plan sponsor. The SEC Release states that the phrase *directed brokerage* "refers to an arrangement whereby an employee benefit plan sponsors requests to its money manager, subject to the manager's satisfaction that it is receiving best execution, to direct commission business to a particular broker-dealer who has agreed to provide services, pay obligations or make cash rebates to the plan." 35 SEC Docket at 712. The DOL has also issued a Technical Release interpreting fiduciary duties under directed commission arrangements. That release states "where a plan sponsor or other plan fiduciary directs the investment manager to execute a specified percentage of the plan's trades or specified amount of the plan's commission business through the particular broker-dealers, consistent with a manager's duty to secure best execution for the transactions." ERISA Tech. Rel. 86-1, 13 Pens. Rep. (BNA) 1007 (May 22, 1986) ("TR 86-1").

175 "The investment manager must 'execute . . .'"
(to end of paragraph): SEC Docket at 712.

176 "The Department of Labor has set forth . . ."
See TR 86-1.

177 "Although this phrase is not defined, . . ."
TR 86-1 at 1008, f.4.

177 "In addition, if a fiduciary . . ."
TR 86-1 at 1008.

178 "Further examples in the Release . . ."
TR 86-1 at 1008, ex. 1, 2.

178 “This particular example . . .”
TR 86-1 at 1008, ex. 3.

179 “If, in the rare case, a fiduciary . . .”
See the discussion of “reasonable efforts” under “Fiduciary Duties,” above.

180 “Such action may involve . . .”
29 C.F.R. § 2509.75-5 FR-10.

181 “Although there are no statutory exemptions . . .”
29 C.F.R. § 2550.408(b)-2(e)(2).

181 “Similar relief was requested . . .”
FIA letter (August 16, 1982).

182 “The Department has stated . . .”
Pens. Plan Guide (CCH), ¶ 16.631, p. 19, 903–39.

182 “This concern is also implicit . . .”
DOL Adv. Op. 82-22A (May 12, 1982); 83-29A (June 13, 1983); and 82-55A (October 15, 1982).

Chapter 11

254 “To a large extent . . .”
For the specific reasons behind this classical view, see John Lintner, “Inflation and Common Stock Prices in a Cyclical Context,” *National Bureau of Economic Research Fifty-third Annual Report* (September 1973).

254 “However, that relationship has not withstood . . .”
See Zvi Bodie, “Common Stocks as a Hedge Against Inflation,” *Journal of Finance*, 31:2 (May 1976).

255 “In consequence, several important members . . .”
See Wayne Angell, “A Commodity Price Guide to Monetary Aggregate Targeting,” The Lehrman Institute, New York (December 1987); Robert H. Heller. “Anchoring the International Monetary System,” The Heritage Lectures, 94, Washington, DC

(1987); Manuel H. Johnson, "Current Perspectives on Monetary Policy," *Cato Journal*, 8:2 (Fall 1987).

255 "This stimulated a great deal of research . . ."

See, for example, Alan C. Garner, "Commodity Prices: Policy Target of Informational Variable?" Federal Reserve Bank of Kansas City (November 1988); International Monetary Fund, "Commodity Price Baskets as Possible Indicators of Future Price Developments," Washington, DC (November 1987); John Rosine, "Aggregate Measures of Price and Quantity Change in Commodity Markets," Board of Governors of the Federal Reserve System, Washington, DC (December 1987); Joseph A. Whitt, "Commodity Prices and Monetary Policy," Federal Reserve Bank of Atlanta (December 1988).

255 "These studies have confirmed . . ."

An interesting consequence of these studies is that the Federal Reserve's monetary policy is now being determined, in part, by movements in commodity prices. Steve Hanke, "Old Wine in a New Bottle," *Friedberg's Commodity and Currency Comments* (March 19, 1989); "Professor Wicksell Revisited," *Friedberg's Commodity and Currency Comments* (October 2, 1989); "On Wicksellian Price Relationships," *Friedberg's Commodity and Currency Comments* (January 20, 1991).

255 "To clarify why holding futures . . ."

For a more detailed discussion of this issue, see Jeffrey Williams, *The Economic Function of the Futures Markets* (1986) and H. Working, "Theory of the Inverse Carrying Charge in Futures Markets," *Journal of Farm Economics* (1948) and "The Theory of Price and Storage," *American Economic Review* (December 1949).

256 "A market is said to be in 'full carry' . . ."

Any time a futures price exceeds a spot price for a full commodity, the market is said to be in contango. Hence, a full carry market is a special case of a contango market.

257 "When that happens, the market . . ."

John Maynard Keynes thought this relationship was "normal" in commodity markets. We now know this to be false at both the theoretical and empirical levels. See Jeffrey Williams, *The Economic Function of Futures Markets* (1986); Lester Telser, "Futures Trading and the Storage of Cotton and Wheat," *Journal of Political Economy,* 66:3 (June 1958); "Reply to Cootner," *Journal of Political Economy,* 68:4 (August 1960).

257 "An asset is an inflation hedge . . ."

Eugene Fama and James D. MacBeth, "Tests of the Multiperiod Two-Parameter Model," *Journal of Financial Economics,* 1 (1974). For several different views on what characterizes an inflation hedge, see Zvi Bodie, "Common Stocks as a Hedge Against Inflation," *Journal of Finance,* 31:2 (May 1976).

257 "Moreover, the price inflation . . ."

For empirical evidence on the cost-of-carry relationship, see Eugene Fama and Kenneth R. French, "Commodity Futures Prices: Some Evidence on Forecast Power, Premiums, and the Theory of Storage," *Journal of Business,* 60:1 (1987): pp. 55–74.

258 "The correlations shown . . ."

The relative weakness of the relationships for the 5- and 10-year CPI-W estimates is not a great surprise, given that the relationship between the CPI-W and CPI-U, as well as that between the CPI-W and PPI, broke down over that period. "CRB Index White Paper: An Investigation into Non-Traditional Trading Applications for CRB Index Futures," Powers Research, Inc., Jersey City, NJ (March 4, 1988).

INDEX

9 780471 529835